Woodbourne Library
Washington-Centerville Public Library
Centerville, Ohio

DISCARD

D1193345

adobe premiere elements 12

CLASSROOM IN A BOOK®

The official training workbook from Adobe Systems

Adobe® Premiere® Elements 12 Classroom in a Book®

© 2014 Adobe Systems Incorporated and its licensors. All rights reserved.

If this guide is distributed with software that includes an end user agreement, this guide, as well as the software described in it, is furnished under license and may be used or copied only in accordance with the terms of such license. Except as permitted by any such license, no part of this guide may be reproduced, stored in a retrieval system, or transmitted, in any form or by any means, electronic, mechanical, recording, or otherwise, without the prior written permission of Adobe Systems Incorporated. Please note that the content in this guide is protected under copyright law even if it is not distributed with software that includes an end user license agreement.

The content of this guide is furnished for informational use only, is subject to change without notice, and should not be construed as a commitment by Adobe Systems Incorporated. Adobe Systems Incorporated assumes no responsibility or liability for any errors or inaccuracies that may appear in the informational content contained in this guide.

Please remember that existing artwork or images that you may want to include in your project may be protected under copyright law. The unauthorized incorporation of such material into your new work could be a violation of the rights of the copyright owner. Please be sure to obtain any permission required from the copyright owner.

Any references to company names in sample files are for demonstration purposes only and are not intended to refer to any actual organization.

Adobe, the Adobe logo, Premiere, Flash, Photoshop, Revel, and Classroom in a Book are either registered trademarks or trademarks of Adobe Systems Incorporated in the United States and/or other countries.

Apple, Mac OS, and Macintosh, and QuickTime are trademarks of Apple, registered in the U.S. and other countries. QuickTime and the QuickTime logo are trademarks used under license. The QuickTime logo is registered in the U.S. and other countries. Microsoft and Windows are either registered trademarks or trademarks of Microsoft Corporation in the U.S. and/or other countries. All other trademarks are the property of their respective owners.

Adobe Systems Incorporated, 345 Park Avenue, San Jose, California 95110-2704, USA

Notice to U.S. Government End Users. The Software and Documentation are "Commercial Items," as that term is defined at 48 C.F.R. §2.101, consisting of "Commercial Computer Software" and "Commercial Computer Software Documentation," as such terms are used in 48 C.F.R. §12.212 or 48 C.F.R. §227.7202, as applicable. Consistent with 48 C.F.R. §12.212 or 48 C.F.R. §§227.7202-1 through 227.7202-4, as applicable, the Commercial Computer Software and Commercial Computer Software Documentation are being licensed to U.S. Government end users (a) only as Commercial Items and (b) with only those rights as are granted to all other end users pursuant to the terms and conditions herein. Unpublished-rights reserved under the copyright laws of the United States. Adobe Systems Incorporated, 345 Park Avenue, San Jose, CA 95110-2704, USA. For U.S. Government End Users, Adobe agrees to comply with all applicable equal opportunity laws including, if appropriate, the provisions of Executive Order 11246, as amended, Section 402 of the Vietnam Era Veterans Readjustment Assistance Act of 1974 (38 USC 4212), and Section 503 of the Rehabilitation Act of 1973, as amended, and the regulations at 41 CFR Parts 60-1 through 60-60, 60-250, and 60-741. The affirmative action clause and regulations contained in the preceding sentence shall be incorporated by reference.

Adobe Press books are published by Peachpit, a division of Pearson Education located in San Francisco, California. For the latest on Adobe Press books, go to www.adobepress.com. To report errors, please send a note to errata@peachpit.com. For information on getting permission for reprints and excerpts, contact permissions@peachpit.com.

Printed and bound in the United States of America

ISBN-13: 978-0-321-94981-3
ISBN-10:   0-321-94981-1

9 8 7 6 5 4 3 2 1

WHERE ARE THE LESSON FILES?

Purchasing this Classroom in a Book gives you access to the lesson files that you'll need to complete the exercises in the book, as well as other content to help you learn more about Adobe software and use it with greater efficiency and ease. The diagram below represents the contents of the lesson files directory, which should help you locate the files you need. Please see the Getting Started section for full download instructions.

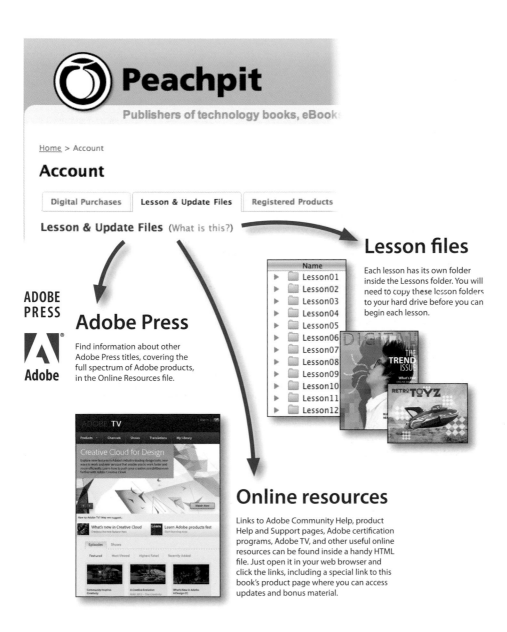

Adobe Press

Find information about other Adobe Press titles, covering the full spectrum of Adobe products, in the Online Resources file.

Lesson files

Each lesson has its own folder inside the Lessons folder. You will need to copy these lesson folders to your hard drive before you can begin each lesson.

Online resources

Links to Adobe Community Help, product Help and Support pages, Adobe certification programs, Adobe TV, and other useful online resources can be found inside a handy HTML file. Just open it in your web browser and click the links, including a special link to this book's product page where you can access updates and bonus material.

CONTENTS

GETTING STARTED

Adobe® Premiere® Elements 12 delivers video editing tools that balance power and versatility with ease of use. Adobe Premiere Elements 12 is ideal for home users, hobbyists, business users, and professional videographers—anyone who wants to produce high-quality movies and DVDs.

If you've used earlier versions of Adobe Premiere Elements, you'll find that this Classroom in a Book covers the updated interface that Adobe Systems introduced in this version, plus new advanced skills and features. If you're new to Adobe Premiere Elements, you'll learn the fundamental concepts and techniques that will help you master this application.

About Classroom in a Book

Adobe Premiere Elements 12 Classroom in a Book is part of the official training series for Adobe graphics and publishing software developed by Adobe product experts. Most lessons in this book include self-paced projects that give you hands-on experience using Adobe Premiere Elements 12. You will almost certainly get the most benefit from working on the lessons in the order in which they occur in the book.

As an overview, in the first two lessons, you'll learn your way around Adobe Premiere Elements and the Adobe Organizer, how to set up a project in Adobe Premiere Elements, and how to customize critical preferences.

In Lesson 3, you'll learn how to capture and otherwise import video into Adobe Premiere Elements. Starting with Lesson 4, you'll open provided projects or create your own from provided contents, and learn how to convert your raw, captured clips into a polished movie.

Note that the project files were created separately for Mac and Windows computers, and were created using prerelease software and content. For this reason, there may be some minor differences between the figures in the book and what you might see onscreen when you're using Adobe Premiere Elements. Throughout the book, we've tried to identify the places you're most likely to see this, but apologize in advance for any differences or inconvenience.

Prerequisites

Before you begin working on the lessons in this book, make sure that you and your computer are ready.

Requirements for your computer

You'll need a maximum of about 4.3 gigabytes (GB) of free space on your hard drive for the lesson files and the work files you'll create. For some lessons, you'll need to have 2GB of RAM installed on your computer. Note that the lessons assume that you have installed all templates and associated content available with the DVD version of Adobe Premiere Elements 12 or via download. If the lesson calls for a template or other content that's not installed on your computer, Adobe Premiere Elements should download it automatically. If this doesn't occur, you should be able to simply choose another template and continue with the lesson.

Required skills

The lessons in *Adobe Premiere Elements 12 Classroom in a Book* assume that you have a working knowledge of your computer and its operating system. This book does not teach the most basic and generic computer skills. If you can answer *yes* to the following questions, you're probably well qualified to start working on the projects in these lessons:

- Do you know how to use the Microsoft Windows Start button and the Windows task bar? On the Mac, do you know how to run applications from the Dock or in the Applications folder? In both operating systems, can you open menus and submenus, and choose items from those menus?

- Do you know how to use My Computer, Windows Explorer, Finder, and/or a browser—such as Chrome, Firefox, Internet Explorer, or Safari—to find items stored in folders on your computer, or to browse the Internet?

- Are you comfortable using the mouse to move the pointer, select items, drag, and deselect? Have you used context menus (which open when you right-click items in Windows or Mac OS, or Control-click items on the Mac if you're working with a single-button mouse)?

- When you have two or more open applications, do you know how to switch from one to another? Do you know how to switch to the Windows or Macintosh desktop?

- Do you know how to open, close, and minimize individual windows? Can you move them to different locations on your screen? Can you resize a window by dragging?

- Can you scroll (vertically and horizontally) within a window to see contents that may not be visible in the displayed area?

- Are you familiar with the menus across the top of an application and how to use those menus?

- Have you used dialog boxes (special windows in the interface that display information), such as the Print dialog box? Do you know how to click arrow icons to open a menu within a dialog box?

- Can you open, save, and close a file? Are you familiar with word processing tasks such as typing, selecting words, backspacing, deleting, copying, pasting, and changing text?

- Do you know how to open and find information in Microsoft Windows or Apple Macintosh Help?

If there are gaps in your mastery of these skills, see the documentation for your operating system. Or, ask a computer-savvy friend or instructor for help.

Installing Adobe Premiere Elements 12

Before you begin using *Adobe Premiere Elements 12 Classroom in a Book*, make sure that your system is set up correctly and that you've installed the required software and hardware. You must purchase the Adobe Premiere Elements 12 software separately. For system requirements and complete instructions on installing the software, visit www.adobe.com/support.

Accessing the Classroom in a Book files

In order to work through the projects in this book, you will need to download the lesson files from peachpit.com. You can download the files for individual lessons, or download them all in a single file.

Your Account page on peachpit.com is where you'll find any updates to the chapters or to the lesson files. Look on the Lesson & Update Files tab to access the most current content. To access the Classroom in a Book files, do the following:

1 Go to www.peachpit.com/redeem, and enter the code found at the back of your book.

2 If you do not have a Peachpit.com account, create one when you're prompted to do so.

3 Click the Lesson & Update Files tab on your Account page. This tab lists downloadable files.

4 Click the lesson file links to download them to your computer.

5 Create a new folder on your hard disk, and name it Lessons. Then, drag the lesson files you downloaded into the Lessons folder on your hard disk.

Additional resources

Adobe Premiere Elements 12 Classroom in a Book is not meant to replace documentation that comes with the program or to be a comprehensive reference for every feature. Only the commands and options used in the lessons are explained in this book. For comprehensive information about program features and tutorials, please refer to these resources:

Adobe Premiere Elements 12 Help and Support: Point your browser to helpx.adobe.com/premiere-elements.html, where you can find and browse Help and Support content on adobe.com.

Adobe Forums: forums.adobe.com lets you tap into peer-to-peer discussions and questions and answers on Adobe products. forums.adobe.com/community/premiere_elements takes you to the forum for Adobe Premiere Elements.

Adobe TV: tv.adobe.com is an online video resource for expert instruction and inspiration about Adobe products, including a How To channel to get you started with your product.

Resources for educators: www.adobe.com/education.edu.html offers a treasure trove of information for instructors who teach classes on Adobe software. Find solutions for education at all levels, including free curricula that use an integrated approach to teaching Adobe software and can be used to prepare for the Adobe Certified Associate exams.

Adobe Premiere Elements 12 product home page: www.adobe.com/products/premiere-elements.html

Free trial versions of Adobe Photoshop Elements 12 and Adobe Premiere Elements 12: The trial version of the software is fully functional and offers every feature of the product for you to test-drive. To download your free trial version, browse to www.adobe.com/downloads.html.

1 THE WORLD OF DIGITAL VIDEO

Lesson overview

This lesson describes how you'll use Adobe Premiere Elements 12 to produce movies and introduces you to the key views, windows, tools, and adjustments within the application. If you're new to Adobe Premiere Elements, you'll find this information useful, but even experienced Adobe Premiere Elements users should invest time in reading this lesson, because the interface and workflow have changed from previous versions.

This lesson will introduce the following concepts:

- The Quick and Expert views, and key similarities and differences between them

- The various windows and panels in the Adobe Premiere Elements interface

- The functions in the Action bar

- Key tools in Adobe Premiere Elements

- What's new in Adobe Premiere Elements 12

 This lesson will take approximately 45 minutes. Download the project files for this lesson from the Lesson & Update Files tab on your Account page at www.peachpit.com, and store them on your computer in a convenient location, as described in the Getting Started section of this book. Your Account page is also where you'll find any updates to the chapters or to the lesson files. Look on the Lesson & Update Files tab to access the most current content.

Adobe Premiere Elements in Quick view

How Adobe Premiere Elements fits into video production

● **Note:** If you have not already downloaded the project files for this lesson to your computer from your Account page, make sure to do so now. See "Getting Started" at the beginning of the book.

Video producers are a diverse group, and each member of that group uses Adobe Premiere Elements differently. At a high level, however, all producers use Adobe Premiere Elements to import and organize footage (video, stills, and audio)—whether from a camcorder, digital camera, or other source—and then edit the clips into a cohesive movie. If you have Adobe Premiere Elements and Adobe Photoshop Elements, you have an extraordinarily flexible and well-featured platform for projects combining still images and video.

From a video perspective, basic editing will include trimming away unwanted sections of your source clips, correcting exposure and adjusting color as needed, and then applying transitions and special effects as well as adding titles. On the audio front, perhaps you'll add narration to your productions or a background music track. When your movie is complete, you might create menus for recording to DVD and/or Blu-ray Discs, and then export the movie for sharing with others via disc (such as DVD or Blu-ray) and/or web or file-based output.

Adobe Premiere Elements facilitates your workflow using an interface with two editing views: Quick and Expert. Quick view aggregates basic features that hobbyists use frequently to quickly edit video footage and share it with others. It's a great workspace for dipping your toes in the video editing waters and learning the basics.

Expert view provides advanced features and tools that professionals can use to accomplish intricate video editing tasks. Although the basic look and feel and workflows are very similar between the two views, Expert view contains more editing effects and more functionality.

The view you use will depend on your experience level with Adobe Premiere Elements and the complexity of your projects. For simple projects, even expert users may choose to use Quick view for its streamlined interface. In contrast, there are some functions, like greenscreen and picture-in-picture effects, that can be accomplished only in Expert view.

New in Premiere Elements 12 is a Guided view that you can use to access tutorials that walk you through functions like trimming your videos, adding titles and narrations, and creating a picture-in-picture effect. This book will identify the guided edits available when relevant to the instructional material presented. Enough talking about it; let's start Adobe Premiere Elements, load some video files, and have a look.

The Adobe Premiere Elements workspace

When you launch Adobe Premiere Elements, a Welcome screen appears. From here, you can open the Organizer or the Video Editor. The Organizer is a great place to start many projects, particularly if you've already captured or transferred the source video footage to your hard drive. It offers excellent tagging and search tools, the ability to view all your media in one place irrespective of its actual location on your hard drive, and the ability to easily share and archive your collections of video and still images. If you also own Adobe Photoshop Elements, it will share the same Organizer, so you can access all your content from either Adobe Premiere Elements or Adobe Photoshop Elements. In addition, you can launch a range of activities and workflows from either application within one common content database.

● **Note:** The Welcome screen that you see may be slightly different than this if you haven't run Adobe Premiere Elements before, but the major buttons and operations will be identical.

Let's load some video files to see how starting projects in the Organizer works. Specifically, let's load the video files from the Lesson01 folder that you copied to your hard drive.

1   Start Adobe Premiere Elements, and click the Organizer button (not the Video Editor button) in the Welcome screen. The Organizer opens. If this is the first time you've worked with Adobe Premiere Elements or the Organizer, it will be empty, and you may be asked to identify folders where your media is located. If you've worked with it previously, it will contain content that you've used before.

2   In the Organizer, choose File > Get Photos And Videos > From Files And Folders. The Get Photos And Videos From Files And Folders dialog box opens.

3 Navigate to your Lesson01 folder.

● **Note:** The Organizer can import video footage directly from all camcorders except for tape-based camcorders, like DV and HDV, and analog camcorders. Footage from these devices must be captured before importing the video into the Organizer. For this reason, if your project involves video from DV, HDV, or analog camcorders that you previously haven't captured to your hard drive, you should start your projects by clicking New Projects in the Welcome screen, as described in "Setting up a new project" in Lesson 2. Otherwise, if you're working with footage from any camcorder or digital camera that stores video onto a hard drive, DVD, SD-card based media, or similar nontape-based storage, you can input that footage directly from the Organizer.

4 Select all files.

5 At the bottom right of the Get Photos And Videos From Files And Folders dialog box, click Get Media. The Organizer loads the video into the Browser pane. If this is the first time you've used the Organizer, you may get a status message stating that the only items in the main window are those you just imported. (If the Welcome dialog box reappears at this point, click Cancel to get out of it.) Click OK to close the message; do not click Show All, which displays the entire catalog.

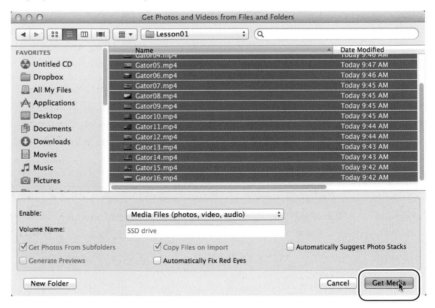

Working in Adobe Organizer

In the Organizer, the main work area is the Browser pane, where you can find, sort, and organize your video, audio, photos, and other media files. You'll learn these operations in Lesson 4; for now, here are a couple of highlights. To make sure your Organizer looks the same as the one I'm working with, do the following:

- In the Organizer menu, choose View > Media Types. Make sure Photos, Video, and Audio are all selected.

- In the Sort By pull-down menu at the top of the Organizer's media browser, make sure Name is selected.

If you click the Tags/Info icon on the lower right, you open the Tags/Information panel, where you can apply tags to your videos to help organize them. You can also right-click any clip in the Browser pane and run the Auto-Analyzer, which applies Smart Tags to the clips. (Smart Tags assist in multiple activities, including creating Instant Movies [Lesson 4], directing Smart Trimming [Lesson 5], and applying SmartFix [Lesson 6].) To run the Auto-Analyzer function, select a clip or clips, right-click, and choose Run Auto-Analyzer.

In addition, if you click Create at the upper right, the Create pull-down menu opens. From this menu you can start a number of types of projects, including InstantMovie and DVD With Menu, as well as a host of photo-related projects. If you click Share to open the Share menu, you can upload video to YouTube or to a mobile phone. And if you click the Editor pull-down menu at the bottom of the Organizer, you can send all selected videos to Adobe Premiere Elements for editing. Let's do that to start your tour of the Adobe Premiere Elements workspace.

1 Press Ctrl+A (Windows) or Command+A (Mac OS) to select all videos currently in the Organizer (only those videos that you just imported should be displayed).

2 In the Tools panel at the bottom of the Organizer, click the triangle next to the Editor icon, and choose Video Editor.

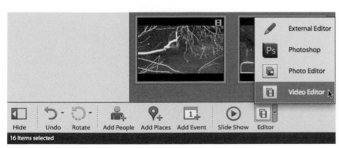

3 If this is the first time you've used this function, you'll see the status message shown below. Click OK to close the message.

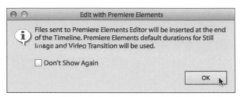

Note: Again, the order of content in your application may be different than that shown onscreen. Don't worry; it doesn't impact the exercise in any way.

4 On the top bar over the Monitor panel, click the Quick button (if necessary) to enter Quick view. Click anywhere in the timeline, and then press the Backslash (\) key to fit the content over the entire Quick view timeline.

The Adobe Premiere Elements workspace is arranged in two main panels: the Monitor panel and the Timeline panel. Simply stated, you build your project in the Timeline panel and preview your work in the Monitor panel. Let's walk through the key components of the interface and take a quick look at the differences between the Quick and Expert views. Although every project is different and every editor works differently, the order of the next few sections will roughly follow that of a typical project.

If you haven't spotted this already, take a quick look at the middle of the silver bar at the top of the Monitor panel. You'll see three buttons: Quick (Quick), Guided (Guided), and Expert (Expert). Click each button to enter its respective view.

Add Media and Project panels

If you don't start your project in the Organizer, you'll probably start by importing content directly into the project, which you can do in either Quick or Expert view by clicking Add Media at the upper left. In both the Quick and Expert views, you have all the import options shown in Quick view. These include importing videos from the Elements Organizer; from a Flip or AVCHD camera; from a DV camcorder, HDV camcorder, or DVD camcorder; from a computer drive or a webcam; importing photos from a camera or devices; and getting videos, photos, and audio from Files and Folders, which you'll use to retrieve files already existing on your hard drive. (These functions are detailed in Lesson 3.)

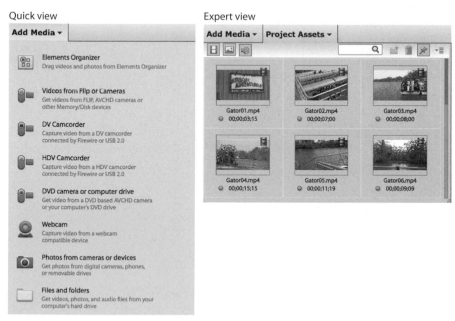

Quick view

Expert view

● **Note:** For Windows users, the Webcam selection will read "Webcam or WDM." WDM stands for WDM-compatible device, which is not available on Mac OS.

In Quick view, all files that you import are immediately inserted into the Quick view timeline, where you can trim unwanted frames, change clip order, and perform other edits. In Expert view, Adobe Premiere Elements stores the files that you import in the Project Assets panel. From there, you can open them in a trim window to remove unwanted frames, and then drag them into the timeline in the desired order, or you can drag them into the timeline and trim them there.

If you want to use a video file or other piece of content twice, in Expert view you can just click to open the Project Assets panel and drag the content back into the timeline. In Quick view, you have to import it again. Or, of course, you could just click into Expert view to make the Project Assets panel available, and then find the content.

This brings up a point that's probably obvious to most readers but worth making anyway: You're not permanently limited in any way by working in Quick view. If you need to perform an edit or access a tool that's available only in Expert view, you can simply click into Expert view. If you generally prefer working in Quick view, you can then click back into Quick view and continue with the project.

Quick view timeline and Expert view timeline

The timeline lets you assemble your media into the desired order and edit clips. It presents all movie components in separate horizontal tracks. Clips earlier in time appear to the left, and clips later in time appear to the right, with clip length on the timeline representing a clip's duration.

There are four tracks in the Quick view timeline: a title track, a single video track, a narration track, and an audio track for background music or other audio files. These four tracks should be sufficient for most projects, including most components of the project that you'll be working on throughout this book.

Quick view

Expert view

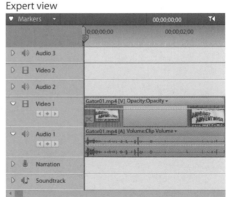

If you need additional tracks for audio, video, or both, switch to Expert view, where you can add dozens of extra tracks. Working in Expert view is also useful in other circumstances, for example, when edits are driven by information shown by the waveform on the audio track (Quick view doesn't show these audio waveforms).

Again, if you perform edits on tracks in Expert view that aren't available in Quick view, like adding audio/video content to tracks above Video 1/Audio 1, that content isn't eliminated if you enter Quick view. Instead, it's preserved and immediately accessible should you reenter Expert view.

Guided view

The Guided view opens up a wizard-based instruction that enables you to perform actual edits on your project. In the prerelease version of Adobe Premiere Elements used to create the projects in this book, there were nine guided edits, the first providing a quick overview of how to edit a project in Adobe Premiere Elements, and the others covering specific functions like trimming, adding transitions, and color correction.

Once you choose a guided edit, you'll see instruction at the upper left side of the workspace, with arrows and highlights pointing you toward the relevant controls. Note that you can choose a guided edit in both Quick and Expert views.

All guided edits are different, but typically you click Next (or Back) to move from step to step. Often, you'll have to perform a function within Adobe Premiere Elements to move to the next step. Work through the Getting Started With Premiere Elements guided edit to learn how guided edits work and for a quick overview of program operation. Feel free to make any changes that you'd like to this project; we won't be working with it any further in this lesson.

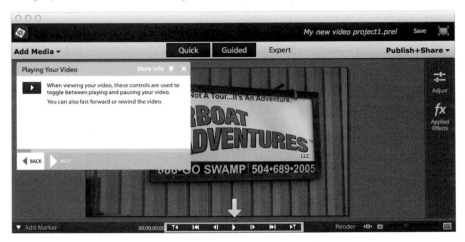

The Monitor panel

The Monitor panel serves multiple purposes. You can navigate to any position in a movie, and preview a section or the entire movie using the VCR-like controls beneath the playback window. Other lessons will detail the Monitor panel's controls and operation; here you can experiment with the playback controls to get a feel for how to use them.

The Monitor panel also offers tools that let you drag one scene onto another to create picture-in-picture effects and add and customize titles. The Monitor panel adjusts its appearance for some editing tasks. For example, when you're creating menus, the Monitor panel switches to become the Disk Layout panel; in title-editing mode, the Monitor panel displays additional tools to create and edit text.

The Adjust and Applied Effects panels

After selecting a clip on the timeline, click the Adjust button (⊞) on the right of the Adobe Premiere Elements window to open the Adjustments panel, which contains the most common adjustments that you'll use in most projects. Then click the double arrow icon (▶▶) at the top right of the panel to close it, or click the Adjust button again. In essence, these adjustments are effects, but because they're so commonly used, they're not stored with the other effects that you must apply manually. Instead, Adobe Premiere Elements applies them via presets identified by simple visuals, which is more efficient. All you have to do is click the Adjust button and make the necessary adjustments, which are detailed in Lesson 6.

When you're working in Quick view, Adobe Premiere Elements provides access to the one-step SmartFix control, as well as Color, Lighting, and Temperature and Tint adjustments for video, and Volume and Balance for audio. In Expert view, these are supplemented by RGB color and Gamma Correction for video and Treble, Bass, and Audio Gain for audio. The other major difference between the two views is that Expert view lets you animate effects, which you accomplish via controls accessed by clicking the Show/Hide keyframe controls icon (◄⏱) in the upper right of the Adjustments panel. You'll learn how to use keyframes in "Working with keyframes" in Lesson 6.

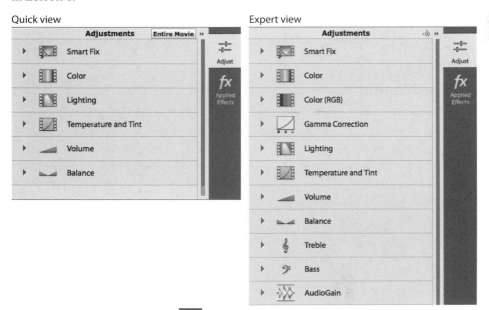

Click the Applied Effects icon (*fx*) beneath the Adjust icon to open the Applied Effects panel, which contains any effects that you've manually applied to the selected clip, plus the very commonly used Motion and Opacity adjustments.

Then click the double arrow icon (▶▶) at the top right of the panel or click the Applied Effects icon again to close it. Note that the Motion effect in particular is one that you'll use in many projects for many different purposes: to create a picture-in-picture, to zoom in or out on a video, or to rotate a video. Remember that it's automatically applied for you and always ready for adjustment in the Applied Effects panel.

Within the Applied Effects panel, the only difference between Expert and Quick views is the ability to keyframe any of the effects in the panel. You can access this capability in Expert view by clicking the Show/Hide keyframe controls icon (◀🕛) at the upper right of the panel.

The Action bar

The Action bar sits at the bottom of the interface, providing access to the Instant Movie panel (⚡ Instant Movie), the Tools panel (✕ Tools), and libraries of content and effects, like transitions (◩ Transitions), titles and text (🔲 Titles & Text), effects (fx Effects), audio (🎵 Audio), and graphics (⛵ Graphics). Click each button to open the respective panel, and then click it again to close the panel. Here's a brief description of each panel:

- **Instant Movie** automatically and quickly steps you through the selection and editing portion of movie creation, as well as adding theme-based effects, titles, transitions, and audio.

- **Tools** contains a range of useful tools that you'll use in many projects and is covered in the next section.

- **Transitions** shows video (both views) and audio transitions (Expert view only) that you can use in your movie by dragging them between two clips on the timeline. In Expert view, you can search for transitions by typing all or part of the name into the search box at the upper right of the panel, browse through all available effects, or filter the panel by type and category. Transitions between clips can be as subtle as a cross-dissolve or quite emphatic, such as a page turn or spinning pinwheel. You'll learn more about transitions in Lesson 7.

- **Titles & Text** shows groups of preformatted title templates you can use in your movie by dragging them onto the title track (Quick view) or any video track (Expert view). In both views, you can browse all available templates or filter the panel by categories. Title templates can include graphic images and placeholder text that you can modify freely, delete from, or add to without affecting the actual templates. You'll learn how to create and customize titles in detail in Lesson 8.

- **Effects** shows video (both views), audio effects (Expert view only), and FilmLooks (both views) that you can use in your movie by dragging them onto any clip in the timeline. In Expert view, you can search for effects by typing all or part of the name into the search box in the upper right of the panel, browse through all available effects, or filter the panel by type and category. Effects in this panel supplement the automatic adjustments available in the Adjust and Applied Effects panels. You can apply video effects to adjust exposure or color problems, add perspective or pixelation, or apply other special effects. Audio effects help you improve the sound quality, add special effects like delay and reverb, and adjust volume or balance. You'll learn about video effects in Lesson 6 and audio effects in Lesson 9.

- **Audio** displays music clips that you can use in your movie by dragging them to the narration or background music track (Quick view) or any audio track (Expert view). You'll learn how to work audio-related features in Adobe Premiere Elements in Lesson 9.

- **Graphics** displays graphics elements that you can drag and drop into the movie track (Quick view) or any video track (Expert view) in your projects. In Quick view, you have access to the 15 commonly used graphics; in Expert view, you have access to dozens more graphics, contained in categories like Animated Objects, Costumes, Baby-oriented clip art, and thought bubbles and similar text-oriented graphics.

Look at the figures on the next page to see the basic differences between Quick view and Expert view discussed in the preceding sections. The figures show the Effects panel, where Quick view offers 20 of the most commonly used effects and FilmLooks; Expert view offers dozens more in well-defined categories. For most productions, the effects and transitions in Quick view are more than adequate. However, if you're scratching your head trying to find the perfect effect to apply to your movie or are searching for a particular effect that you've used in the past, switch over into Expert view.

In addition, when in Expert view, some (but not all) of the panels in the Action bar have search functions accessible by clicking the magnifying lens (🔍) at the upper right of the panel. This search function is not available in Quick view.

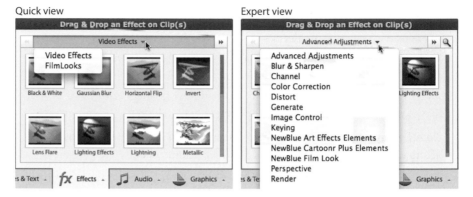

The Tools panel

The Tools panel contains a range of useful tools that you'll use in many projects. To open the panel, click Tools (✕ Tools) in the Action bar at the bottom of the Adobe Premiere Elements window. To close the panel, click the triangle next to the Tools icon (▲) or just click Tools again.

In Quick view, the Tools panel contains the following tools:

- **Adjustments:** For opening the Adjustments panel described earlier in the lesson.

- **Freeze Frame:** For capturing a frame from a video and using it in your project. You'll learn how to use this function in "Exporting a frame of video as a still image" in Lesson 11.

- **Movie Menu:** For adding menus to DVDs, Blu-ray Discs, and web DVDs, a function detailed in Lesson 10.

- **Narration:** For adding narration to your project, a function described in "Adding narration" in Lesson 9.

- **Pan & Zoom:** For adding pan-and-zoom effects to pictures and videos, which you'll learn to use in "Creating a Pan & Zoom effect" in Lesson 6.

- **Smart Mix:** For managing the audio levels of foreground and background audio. This function is detailed in "Adjusting project volume with Smart Mix" in Lesson 9.

- **Smart Trim:** For identifying and trimming out low-quality regions within your clips, which you'll learn about in "Working in Smart Trim mode" in Lesson 5.

- **Time Remapping:** For implementing fine control of fast- and slow-motion effects applied to your clips, which is covered in Lesson 6.

- **Motion Tracking:** For following objects in your footage and attaching graphics to them, covered in Lesson 6.

In Expert view, you also have access to the following tools:

- **Audio Mixer:** Another tool for managing audio levels over multiple tracks, which is detailed in "Working with the Audio Mixer" in Lesson 9.

- **Time Stretch:** Another tool for controlling the speed of your clips, also covered in Lesson 6.

Publish+Share panel

After you're finished editing and are ready to share your movie with the world, click the Publish+Share button (**Publish+Share ▾**) to open the Publish+Share panel. The Publish+Share panel shows buttons for accessing all the different methods for exporting and sharing your movie: Private Web Gallery, Social Websites, Disc, Web DVD, Computer, and Mobile Phones and Players. This panel is identical in Quick and Expert views.

Information and History panels

The Information panel displays information about a selected clip in the My Project panel. Among other things, the Information panel can be helpful in identifying the resolution, frame rate, and duration of a clip.

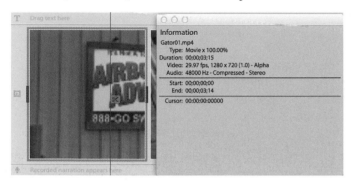

▶ **Tip:** In addition to the History panel, Adobe Premiere Elements supports multiple undos by choosing Edit > Undo or by pressing Ctrl+Z (Windows) or Command+Z (Mac OS). Each time you press Ctrl/Command+Z, you're undoing another step and working back through your edits in order, starting with the most recent. You can redo a step by choosing Edit > Redo or pressing Ctrl+Shift+Z (Windows) or Command+Shift+Z (Mac OS).

1 To open the Informaton panel, choose Window > Info. You can then drag the panel by its title bar to reposition it on the screen, if necessary.

2 Click to select a clip in the Timeline or Project Assets panel. The Information panel displays the clip's name, type, start and end points, duration, video and audio attributes, and location in the timeline, as well as the position of the cursor.

The History panel (Window > History) keeps a running list of every step you take during a project and adds each action to the bottom of that list. To undo an editing step, click it in the History panel. To undo multiple steps, click the earliest step that you'd like to undo; Adobe Premiere Elements will undo all editing steps after that point.

These are the most prominent panels and workspaces within Adobe Premiere Elements. By now, you should be familiar with the general project workflow of Adobe Premiere Elements, the key interface elements and functions, and the major differences between Quick and Expert views.

What's new in Adobe Premiere Elements 12

Let's briefly cover some of the new features in Adobe Premiere Elements 12. You've already seen the most significant one: guided edits. Here are some additional highlights.

Motion Tracking

Motion tracking lets you track an object in the video (like an alligator shown below), and then attach a graphic to that object (in this case, the thought bubble). Apparently, the alligator is having second thoughts about kissing the fair maiden. You'll learn how to apply motion tracking in Lesson 6.

Adjustment Layers

Adjustment layers let you apply a single effect—like a movie look—to multiple clips. For example, in the figure below, the effect is applied to the adjustment layer, which then applies it to all the clips below. It's a great technique for applying effects like color correction to all clips shot in the same location, or to create a common look or feel for your entire movie. You'll learn how to apply and configure adjustment layers in Lesson 6.

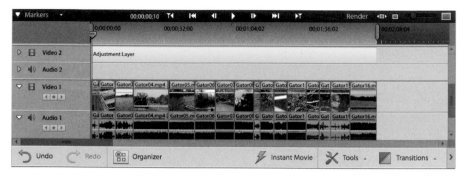

Scores

Scores are background audio tracks that adjust to the length of your production. Like all background music, they are meant to enhance the atmosphere of the video and add a polished touch. Here, you see the score Rockabilly Rumble (with which you'll become intimately familiar as you work through this book) being added to the project.

Integration with Adobe Revel

Adobe Revel™ is a photo and video app for Mac, iPad, and iPhone. Upload to the web-based service once, and you can edit your photos and videos online, and share them to various picture- and video-sharing sites on the Internet. Best of all, all content and edits are shared across all of your devices, so you always have the latest version, no matter which device you're using. We'll cover exporting to Adobe Revel in Lesson 11.

Review questions

1 What are the major differences between Quick and Expert views?

2 What types of projects should you consider starting from the Organizer, and why?

3 What types of effects are in the Adjust panel, and why?

4 Where are Motion adjustments located in the new Adobe Premiere Elements interface?

5 What are guided edits?

Review answers

1 Quick view is a streamlined interface that gives you access to the most commonly used editing options, whereas Expert view provides all the functionality in Adobe Premiere Elements. Quick view shows only four tracks, supplies only the most commonly used transitions and effects, and doesn't offer functionality like keyframing or greenscreen overlays. There's also no Project Assets panel in Quick view, so all the content you import into a project is immediately placed on the Quick view timeline.

2 Any project that doesn't involve capture from tape should start from the Organizer. Starting work in the Organizer provides faster access to tagging and sorting tools and direct access to production activities, like creating an Instant Movie.

3 The Adjust panel contains the most commonly used color, lighting, and temperature and tint adjustments for video, and volume and balance for audio. These effects are automatically placed in the Adjust panel for efficiency's sake; because they're used so frequently, editors don't need to apply them manually.

4 The motion adjustments are in the Applied Effects panel in both Quick and Expert views.

5 Guided edits are wizards within Adobe Premiere Elements that guide the user through certain edits.

2 GETTING READY TO EDIT

Lesson overview

Now that you're familiar with the Adobe Premiere Elements interface, you'll learn how to create a project, set relevant user preferences, and configure the interface to your liking. Note that once you choose a project-settings preset and start editing, you can't change the setting. In some instances you may have to abandon the initial project and start again using a different setting to achieve the results you desire. Invest a little time here to understand how Adobe Premiere Elements works with project settings, so you can get your project done right the first time.

In this lesson, you'll learn to do the following:

- Set your Adobe Premiere Elements startup preferences

- Create a new project

- Choose the optimal settings for your project

- Set preferences for auto save, scratch disks, and the user interface

- Customize window sizes and locations in the workspace

- Restore the workspace to its default configuration

- Enter and work in a dual monitor workspace

 This lesson will take approximately one hour. Download the project files for this lesson from the Lesson & Update Files tab on your Account page at www.peachpit.com, and store them on your computer in a convenient location, as described in the Getting Started section of this book. Your Account page is also where you'll find any updates to the chapters or to the lesson files. Look on the Lesson & Update Files tab to access the most current content.

Customizing Adobe Premiere Elements' interface
in Quick view

Setting startup preferences

● **Note:** If you have not already downloaded the project files for this lesson to your computer from your Account page, make sure to do so now. See "Getting Started" at the beginning of the book.

In preparation for using Adobe Premiere Elements, let's set your preference for what happens when you actually run the program from the Startup menu, Applications folder, or Dock. By default, the Welcome screen appears, which enables you to run either Adobe Premiere Elements or the Adobe Organizer. If you want one program or the other to appear when you start the program, follow this procedure.

1   Launch Adobe Premiere Elements. If it is already open, choose Help > Welcome Screen from the Adobe Premiere Elements main menu to return to the Welcome screen. When the Welcome screen appears, click the Options button at the upper right to open the Options menu.

2   From the On Start Always Launch pull-down menu, choose the desired option. For now, you might want to leave the Welcome Screen open, but later you may choose to run the Video Editor straight away.

3   Click Done to close the Options menu. The next time you run the program, your selected option will launch automatically.

To reverse this decision and open the Welcome screen when you first run the program, choose Help > Welcome Screen in the Adobe Premiere Elements main menu. The Welcome screen appears so you can change your startup preference.

Setting up a new project

Adobe Premiere Elements can work with video from any source, from DV camcorders shooting 4:3 or 16:9 (widescreen) standard-definition (SD) video to the latest AVCHD and Digital Single Lens Reflex (DSLR) cameras. For the best results, you should use a project-settings preset that matches your source footage. Fortunately, Adobe Premiere Elements makes that very simple.

There are (at least) three ways to open Adobe Premiere Elements to a new project:

- Run Adobe Premiere Elements, and choose Video Editor > New Project from the Welcome screen.

- If you've elected to bypass the Welcome screen (as shown earlier) and launch the Video Editor or the Organizer when the application first starts, it opens to a new project.

- With Adobe Premiere Elements open, choose File > New > Project from the main menu (Expert view) or File > New Project (Quick view).

When you choose either of the first two options above, Adobe Premiere Elements deploys the project-settings preset from the last project that you worked on, which may or may not be the optimal setting. Only the third option—when you start a new project from within Adobe Premiere Elements—opens the New Project dialog box shown below, which allows you to choose a project-settings preset and, if desired, force the selected project settings on the project. We'll return to this dialog box after discussing how you can determine optimal project settings and what happens when you first add content to a project.

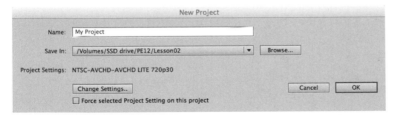

Getting started

Let's load a project to make sure that you're looking at the same content and screens shown in the exercises in this book.

1 Make sure that you have correctly copied the Lesson02 folder from your Account page onto your computer's hard drive. For more information, see "Copying the Classroom in a Book files" in the Getting Started section at the beginning of this book.

2 Launch Adobe Premiere Elements.

3 In the Welcome screen, click Video Editor, select Existing Project, and click the Open folder.

The Open Project dialog box opens.

● **Note:** Depending on the operating system you are running and the options you've chosen, the extension .prel may not be visible. If not, just choose the respective filename for the operating system that you're running, and don't worry about the .prel extension.

4 In the Open Project dialog box, navigate to the Lesson02 folder you downloaded to your hard drive. Select the file Lesson02_Start_Win.prel (Windows) or Lesson02_Start_Mac.prel (Mac OS), and then click Open. If a dialog box appears asking for the location of rendered files, click the Skip Previews button.

Your project file opens.

5 Choose Window > Restore Workspace to ensure that you start the lesson with the default window layout.

6 If you're not already in Expert view, click the button Expert (Expert) at the top of the Project window.

We'll look at the Project window in Expert view in the next section.

Finding the optimal project setting

99% of the time, you won't need the information contained in this section, because Adobe Premiere Elements automatically uses the optimal project settings. But if you want to be able to diagnose and resolve the issues in the unlikely event that you do have a problem, read on.

Briefly, the project settings are the palette within which Adobe Premiere Elements creates your project. More specifically, a project-settings preset defines configuration options for items like video resolution and frame rate. All content added to a project is conformed to that setting. Although you can add files of any configuration to a project using any project settings, Adobe Premiere Elements works most efficiently when the project settings match those of the content you're editing.

Why? Because this way, Adobe Premiere Elements can work with your source footage natively, without having to change it to the configuration of the project settings. As an example, the bulk of the footage in the projects provided for this book has a resolution of 1280x720 and a frame rate of 30 frames per second (fps). This means that it matches the NTSC-AVCHD-AVCHD LITE 720p30 preset you see in the Project settings dialog box on the next page. In essence, when you use this setting, the timeline itself is configured for a resolution of 1280x720 and a frame rate of 30 fps.

What happens if you add footage to the timeline that doesn't conform to that setting? Adobe Premiere Elements has to render that footage to the configuration of the timeline before playing it in the Preview window. Rendering can involve significant CPU resources and can slow down playback. For this reason, you experience the most responsive editing when you work with footage that matches the project settings.

Mismatches between content and project settings can also cause Adobe Premiere Elements to letterbox your footage. Sometimes you may want or need to use letterboxes, but in many instances, the presence of letterboxes indicates that you're using the wrong project settings. As mentioned earlier, because you can't change project settings after you start editing, it's best to diagnose and resolve these issues before you invest substantial time in the project.

Let's spend a bit of time examining the sample project below. It's a simple project that uses the NTSC-AVCHD-AVCHD LITE 720p30 project-settings preset, which is used in all projects in this book. Note that the project is in Expert view, which is necessary to see the detail in the Timeline.

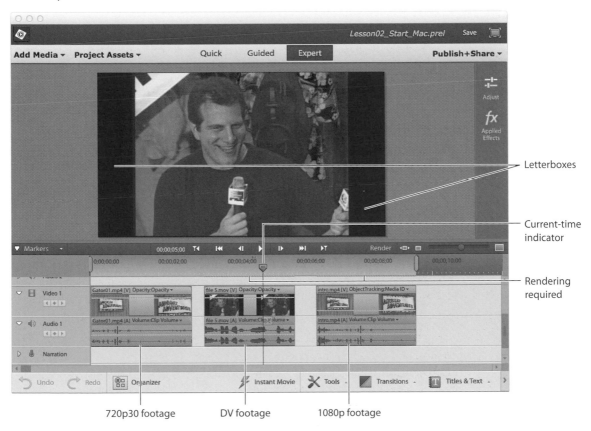

The first video on the timeline is one of the video files you'll be working with throughout the book; the second is a DV file; the third is the original 1920x1080 file shot in AVCHD to produce Gator01.mp4. Note the thin orange lines on the top of the timeline above the second and third clips. These lines tell you that Adobe Premiere Elements has to render the clip before previewing. There is no similar orange line above the first clip, which means that no rendering is required.

Also note that the current-time indicator (CTI), which determines which frame in the project is displayed in the Monitor panel, is over the DV file. As you can see, when the 4:3 DV is displayed in the Monitor panel of the 16:9 720p project, letterboxes appear on the sides. If you move the CTI over either of the other two files, the letterboxes will disappear.

How can you see which project-settings preset Adobe Premiere Elements is currently using? From the Adobe Premiere Elements main menu, choose Edit > Project Settings > General to open the Project Settings dialog box shown below. This dialog box reveals the key configuration options contained in the project-settings preset. Unfortunately, there's no direct reference to the actual project settings used, so you can't tell which project-settings preset resulted in this configuration. Specifically, although this project was created with the NTSC-AVCHD-AVCHD LITE 720p30 format, that fact is not obvious from the information shown in the Project Settings dialog box.

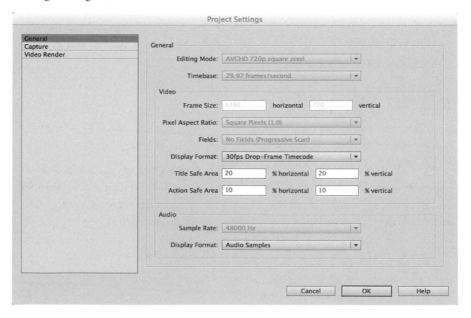

Fortunately, there's a way to identify the current setting that Adobe Premiere Elements is using, described later in this lesson in the section "Identifying the right project setting." In the meantime, let's agree that the optimal project preset would ensure that no orange lines appear above content in the timeline when it's first imported into the project and that no letterboxes appear (unless desired). And as it happens, that's the project-settings preset that Adobe Premiere Elements automatically applies in most instances. To see how that works, read on.

How Adobe Premiere Elements chooses the project setting

Let's return to where we started. No need to follow along in the application; we're discussing theory here. As discussed in Lesson 1, there are (at least) three ways to open Adobe Premiere Elements to a new project:

- Choose Video Editor > New Project from the Welcome screen in Adobe Premiere Elements.

- Bypass the Welcome screen; Adobe Premiere Elements launches a new project automatically.

- Within Adobe Premiere Elements, choose File > New > Project (Expert view) or File > New Project (Quick view).

When you start a new project using either of the first two techniques, Adobe Premiere Elements simply uses the project-settings preset from the previous project. With the third technique, it uses the project-settings preset selected in the New Project dialog box.

However, by default, Adobe Premiere Elements will change the project settings when you import content into the project in these instances:

- If you import only a single clip, Adobe Premiere Elements switches the project settings to the settings of that clip.

- If you import multiple clips that all share the same settings, Adobe Premiere Elements switches the project settings to those matching properties.

- If you import multiple clips with various settings, Adobe Premiere Elements switches the project settings based on the first clip's settings.

We found that this paradigm worked flawlessly when importing disk-based clips or when importing file-based video from DSLRs and AVCHD camcorders. So, if you're working with file-based content from your hard drive or from a camera, you should never have to worry about choosing the right preset as long as the first files that you load in the project are the predominant format used in the project. However, you will run into problems if you first load a file that's not the predominant format.

For example, referring to the project you just opened, if the first file you loaded into the project was the DV file, Adobe Premiere Elements would automatically apply the DV Project Settings preset without asking any questions; it just conforms the setting. If you subsequently

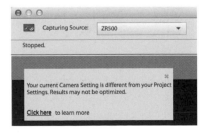

loaded the AVCHD file that you wanted the setting to match, Adobe Premiere Elements would not do so; it would continue to use the DV preset.

There is a way to force Adobe Premiere Elements to use the selected project settings (discussed in the next section), but otherwise, Adobe Premiere Elements will automatically choose the project settings using the rules just described. The only time the program doesn't conform the project settings to the video that you input is when you're capturing from tape-based devices like DV and HDV. In these instances, if the selected preset doesn't match the footage captured from tape, you'll see the error message shown above in the Capture panel.

If you capture the video anyway, you'll have a mismatch between the captured footage and project settings, which means orange lines over the timeline, letterboxes, or both. So if you ever see this error message and want the project settings to conform to the footage you're about to capture, exit the capture screen, start a new project, and choose the project-settings preset that conforms to the tape-based video you're about to import. The next section details how to do this.

In addition, if you ever load your initial files and see letterboxing or the render bar, you'll have to identify the right project setting using the information you'll learn in the section "Identifying the right project setting," and then manually choose your project setting, as you'll learn in the next section.

Manually choosing a project setting

Manually choosing a project-settings preset might be necessary to address the capture issue addressed in the preceding section. Here also, you'll learn how to force Adobe Premiere Elements to use a selected project-settings preset, which might be necessary if the first content you import into a project is different from your main content.

Again, to manually select project settings, you must have Adobe Premiere Elements running; otherwise, you won't see the New Project dialog box.

1 From the main menu, choose File > New > Project (Expert view) or File > New Project (Quick view).

2 Make sure the project settings in the New Project dialog box match those in the image below. If so, proceed to step 4. If not, click the Change Settings button to open the Change Settings dialog box.

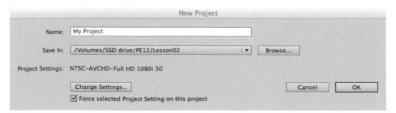

3 In the Change Settings dialog box, click the preset that matches your content. Note that the selected preset isn't the right preset for the provided source footage. For that, use the AVCHD LITE 720p30 preset found in the AVCHD folder [NTSC > AVCHD].

4 After choosing a preset, click OK to close the Change Settings dialog box and return to the New Project dialog box.

● **Note:** For more information on a preset, click the setting; Adobe Premiere Elements will display technical details in the Description field.

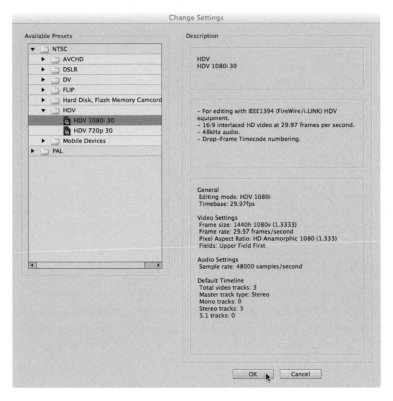

5 Select the Force Selected Project Settings On This Project option at the bottom of the screen to force Adobe Premiere Elements to use the selected preset.

6 Choose a name and storage location for the new project. Then click OK to save the new project file.

After you choose a setting, Adobe Premiere Elements automatically uses the same setting for all future projects until you change it manually or it gets changed automatically by Adobe Premiere Elements. When you do change formats, be on the lookout for rendering lines on the timeline and for letterboxes that may indicate a content/project settings mismatch, particularly when you're capturing from tape.

Identifying the right project setting

Of course, the aforementioned information assumes that you know which are the "right" project settings for your footage. How can you figure this out? There are two ways: the easy way and the hard way.

The easy way is to let Adobe Premiere Elements tell you. To do this, find a video file in the format in which you plan to edit. Start a new project (File > New > Project), import the file (see "Importing content from your hard drive" in Lesson 3), and then save the project (File > Save). Then start a new project (File > New > Project), and note the project settings in the New Project dialog box. That's the preset you should use for future projects with that type of content.

Note that sometimes this preset may be named differently from the content that you're using. For example, you might import DSLR footage and find that, by using this technique, Adobe Premiere Elements used an AVCHD preset. No worries; if you use this technique, you should end up with a preset that won't have to render your content before previewing (so no orange lines and no letterboxes).

What's the hard way? Reviewing your camera's documentation and configuration screens to identify the parameters of your source footage, and then manually determining the right preset from that information. See the next section for more information.

Choosing the correct setting

Adobe Premiere Elements offers dozens of project settings. By far the easiest way to choose the right preset is to make sure that the first clip you import into your new project is in the predominant format, and let Adobe Premiere Elements choose the right project settings. If this doesn't work for you and you need to choose your project settings manually, consider these factors:

- **Source:** Choose the source first. For NTSC (North American) camera sources, Adobe Premiere Elements has presets for AVCHD, DSLR, DV, FLIP, Hard Disk and Flash Memory Camcorders, HDV cameras, and Mobile Devices. (Available PAL sources include all of these as well, except for FLIP and Mobile Devices.) So, again, first find the presets that relate to your source.

- **Resolution:** Next, consider the resolution of the video, which is typically 1080i or 1080p (1920 horizontal, 1080 vertical, interlaced [i] or progressive [p]—see the following figure); 720i or 720p (1280h, 720v); 720h 480v resolution for DV; and sometimes 480p, which is 640h, 480v resolution. Find a preset that matches your source.

  Complicating the resolution factor is the issue of pixel aspect ratio, which affects AVCHD and HDV camcorders as well as DV sources. Specifically, all HDV camcorders that shoot in 1080i or 1080p actually capture video at 1440x1080 resolution and then stretch the video to 1920x1080 during display. For that reason, the HDV 1080i 30 HDV preset shows a frame size of 1440h, 1080v and a pixel aspect ratio of 1.333. This tells Adobe Premiere Elements to stretch the 1440 horizontal resolution by 1.333 to display it correctly on the timeline. Although this may seem confusing at first, don't worry: This distinction never causes any problems, because Adobe Premiere Elements knows that all HDV 1080 video is stored in this manner and handles it appropriately.

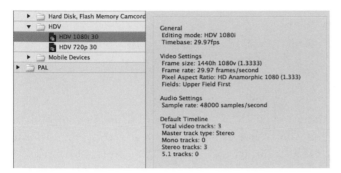

On the other hand, when you're shooting 1080i or 1080p video, all AVCHD camcorders display the video at 1920x1080 resolution. But, again, don't worry: Like HDV, "HD" AVCHD video is stored by the camcorder at a resolution of 1440x1080, and each horizontal pixel is stretched by a factor of 1.33 during display to achieve full resolution. In contrast, "Full HD" AVCHD video is captured at 1920x1080 resolution, so no stretching is required to produce the full 1920x1080 display. If you're shooting in AVCHD, check the specs of your camcorder to determine if you're shooting in Full HD or just HD.

Additionally, all DV video is shot at 720x480 resolution, but 4:3 video has a pixel aspect ratio of .9091, which means that the pixels are shrunk about 10% during display, achieving the 4:3 aspect ratio. Widescreen DV video has a pixel aspect ratio of 1.2121, so the video is stretched during display, achieving the 16:9 aspect ratio. This is seldom confusing, because you'll probably know whether you shot in 4:3 or widescreen, and you can choose the preset accordingly.

• **Progressive or interlaced:** After you identify the right resolution and aspect ratio, you must determine whether the video is interlaced or progressive. Technically, interlaced video presents each frame in two fields—one consisting of the odd lines and the other of the even lines. Progressive video displays all lines in a frame simultaneously with no fields. Older TV content is almost always interlaced, whereas film-based movies are always progressive. Most modern camcorders shoot in both modes (or at least shoot "natively" in one mode and simulate the other mode); check the settings on your camcorder to see if you've shot in progressive or interlaced, and then choose your preset accordingly. As a rule, I usually shoot in interlaced format when shooting for DVD distribution and shoot in progressive for content bound primarily for web or computer viewing.

- **Frames per second:** Most camcorders can shoot at multiple speeds, including 23.976 fps, 24 fps, 29.97 fps, 30 fps, 59.94 fps, and 60 fps. Again, check the settings on your camcorder to see which frame rate you've used, and then choose your preset accordingly.

Once you understand and incorporate all these factors into your preset selection, you should be able to choose the right preset, if it's available. What do you do if you can't find a preset that matches the precise specs that you shot in? Try to find a pre-set from a different format that matches your specs. In particular, there are lots of AVCHD presets in multiple configurations, so if you're shooting in HDV and can't find a matching preset in that category, look in AVCHD.

Load the preset, drag in your content, and if there are no orange rendering lines or letterboxes, you're home free. If there are, choose another preset, and try again.

Working with project preferences

● **Note:** Adjusting these default durations will impact only edits made after the adjustment. For example, if you change the Still Image Default Duration to 120 frames, Adobe Premiere Elements will assign this duration to all still images added to the project thereafter, but won't change the duration of still images already inserted into the project.

For the most part, once you have the right project settings selected, you can jump in and begin editing with Adobe Premiere Elements. However, at some point you may want to adjust program preferences that impact your editing experience. Here we'll walk through the preferences that will prove relevant to most video editors.

1   Choose Edit > Preferences > General (Windows) or Adobe Premiere Elements Editor > Preferences > General (Mac OS) to open the General Preferences panel. You'll find multiple preferences in this panel; most important are the Video and Audio Transition Default Duration and the Still Image Default Duration. The latter controls the duration of all still images added to your project. As a rule, I typically use a 30-frame transition for DVD-based projects, which is one second long for 30fps footage, but I often shorten it for web-based video where one-second transitions can cause obvious artifacts.

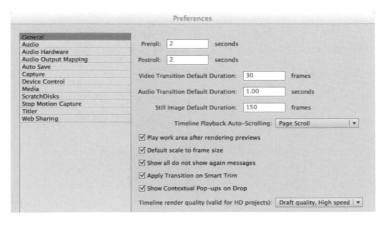

If you plan to use Smart Trim (covered in "Working in Smart Trim Mode" in Lesson 5), you should also decide whether or not to apply transitions to trims made in that mode (the default is to apply them).

2   Click Auto Save on the left to view Auto Save preferences. Although five is typically a sufficient number for Maximum Project Versions, you might consider shortening the 20-minute Auto Save duration if your computer environment has proven unstable.

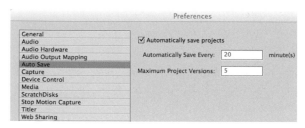

3   Click ScratchDisks. The ScratchDisks preferences identify the folders used to store audio and video clips that Adobe Premiere Elements creates while producing your project. This includes clips captured from your camcorder, video and audio previews, and media encoded for recording onto DVD or Blu-ray Disc. By default, Adobe Premiere Elements stores most of this content in the same folder as the project file. As a result, when you're done with a project, you can delete the project folder, if desired, and reclaim the disk space. The one exception is the media cache, which is stored in a centralized location.

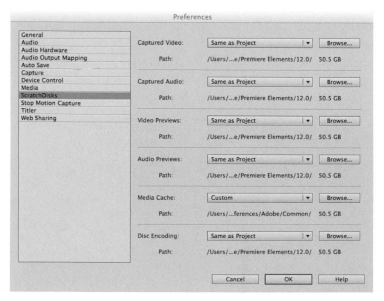

4 Click Media to manage the media cache database. According to Adobe Premiere Elements Help, the media cache contains files that the program creates "to improve performance when reading media files." Files in the media cache accumulate quickly, and because there is no mechanism to automatically delete them, they can quickly consume gigabytes of disk space. To manually delete these files, click the Clean Now button in the Media Preferences dialog box. A good time to do this is just after you finish a large project; if you remove these files while working on a project, it could slow performance until Adobe Premiere Elements re-creates them. Otherwise, you can limit the cache size via the Set Media Cache Size slider, or elect to delete the entire database monthly by clicking the Automatically Clean Once a Month checkbox.

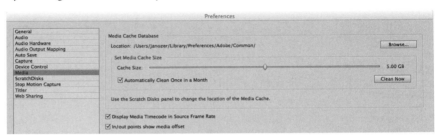

5 When you're ready, click OK on the bottom right to close the Preferences dialog box.

The preceding preferences are the most critical to consider before starting your first project. With these configured, let's explore other options for customizing your workspace.

Better saved than sorry

With Auto Save enabled, Adobe Premiere Elements automatically saves a copy of your project at the specified duration, which you can customize. You can also change the number of separate projects that Adobe Premiere Elements saves.

Adobe Premiere Elements saves all Auto Save files in a separate subfolder titled Premiere Elements Auto-Save, which is located in the folder containing your current project file.

It's good practice to manually save your project periodically during editing to preserve your work in the event of a power outage or other random crash. Should a crash occur, you may be able to recover some of the editing that you've done subsequent to your last manual save by loading the most recent project automatically saved by Adobe Premiere Elements.

You load these projects just like any other project: Choose File > Open Project, navigate to the Adobe Premiere Elements Auto Save folder, and select the newest project file.

Customizing the workspace

If you don't have a project open in Adobe Premiere Elements, go ahead and reopen the Lesson02 project file as a visual aid while we talk about "having it your way." As you can see, the default Adobe Premiere Elements application is contained in a single window, with movable panels and windows so you can customize the interface to your liking. What you see in the figure below is shown in Quick view, so click the Quick button (Quick) if necessary to change over.

In both Quick and Expert views, the interface has two major permanent components: the Monitor panel and the Timeline panel. Click the icon or button to open the panels on the left, right, and bottom, and then click them again to close them.

1   With Adobe Premiere Elements open, notice the double-headed arrow on the very bottom right of the application. You can click and drag this handle to increase and decrease the height and/or width of the application window.

2   To adjust the respective size of the Monitor panel and Timeline panel, hover your pointer over the dividing line between the two components until it changes to a two-headed arrow, and then drag it up or down in the desired direction.

3   To adjust the respective size of the Monitor panel and the Adjust or Applied Effects panel, hover your pointer over the dividing line between the two panels until it changes to a two-headed arrow, and then drag it to the left or right in the desired direction.

4   To reset the interface to its default layout, choose Window > Restore Workspace. Notice how everything snaps back to its original position.

Configuring your dual monitor workspace

If you're running Adobe Premiere Elements on a computer with two monitors, you can detach the Monitor panel and Timeline panel, and run them on separate monitors. Here's the procedure.

1   In Expert view, choose Window > Dual Monitor Workspace. Adobe Premiere Elements separates the Monitor panel and the Timeline panel into two separate windows.

2   Drag each window onto a monitor, and drag the edges to resize as desired.

3   Choose Window > Restore Workspace to return to the default workspace layout.

Review questions

1 What's the most important factor to consider when you're choosing a project-settings preset?

2 Why is it so important to choose the right project-settings preset at the start of the project?

3 How can you tell if your project settings don't match your content?

4 What is Auto Save, and where do you adjust the Auto Save defaults in Adobe Premiere Elements?

5 What is the media cache, and why is it important?

6 What command do you use for restoring your workspace to the default panel configuration?

Review answers

1 Proper settings are the most important factor. Choose a setting that matches the primary video that you will use in the project. For example, if you're shooting in 720p30 AVCHD, you should use the 720p30 LITE AVCHD project-settings preset.

2 It's critical to choose the right setting when starting a project because, unlike most Adobe Premiere Elements configuration items, you can't change the project settings after you create the project. In some instances, you may have to start the project over, using the correct setting to produce optimal results.

3 Your project settings don't match your content when there are orange rendering lines above the content when it's immediately loaded into the program and/or when there is letterboxing.

4 The Auto Save function in Adobe Premiere Elements automatically saves a copy of the project file at specified intervals, guarding against loss of work due to power outages or other random crashes. You can adjust the Auto Save defaults in the Preferences panel.

5 The media cache is where Adobe Premiere Elements creates and stores files that help improve preview and other aspects of program performance. It's important because the media cache is in one centralized location and can grow quite large over time. You can delete the media cache in the Media tab of the Preferences panel.

6 Choose Window > Restore Workspace.

3 VIDEO CAPTURE AND IMPORT

Lesson overview

This lesson describes how to capture and import video from your camcorder and other devices for editing in Adobe Premiere Elements, and introduces the following key concepts:

* Using the Video Importer to import video from a DSLR or smartphone, an AVCHD or DVD camcorder, or a non-copy-protected DVD

* Connecting a camcorder to your PC

* Capturing video from a DV/HDV camcorder

* Importing audio, video, or still images from your hard drive into an Adobe Premiere Elements project

There are several differences between the capture and import operations in Quick and Expert views. Most notable is that when you're adding media in Quick view, the new media is inserted directly into the Quick view timeline. When you're adding media in Expert view, the media is inserted into the Project Assets panel unless you opt to add the imported media to the timeline. You'll learn about other differences in the relevant sections.

This lesson will take approximately one hour. Download the project files for this lesson from the Lesson & Update Files tab on your Account page at www.peachpit.com, and store them on your computer in a convenient location, as described in the Getting Started section of this book. Your Account page is also where you'll find any updates to the chapters or to the lesson files. Look on the Lesson & Update Files tab to access the most current content.

Capturing video from a Canon Vixia camcorder

Capturing video with Adobe Premiere Elements

● **Note:** If you have not already downloaded the project files for this lesson to your computer from your Account page, make sure to do so now. See "Getting Started" at the beginning of the book.

Adobe Premiere Elements users begin their projects using video shot with a large and ever-increasing range of devices. As of this writing, the most common sources are an AVCHD, DV, or HDV camcorder; video captured with a digital still camera or DSLR camera; video taken with a smartphone; or even video imported from a previously created DVD.

● **Note:** Whatever the source, Adobe Premiere Elements includes all the tools necessary to capture or import your footage so you can begin producing movies. Although the specific technique will vary depending on the source, Adobe Premiere Elements guides your efforts with device-specific interfaces. All you have to do is connect the device to your computer as described in this lesson, and then choose the appropriate icon from the Add Media panel.

Adobe Premiere Elements has two basic interfaces for capturing or importing video. After a quick overview of these interfaces, this lesson will detail how to capture video from a DSLR AVCHD camcorder, an iPhone, or any other device that stores video on a hard drive, on CompactFlash media (such as an SD card), or on optical media. Then we'll discuss how to capture video from a tape-based camcorder. All the concepts in this section and the specific Adobe Premiere Elements features that support them are described in more detail in the Adobe Premiere Elements User Guide.

● **Note:** Adobe Premiere Elements lets you add video, audio, graphics, and still images to your project from numerous sources. In addition to capturing footage, you can import image, video, and audio files stored on your computer's hard drive, card readers, mobile phones, DVDs, Blu-ray Discs, CDs, digital cameras, other devices, or the Internet.

Capture interfaces

When you shoot video, it's stored locally on your camcorder, whether on tape, SD media, a hard drive, or even an optical disc such as a DVD. Before you can edit your movie in Adobe Premiere Elements, you must transfer these clips to a local hard drive. In addition to capturing or importing video from a device, you may have existing content on your hard drive to import into a project.

Tape and live capture vs. clip-based import

Adobe Premiere Elements provides three interfaces for accomplishing captures and imports. If you're importing video clips from a DSLR, smartphone, AVCHD camcorder, or optical media, you'll use the Video Importer. In the example below, you'll see three sources connected to the computer: the SD card from a Canon DSLR, a Panasonic AG-HMC150 AVCHD camcorder, and an iPhone. You use the same interface to capture from all three sources. Again, to open the appropriate interface, just connect your device and click the appropriate icon in the Add Media panel; Adobe Premiere Elements will do the rest.

If you're capturing video footage from a tape-based camcorder such as a DV or HDV model, or live from a webcam, you'll use the Capture panel, as shown below.

For audio, video, or still image files already on your computer's hard drive, click the Files And Folders icon in the Add Media panel, navigate to the files, and select them as you normally would. Details concerning this procedure are at the end of this lesson.

Using the Video Importer

As mentioned above, you'll use the Adobe Premiere Elements Video Importer to import video clips from AVCHD and DVD-based camcorders, smartphones, and DSLR and other digital cameras that also capture video. You'll also use the Video Importer to import videos from non-copy-protected DVDs. In essence, if the video is stored on a hard drive, SD card, optical disc, or other storage media other than tape, you'll import it with the Video Importer.

In this exercise, you'll use the Video Importer to (what else?) import video from an SD card containing footage from a DSLR camera. Although some DSLR cameras and other devices let you capture footage directly from the camera, a good rule of thumb

Note: I use an inexpensive card reader from Panasonic, although any card reader should do.

is that if the video is stored on an SD card, remove the SD card from the device and capture directly from that. It's consistently, necessarily faster, safer, and simpler.

If you don't have a DSLR camera, you can follow along using video captured on an AVCHD camcorder or other digital still camera, a smartphone, or even a non-encrypted DVD, such as one that you've previously produced with Adobe Premiere Elements. Note that Adobe Premiere Elements will not import video from DVDs that are encrypted, such as most Hollywood DVD titles.

Note: If you're capturing from a device rather than an SD card reader, the connection procedure will vary by device: Some AVCHD camcorders require you to set the camcorder to PC mode before connecting the USB 2.0 cable; others, the reverse. Check the documentation that came with your camcorder for additional details.

1   Connect your video source (or SD card recorded therein) to your computer via the USB 2.0 or 3.0 port, or insert the SD card directly into the SD card slot in your computer if it has one available.

2   If you're capturing from a camcorder, turn on the camcorder, and set it to PC mode, or whichever mode is used to transfer video from the camcorder to your computer.

3   Launch Adobe Premiere Elements. Click New Project in the Welcome screen to start a new project. If Adobe Premiere Elements is already running, choose File > New Project, save your current project if desired, choose a project name, and then click OK to save the new project.

Note: Adobe Premiere Elements will conform your project setting to the first video imported into the project, so you don't need to worry about choosing the correct setting in the New Project dialog box. If you want your project setting to be different from the video that you're importing, choose File > New Project to open the New Project dialog box, click the Change Settings button (if necessary) to choose the desired setting, and select the Force Selected Project Setting On This Project option. Then click OK to open the new project.

4   In the upper left of the Adobe Premiere Elements window, click Add Media (**Add Media ▾**) to open the Add Media panel.

5 In the Add Media panel, click Videos From Flip Or Cameras (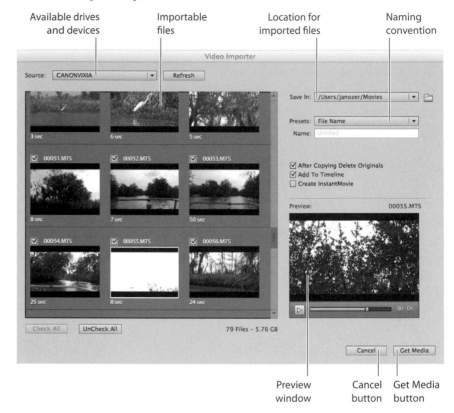).

The Video Importer opens.

● **Note:** What you're seeing here shows Expert view. In Quick view, the Add To Timeline option won't be available, because all files are added to the Timeline automatically.

Available drives and devices · Importable files · Location for imported files · Naming convention

Preview window · Cancel button · Get Media button

6 For Source, choose the drive or device from the pull-down menu.

After you choose the drive or device, Adobe Premiere Elements populates the Video Importer with thumbnails of all available video files.

7 Double-click a video file to preview it. Adobe Premiere Elements conforms the audio and loads it in the preview window on the lower right. Click the Play/ Pause button to play the file.

8 To specify a location for the saved files, do one of the following:

- To save files to the default location—the location where you previously stored files captured by the Video Importer—leave the location unchanged.

- To specify a new location for saving the files, click the folder icon to open the Browse For Folder window (Windows) or Open dialog box (Mac OS), and choose a folder, or click Make New Folder (Windows) or New Folder (Mac OS) to create a new folder.

9 In the Presets pull-down menu, choose one of four naming options:

- **File Name** uses the original filenames created by the camera.

- **Folder Name-Number** names each file with the folder name plus an incremental number.

- **Date-File Name** names each file with the date plus the original filename.

- **Custom Name-Number** adds a custom name and incremental number to each file.

10 Type the desired name into the Name text field. For example, if your project is about a boat ride in the bayou, like the project you'll be starting in Lesson 4, you could name your files Gator01, Gator02, and so on.

11 In the thumbnail area, select individual files to add to the Media panel. (By default, all files are selected.) Only selected files are imported. Click a check box to deselect it.

Note the Check All and UnCheck All buttons at the bottom of the window, which often can speed your selection.

12 Note the options to the right of the thumbnail area:

- To delete files from your camera or SD card after copying, select After Copying Delete Originals.

- To add imported files directly to the timeline, select Add To Timeline. Note that this option won't be available when you're importing in Quick view, where all imported files are added to the timeline automatically.

- To create an InstantMovie from the imported footage, select Create InstantMovie. You will learn about InstantMovies in Lesson 4.

13 Click Get Media to transfer the media to the destination location—typically, your hard drive. You can click Cancel in the Copying Files dialog box at any time to stop the process.

● **Note:** If you've already imported the selected files to your hard drive and you try to import one or more of these files again, Adobe Premiere Elements will display an error message. If these files are not currently imported into the project, you can add them by choosing Add Media > Files And Folders (see "Importing content from your hard drive" at the end of this lesson).

Capturing stop-motion and time-lapse video

Using stop-motion and time-lapse video, you can make inanimate objects appear to move (stop motion) or show slow-moving objects move and change in seconds (time lapse). In these modes, you capture single video frames at widely spaced time intervals for later playback at normal frame rates. For more information on either of these functions, see Adobe Premiere Elements Help.

Converting analog video to digital video

Before DV camcorders were widely manufactured, most people used camcorders that recorded analog video onto VHS, 8mm, or other analog tape formats. To use video from analog sources in your Adobe Premiere Elements project, you must first convert (digitize) the footage to digital data, because the program accepts direct input only from digital sources. To digitize your footage, you can use either your digital camcorder or a standalone device that performs analog-to-digital (AV DV) conversion.

You can perform a successful conversion using the following methods:

- **Output a digital signal.** Use your digital camcorder to output a digital signal from an analog input. Connect the analog source to input jacks on your digital camcorder, and connect the digital camcorder to the computer. Not all digital camcorders support this method. See your camcorder documentation for more information.

- **Record analog footage.** Use your digital camcorder to record footage from your analog source. Connect your analog source's output to the analog inputs on your digital camcorder. Then record your analog footage to digital tape. When you are finished recording, Adobe Premiere Elements can then capture the footage from the digital camcorder. This is a very common procedure. See your camcorder documentation for more details on recording from analog sources.

- **Capture sound.** Use your computer's sound card, if it has a microphone (mic) input, to capture sound from a microphone.

- **Bridge the connection.** Use an AV DV converter to bridge the connection between your analog source and the computer. Connect the analog source to the converter and connect the converter to your computer. Adobe Premiere Elements then captures the digitized footage. AV DV converters are available in many large consumer electronics stores.

Note: If you capture using an AV DV converter, you might need to capture without using device control.

—From Adobe Premiere Elements Help

Capturing tape-based or live video

If you're capturing from a DV or HDV camcorder or a webcam, you'll use the Capture panel, which you access by clicking Add Media (**Add Media ▾**) to open the Add Media panel and then clicking DV Camcorder (█▬), HDV Camcorder (█▬), or Webcam or WDM (the latter Windows only) (◉) to match your source input. This exercise discusses some preliminary concepts relating to these devices, and then details the procedure.

Connecting your device

The best way to capture DV or HDV video is to connect the camcorder to a computer via an IEEE 1394 port. Adobe Premiere Elements supports a wide range of DV devices and capture cards, making it easy to capture DV source files. What can get complicated is the range of connection types, primarily on your computer. In virtually all instances, you'll see one of the three types shown below.

● **Note:** Although it's extremely rare, sometimes when connecting your computer to your camcorder via an IEEE 1394 connector, an electrical charge from the computer can damage the camcorder. To minimize this risk, always turn off both devices before capture, connect the IEEE 1394 cable, turn on your computer, and then turn on the camcorder.

4-pin IEEE 1394 400

6-pin IEEE 1394 400

9-pin IEEE 1394 800

First, some background. The initial IEEE 1394 standard had a maximum speed of 400 megabits per second (Mbps) and was known as IEEE 1394 400. This standard was used for years by Windows and Macintosh computers alike, as well as all DV and HDV camcorders. As shown above left and above middle, IEEE 1394 had two connectors: a 4-pin connector and a 6-pin connector.

Virtually all prosumer camcorders used the 4-pin connector, so any cable used for video acquisition had to have at least one 4-pin connector. Most desktop computers and workstations use 6-pin connectors, and most video producers worked on this class of machine, so the typical cable used

by video producers was a 4-pin to 6-pin cable. Although you can pay $20 or more for such a cable, if you shop wisely, you can find one for under $5.

As notebooks became more powerful, many editors started producing on these as well. In the Windows world, your notebook probably has a 4-pin IEEE 1394 connector; if so, you need a 4-pin to 4-pin IEEE 1394 connector. These are less common, but you can still find them for well under $12 if you shop around.

In 2002 came IEEE 1394 800, which ran at 800Mbps. The target for this standard was primarily computer peripherals, and few, if any, camcorder vendors adopted it. However, in 2009 Apple started using IEEE 1394 800 ports on its Mac computers, which used the 9-pin connector. IEEE 1394 is backward-compatible to slower speeds, so this caused no serious compatibility issues, but traditional 4-pin and 6-pin cables no longer worked.

If you have a Mac with an IEEE 1394 connector, you have two options. You can buy a custom cable with a 9-pin 800 connector on one end and the required 4-pin or 6-pin 400 connector on the other. Or you can buy an adapter like the one shown below, which has a 6-pin 400 connector on one end and a 9-pin 800 connector on the other. These cost less than $5 each, so consider buying more than one; they're about the size of a USB key and are easily misplaced.

Note that in addition to IEEE 1394 ports, some DV and HDV camcorders also have USB 2.0 ports. USB 2.0 is a high-speed transfer protocol similar to IEEE 1394. When present on a DV/HDV camcorder, the USB 2.0 connector is typically used for transferring to the computer only digital still images, rather than tape-based video shot by the camcorder. When both connectors are present, use the IEEE 1394 connector for video capture.

System setup

Before you attempt to transfer video from a DV/HDV camcorder, make sure your system is set up properly for working with digital video. Here are some general guidelines for ensuring that you have a DV-capable system.

- **IEEE 1394 port:** Make sure your computer has an IEEE 1394 port. This port may either be built into your computer or available on a PCI or PC card (often referred to as capture cards) that you install yourself. Many currently manufactured computers include onboard IEEE 1394 cards.

- **High data transfer rate:** As long as your computer was manufactured in the last five years or so, your hard drive should be fast enough to capture the 3.6 megabytes per second required by DV and HDV footage. If you're working with an older computer, check your computer's or hard drive's documentation to confirm that it can sustain storage at this rate.

- **Extra storage:** Consider using a secondary hard drive for extra capacity during capture and production and to enhance capture performance. In general, most internal hard drives should be sufficiently fast for capture and editing. However, external drives that connect via USB 2.0 and IEEE 1394, although excellent for data-backup chores, may be too slow for video capture. If you're looking for an external drive for video production, a technology called eSATA offers the best mix of performance and affordability, but you may have to purchase an internal eSATA adapter for your computer or notebook.

- **Sufficient hard drive space:** Make sure you have sufficient drive space for the captured footage. Five minutes of digital video consumes about 1 gigabyte (GB) of hard drive space. The Capture panel in Adobe Premiere Elements indicates the remaining space on your hard drive. Be certain beforehand that you will have sufficient space for the intended length of video capture.

- **Defragment:** Make sure you periodically defragment your hard drive. Writing to a fragmented disk can cause disruptions in your hard drive's transfer speed, causing you to lose or drop frames as you capture. You can use the defragmentation utility included with Windows or purchase a third-party utility.

Capture options

When you're capturing from tape, options in Quick and Expert views differ, primarily in regard to scene detection. Specifically, you can enable scene detection in Expert view, but not in Quick view.

What is scene detection, and how does it work? During capture, Adobe Premiere Elements can split the captured video into scenes, which makes it much easier to find and edit the desired content. Adobe Premiere Elements can use one of two scene-detection techniques to detect scenes: Timecode-based and Content-based.

Timecode-based scene detection is available only when capturing DV source video. As the name suggests, this technique uses timecodes in the video to break the capture clips into scenes. Specifically, when you record DV, your camcorder automatically records a time/date stamp when you press Stop or Record. During capture, Adobe Premiere Elements can create a new scene each time it detects a new time/date stamp, and creates a separate video file on your hard drive for each scene.

Content-based scene detection, which is your only option for HDV or webcam videos, analyzes the content after capture to identify scene changes. For example, if you shot one scene indoors and the next outdoors, Adobe Premiere Elements would analyze the video frames and detect the new scene.

When detecting scenes using Content-based scene detection, Adobe Premiere Elements stores only one video file on your hard drive, and designates the scenes in the Project Assets panel and Timeline panel. After capture, while scanning the captured video for scene changes, Adobe Premiere Elements displays a status panel describing the operation and apprising you of its progress.

The panel shown at right displays the capture options in Expert view. None of these options appear in Quick view. Unless you're filming one long event, like a ballet or play, I recommend always capturing with scene-detection enabled. When you're working with DV, I recommend using Timecode-based scene detection, because it's faster and more accurate.

In addition, when you're capturing in Quick view, all clips are automatically added to the timeline, so the Capture To Timeline option does not appear. In Expert view, you can select the Capture To Timeline option to achieve the same result.

About timecode

When capturing video, it's important to understand the basics of timecode. Timecode numbers represent the location of a frame in a video clip. Many camcorders record timecode as part of the video signal. The timecode format is based on the number of frames per second (fps) that the camcorder records and the number of frames per second that the video displays on playback. Video has a standard frame rate: either 29.97 fps for NTSC video (the North American and Japanese TV standard) or 25 fps for PAL video (the European TV standard). Timecode describes a frame's location in the format of hours:minutes:seconds:frames. For example, 01;20;15;10 specifies that the displayed frame is located 1 hour, 20 minutes, 15 seconds, and 10 frames into the scene.

—From Adobe Premiere Elements Help

Capturing clips with device control

When you're capturing clips, *device control* refers to the ability to control the operation of a connected video deck or camcorder using controls within Adobe Premiere Elements rather than those on the connected device. This mode of operation is more convenient, because Adobe Premiere Elements offers controls like Next Scene or Shuttle that your camcorder may not offer.

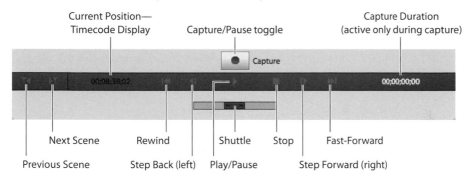

Current Position—
Timecode Display

Capture/Pause toggle

Capture Duration
(active only during capture)

Next Scene   Rewind   Shuttle   Stop   Fast-Forward

Previous Scene   Step Back (left)   Play/Pause   Step Forward (right)

You probably know most of these controls; they're similar to your camcorder or VCR. You may not be familiar with the Shuttle control, which you can drag with your pointer to the left or right to rewind or fast-forward the video. This control is position-sensitive; the farther you drag the shuttle widget from the center, the faster the tape fast-forwards or rewinds. The Previous Scene and Next Scene controls use timecode-based scene detection to advance backward or forward to the previous or next scenes.

Adobe Premiere Elements should be able to establish device control with all DV and HDV camcorders, but it's not available when capturing from webcams, a WDM Device (Windows)/Webcam (Mac OS), or analog camcorders. You can still capture video from these sources without device control, but the capture procedure is slightly different. Procedures for capturing with and without device control are detailed in the following section.

> **Note:** This exercise assumes that you have successfully connected an HDV camera to your computer and that you have footage available to capture. If this is not the case, you can still open the Capture panel to review the interface; however, you will not be able to access all the controls.

Capturing with the Capture panel

With the preceding information in this lesson as a prologue, let's look at the process for capturing video in Adobe Premiere Elements via the Capture panel.

1 Connect the HDV camcorder to your computer via an IEEE 1394 cable.

2 Turn on the camera and set it to playback mode, which may be labeled VTR, VCR, or Play.

Note: If your DV camera is connected but not turned on, the Capture panel will display Capture Device Offline In the status area. Although it is preferable to turn on your camera before launching Adobe Premiere Elements, in most cases turning on your camera at any point will bring it online.

Note: When capturing DV and webcam footage, you will see video in the Preview area of the Capture panel.

3 Launch Adobe Premiere Elements. Click New Project in the Welcome screen to start a new project. If Adobe Premiere Elements is already running, choose File > New Project, save your current project if desired, and then choose a project name and the appropriate preset. Then click OK to save the new project.

4 In the upper left of the Adobe Premiere Elements window, click Add Media (**Add Media ▾**) to open the Add Media panel.

5 In the Add Media panel, select HDV Camcorder ( ) to follow along with this procedure. The Capture panel appears. Note that there will be no preview on your computer when capturing HDV video and that you will have to watch the LCD screen on your camcorder to determine when to stop capture.

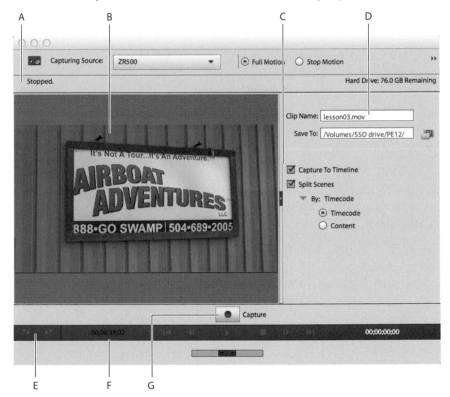

A. **Status area**—Displays status information about your camera.

B. **Preview area**—Displays your current video as played through your camera (DV and webcam only, not HDV).

C. **Capture settings**—Enables you to change the capture settings.

D. **Clip Name**—By default, Adobe Premiere Elements uses the project name to name the AVI or MOV movie clips.

E. **Device controls**—Contains buttons used to directly control your camera.

F. **Current position**—Timecode display. Shows you the current frame of your video, measured in the format of hours; minutes; seconds; frames.

G. **Capture/Pause button**—Starts and stops video/audio capture.

6 In the upper right area of the Capture panel, enter the desired names and locations for the captured files. Note that Adobe Premiere Elements defaults to the project name for Clip Name and uses the folder where you stored your project file for the default Save To location. If desired, change any of the default Capture settings.

● **Note:** If you receive the error message "Recorder Error—frames dropped during capture," or if you're having problems with the device control, it's likely that your hard drive is not keeping up with the transfer of video. Make sure you're capturing your video to the fastest hard drive available, for example an external IEEE 1394 drive rather than a hard drive inside a laptop computer.

● **Note:** When capturing without device control, use the camcorder's playback controls to navigate to a position about 20 seconds before the first scene you want to capture. Click Play, and about 10 seconds before the actual scene appears, click the Capture button (●). Adobe Premiere Elements will start capturing the video, and you should see a red box around the preview screen in the capture window. Capture the desired scenes, and about 10 seconds after the last target frame, click the Pause button (❚❚) to stop capture.

7 At the bottom of the Capture panel, use the navigation controls to navigate to the first scene you'd like to capture.

8 Click the Capture button (●). Adobe Premiere Elements automatically starts playing video on the DV camcorder, captures each scene as an individual movie clip, and adds it to your project.

9 After clicking the Capture button, the button becomes the Pause button (❚❚). To stop capturing video, click the Pause button, or press the Esc key on your keyboard. If enabled, the Auto-Analyze window will appear as Adobe Premiere Elements analyzes the clip and then close. Any clips you have already captured will remain in your project.

10 After you've finished capturing your video, close the Capture panel. If you captured in Quick view, your captured clips appear in the Quick view timeline. If you captured in Expert view, your captured clips appear in the Project Assets panel, and if you enabled Capture To Timeline, Adobe Premiere Elements will also place each clip into your sceneline in sequential order.

● **Note:** If you see the error message shown below, it means that your project setting doesn't conform to the video that you're about to capture. To fix this, choose File > New Project, and then click the Change Settings button to choose the appropriate setting (HDV for HDV footage, or DV for DV footage). Click OK to open the new project.

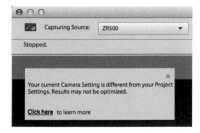

Importing content from your hard drive

Follow this procedure to import audio, video, or still-image content that's already on your hard drive.

1 In the upper left of the Adobe Premiere Elements window, click Add Media (**Add Media ▾**) to open the Add Media panel.

2 In the Add Media panel, select Files And Folders (⬜). The Capture panel appears.

Adobe Premiere Elements opens the Add Media dialog box.

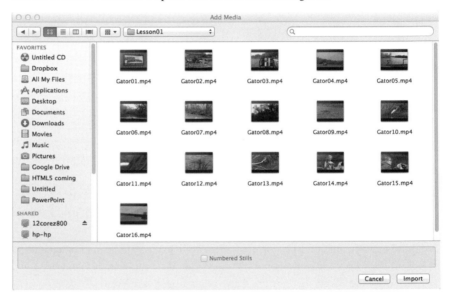

3 To change to a new disk or folder, click the Look In (Windows)/Folder (Mac OS) menu, and navigate to a new location.

4 To display only certain files types in the dialog box, click the Files Of Type pull-down menu (Windows only), and choose the desired file type. The dialog box displays only files of the selected type.

5 To import files, choose them in the dialog box as you normally would, and click Open (Windows)/Import (MacOS).

Files that you import in Quick view are inserted at the end of the timeline. Files inserted in Expert view are added to the Project Assets panel.

Review questions

1 How do you access the Capture panel in Adobe Premiere Elements?

2 Why is having a separate hard drive dedicated to video a good idea?

3 What is scene detection, and how would you turn it on or off if you wanted to?

4 What is the Video Importer, and when would you use it?

5 What is device control?

Review answers

1 Click Get Media from the Organize Workspace, and then click the appropriate capture icon.

2 Video files take up large amounts of space compared to standard office and image files. A hard drive stores the video clips you capture and must be fast enough to store your video frames. And although office-type files tend to be fairly small, they can clutter a hard drive when scattered throughout the available space; the more free, defragmented space you have on a hard drive, the better the performance of real-time video capture will be.

3 Scene detection is the program's ability to detect scene changes in your video (based on timecode or by content) during video capture and save each scene as an individual clip in your project. You can select or deselect Timecode-based or Content-based in the Capture panel menu.

4 The Video Importer is a feature of Adobe Premiere Elements that enables you to import media from AVCHD camcorders, digital still cameras, mobile phones, other portable media devices, and DVDs, whether from a camcorder or PC DVD drive.

5 Device control is the ability of Adobe Premiere Elements to control the basic functions of your digital video camera (such as play, stop, and rewind) through the interface in the Capture panel. It's available on most DV and HDV camcorders.

4 ORGANIZING YOUR CONTENT

Lesson overview

Fast and efficient movie production requires organization before and during the edit. When you're working with content from multiple sources and dates, Adobe Organizer is a very powerful tool for categorizing content and quickly finding video, audio clips, and pictures to use in your projects. In this lesson, you'll learn how to do the following:

- Create places in the Organizer and associate your content with those places

- Use Smart Events to quickly find content from specific dates

- Create events in the Organizer and associate your content with those events

- Rate your clips and find clips based on those ratings

- Create and use keyword tags to find your content

- Use the Auto-Analyzer to split your video into scenes and rate it qualitatively

- Transfer clips from the Organizer to Adobe Premiere Elements

This lesson will take approximately two hours. Download the project files for this lesson from the Lesson & Update Files tab on your Account page at www.peachpit.com and store them on your computer in a convenient location, as described in the Getting Started section of this book. Your Account page is also where you'll find any updates to the chapters or to the lesson files. Look on the Lesson & Update Files tab to access the most current content.

Geotagging content in the Organizer

Getting started

● **Note:** If you have not already downloaded the project files for this lesson to your computer from your Account page, make sure to do so now. See "Getting Started" at the beginning of the book.

Before you start working with the footage, let's review a final version of the movie you'll be creating. Make sure that you have correctly copied the Lesson04 folder from your Account page onto your computer's hard drive. See "Copying the Classroom in a Book files" in the Getting Started section at the beginning of this book.

1 Launch Adobe Premiere Elements. If it is already open, choose Help > Welcome Screen in the Adobe Premiere Elements main menu to return to the Welcome screen.

2 In the Welcome screen, click Video Editor, select Existing Project, and click the Open icon.

3 In the Open Project dialog box, navigate to the Lesson04 folder you copied to your hard drive. Within that folder, select Lesson04_Start_Win.prel (Windows) or Lesson04_Start_Mac.prel (Mac OS), and then click Open. If a dialog box appears asking for the location of rendered files, click the Skip Previews button.

Your project file opens.

4 Choose Window > Restore Workspace to ensure that you start the lesson with the default panel layout.

Viewing the completed movie before you start

To see what you'll be creating in this lesson, take a look at the completed movie. You must be in Expert view to open the Project Assets panel to view the movie; if you are not, click Expert at the top of the Monitor panel (Expert) to enter that view.

1 At the upper left side of the Adobe Premiere Elements window, click the Project Assets button (Project Assets ▾) to open that panel. Locate Lesson04_Movie.mov (which should be the only file), and then double-click it to open the video into the preview window.

2 Click the Play button to watch the video about a boat ride in the bayou, which you'll build in this lesson.

3 When you're finished, close the preview window.

Working in the Project Assets panel

The Project Assets panel contains all the content that you've input into your project, and is available only in Expert view. As with all panels, you click the Project Assets button (**Project Assets ▾**) to open it, and then click the button again to close it.

The Project Assets panel's role is to help you organize and find files using different search methods. Let's load some files into the project so you can work with them in the Project Assets panel.

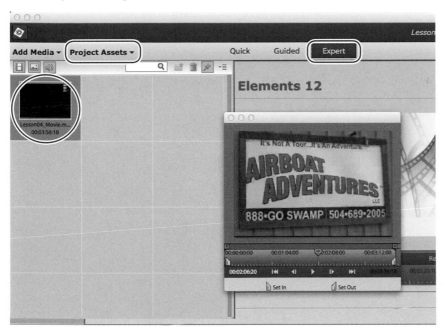

Loading files in the Project Assets panel

Again, if you don't see the Project Assets panel, click Expert at the top of the Monitor panel (**Expert**) to enter that view.

1 Click Add Media (**Add Media ▾**) to open the Add Media panel.

2 Click Files And Folders (▢) to open the Add Media dialog box.

3 Navigate to the Lesson04 folder. While pressing the Ctrl key (Windows) or Command key (Mac OS), select the movie clips Gator01.mp4 to Gator16.mp4, all digital pictures from Picture 1.jpg to Picture 8.jpg, and the single audio clip, narration.wav. Then click Open (Windows) or Import (Mac).

Controls in the Project Assets panel

You can use controls in the Project Assets panel to create titles, black videos, bars and tones, and color mattes. In this section, you'll learn how to use the basic tools in the Project Assets panel to find the desired file.

You can do either of the following in the Project Assets panel to view your files:

- Grab the handle on the extreme lower right of the panel to expand it vertically and horizontally.

- Browse through the entire catalog by using the scroll bar at the right side of Project Assets panel.

Note: Ignore minor differences between this image and what you're seeing onscreen. In particular, the duration of the narration will almost certainly be different. This won't affect the information you'll learn in this lesson or the functionality of the exercises.

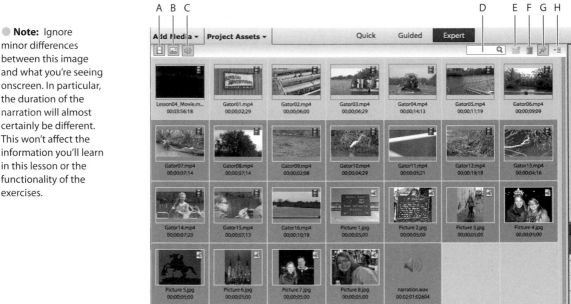

A. Show/Hide Video
B. Show/Hide Still Image
C. Show/Hide Audio
D. Search

E. Go up one folder level
F. Clear
G. Pin view
H. Project Assets menu

Let's work through some of the most common functions of the Project Assets panel.

1 At the upper left of the Project Assets panel, experiment by clicking the Show/Hide Video (🖬), Show/Hide Still Image (🖾), and Show/Hide Audio (🔊) buttons. For example, click the Hide Still Image and Hide Audio buttons so only video files appear in the Project Assets panel. This is a very simple technique for quickly finding the video content that you're looking for.

2 From the Project Assets panel menu, choose View > List View to display the content in this view. Once in List view, click and drag the bottom right corner to expand the window so all the columns are visible. You can sort your content by clicking the column head of any column. The arrow in the column you choose shows whether the data is sorted in ascending or descending order. For example, click the Name column head to see how it sorts the content, and then click the Media Duration column head. The column with the arrow showing is the column currently being used to sort the content.

3 In the Project Assets panel menu, choose New Folder to create a folder to organize your videos. Adobe Premiere Elements creates a folder named Folder 01, with the text highlighted so it's easy to change the name. Type in the word **Video** and press Enter or Return, replacing the default name Folder 01.

4 Select all video files, and drag them into the new folder. Click the triangle next to the Video folder to close it. Now your Project Assets panel is a whole lot tidier. When you're working with large projects with multiple video, still image, and audio files, creating folders is the best strategy for organizing your content and making it easy to find.

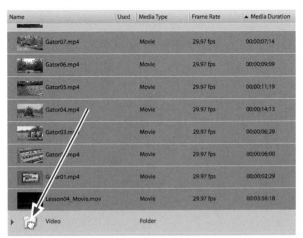

Note: On Windows, you can also create a Universal Counting Leader—a vestigial feature typically used only when writing video back to analog tape.

5 From the Project Assets panel menu, choose New Item to view the new items that you can create from this menu. We'll cover adjustment layers in Lesson 6 and titles in Lesson 8. Bars And Tone is a vestigial concept that is useful for analog projects but has little application for most digital video-based projects. Creating black video and color mattes is useful when you need colored or black backgrounds for titles or other movie elements. When you choose any of these items, Adobe Premiere Elements will open a format-specific dialog box for creating the content and inserting it into the Project Assets panel.

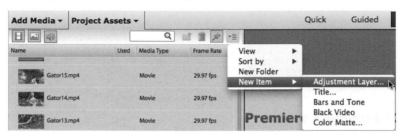

6 Double-click Gator01.mp4 in the Videos folder of the Project Assets panel to open it in the preview window. (If necessary, click and drag the bottom-right corner of the Project Assets panel to make the preview window visible.) The preview window lets you play your content using VCR-like controls before you add it to your project. You can also trim frames from the start and end of a video before adding it to your project. Although you can also trim frames in the timeline, you may prefer to do this in the preview window.

7 Trim a few frames from the clip: In the Preview window, drag the current-time indicator (CTI) to the right until the timecode beneath the video reads 00;00;00;22, which is 22 frames in from the start of the clip and the point at which the zoom-in starts. Note that you can also use the Left and Right Arrow keys on your keyboard for precise positioning of the current-time indicator.

Note: Rather than moving the CTI to the desired location and choosing Set In point or Set Out point, you can simply drag the In point handle or Out point handle to the desired location.

8 Click the Set In icon ( ) to set the In point, or press the letter I on your keyboard. In essence, you've told Adobe Premiere Elements to ignore the first 22 frames when you add the clip to the project, and to start at frame 23. Of course, the edit is *nondestructive*, so you haven't actually deleted any frames from the video file on your disk. You can always undo this later and show the frames that you just trimmed.

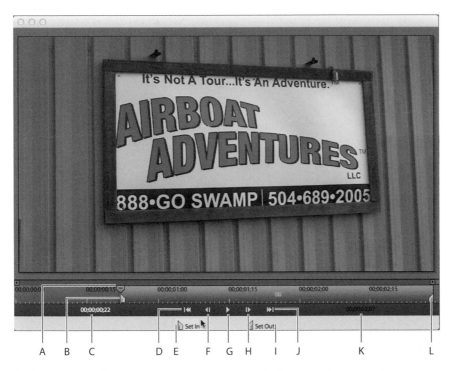

A. Current-time indicator

B. In point handle

C. Current time in movie

D. Rewind

E. Set In point (I)

F. Step Back (Left Arrow key)

G. Play/Pause toggle (spacebar)

H. Step Forward (Right Arrow key)

I. Set Out point (O)

J. Fast-Forward

K. Clip duration

L. Out point handle

9 In the Preview window, drag the current-time indicator to the right until the timecode beneath the video reads around 00;00;02;15, which is where the zoom-in ends. Click the Set Out icon (Set Out) to set the Out point, or press the letter O on your keyboard. You've just set the Out point, essentially trimming out all video frames to the right of that point of the video.

10 Click and drag Gator01.mp4 in the preview window to the start of the Video 1 and Audio 1 tracks on the timeline as shown below, and release. You've just added the trimmed video to the timeline. Click No if Adobe Premiere Elements asks if you want to fix any quality issues in the clip or any other questions.

● **Note:** When you set In and Out points in the preview window, they're automatically applied when you drag the clip into the timeline; they aren't retroactively applied to clips already in the timeline. You'll learn how to trim clips in the timeline in the next lesson.

11 Close the preview window, and click the Project Assets button (Project Assets ▾) to close the Project Assets panel. Make sure that the current-time indicator in the timeline is at the start of the clip, click anywhere in the timeline, and then press the spacebar to play the clip. Note that it starts and ends on the trimmed frames.

Tagging in the Organizer

The Project Assets panel is great for quickly finding clips, but the Organizer is the best tool in Adobe Premiere Elements for serious organization and search-and-retrieval work. You can open the Organizer by clicking the Organizer icon (🖳) in Adobe Premiere Elements Action bar. In this exercise, you'll learn how to perform manual tagging and Smart Tagging in the Organizer, and then how to search for clips using those tags in the Organizer.

Note that the contents of the Organizer will depend upon many circumstances, including which lessons you've performed, whether you've imported content into the Organizer from Photoshop Elements, and other factors. To make your Organizer look like the next figure, take the following steps:

1   On the extreme lower left of the Organizer, click the Show icon (), which reveals the folders on the upper left. (If Show is already selected, you'll see the Hide icon in this location.) Click Folder 4, which opens just the contents from that folder in the Organizer. Make sure that you have the Media tab selected on the top to see what's showing in the figure below.

2   On the extreme lower right of the Organizer, click the Tags/Info icon ( ), which opens the Tags and Information panels on the right of the Organizer's interface.

3   Choose View > Media Types, and make sure Photos, Video, and Audio are all selected.

4   Choose View > Details.

5   Choose View > File Names.

6   In the Sort By menu at the top of the Media browser, choose Name.

People, Places, and Events   Star ratings   Manual tagging with keyword tags

● **Note:** Your screen may not match perfectly what's shown on the page, but the minor differences shouldn't keep you from completing any exercises.

Show/Hide folders toggle   Media Browser   Smart Tagging   Tags/Info toggle

● **Note:** You can play any video file, or view any still image, in the Organizer by double-clicking the video or still image in the browser and then clicking the Play button in the Preview window that appears. Close the window to return to the Media Browser. Still images are displayed in an expanded window in the Media Browser; click Grid (Grid) on the left of the toolbar immediately above the image to return to the Media Browser.

Note: The Adobe Organizer can display all clips in a Timeline view (in Media view, choose View > Timeline) that displays content by date, which can be a convenient way to find some clips. In this view you can click any clumps of sequential clips in the timeline, and they appear in the Media Browser. Of course, you need clips in the Organizer for there to be any clumps, so until you populate the Organizer, this view won't provide that much value.

There are three ways that the Adobe Organizer helps you organize your clips: by categorizing them into People, Places, and Events; by giving them star ratings on a scale from 1 to 5; and by manually tagging them with keywords and via smart tags. We'll give you a quick introduction to each technique, and then you'll learn how to use them all.

In Adobe Premiere Elements 12, the Organizer's interface has been optimized for three views, as shown on the top toolbar: People, Places, and Events. By associating your video clips with one or more of these categories, you can easily find all clips associated with a person, place, or event. We'll demonstrate how to associate your clips with a place or an event, but not a person, primarily because face recognition—a great feature that the Organizer uses to automate the process of people tagging your still images—is not available for video.

The star ratings system allows you to review and rate all your clips on a scale from 1 to 5; you can later search for only those clips that you rated 4 or higher, for example—an easy way to find high-quality clips and/or eliminate poor-quality clips.

Keyword tagging allows you to tag a clip by person, location, event, or other classifications, and includes customizable categories.

When you run the Auto-Analyzer on a clip, Adobe Premiere Elements analyzes the video to detect scenes based on content, and rates the content qualitatively, a process known as Smart Tagging. This allows you to hunt for scenes that contain faces and identify scenes that are out of focus, shaky, underexposed, or overexposed. Using this qualitative data, Adobe Premiere Elements then categorizes all clips as high, medium, or low quality. This serves a valuable triage function that later helps you search for the best clips for your movie. This analysis is also used for features like Smart Trimming and Smart Fix, as discussed in Lesson 6.

For example, if you shot an hour of video on your last vacation, Smart Tagging allows you to identify medium-and-higher quality clips containing faces (presumably family members) and to produce a movie containing only these clips. What would literally take you hours to accomplish manually, Smart Tagging can produce in a few moments.

Using all these tags in any combination, you can hunt for clips to manually add to your projects, or you can create an InstantMovie, which is a professional-looking edited movie complete with titles, soundtrack, effects, and transitions. You'll create an InstantMovie in the last exercise in this lesson.

Tagging clips to Places

The content we're using in this book was shot in two different places: The still images are from New Orleans; the videos from Airboat Adventures in Lafitte, Louisiana.

You'll use this content to create two Places in the Organizer—one for the videos, the other for the still images—and associate some content with each Place. Then, working from the Organizer's Google Maps view, you can click a place and see all clips associated with that place.

1 On the Organizer's top toolbar, click Places (**Places**).

2 On the Organizer's bottom toolbar, click Add Places ().

3 In the Add Places Search field, type **Lafitte Louisiana**, and click Search. Note that if you were typing in a street address, you would type in the address as you would on an envelope. For example, if you shot video at the White House in Washington, DC, you could either type in **The White House** or **1600 Pennsylvania Avenue, NW Washington, DC 20500**.

4 In the Organizer, click Lafitte, LA, USA.

5 Hold down the Ctrl key (Windows) or Command key (Mac OS) and, in the media bar at the top of the Add Places dialog box, click all the videos associated with that location. This should total 17 videos: 16 Gator clips and Lesson4_Movie.mov.

6 Release the Ctrl or Command key, and click the green checkmark. Adobe Premiere Elements will associate the selected content with that place.

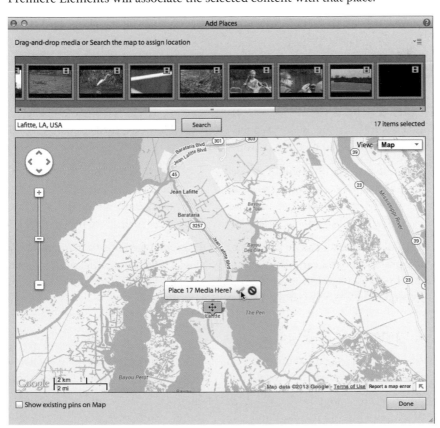

7 At the bottom right of the Add Places dialog box, click Done. The Organizer creates the place.

● **Note:** In addition to the Map view, Places has a List view, which might provide better precision for certain search functions.

8 Repeat the process for the images. Click Add Places again, type **New Orleans** in the Search field, and click the location that the Organizer finds. Hold down the Ctrl key (Windows) or Command key (Mac OS), select all the images, and then click the green checkmark. Click Done when you're finished.

You should now have at least two places identified and content associated with each. Let's see how this will help you find your content for future projects.

In the Organizer's top toolbar, click Media (**Media**) to exit Places view, and then click Places (**Places**) to return to that view. If the map isn't displayed on the right, click the Map icon (🌐) in the lower right corner of the Organizer window.

You may have to adjust the navigational and sizing controls on the upper left of the map, but you should be able to approximate the view shown above. Double-click either icon, and the Organizer will display the content from that location in the Media browser. Single-click the icon, and the Organizer will display all content, with the content from that location highlighted. If you hover your pointer over the blue icon in each video or still image, you'll notice that it's been tagged to the respective places.

Tagging clips to Events

The Organizer has a Smart Events feature that you can use to find content without any tagging on your part. To see this function in action, click Events (**Events**), and then select Smart Events in the Events top toolbar. This shows all content grouped by date in the Media browser, which you can navigate through using the vertical scroll bar on the right. Or you can narrow your search by choosing a year, month, and/or day using the calendar.

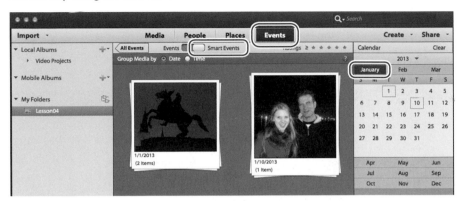

Sometimes, however, you'll want to manually organize clips into Events—perhaps because, like our trip to New Orleans, the event took place over multiple days. Or maybe you shot video and pictures at more than one event on a particular day and need to break them into multiple events, like a wedding ceremony and wedding reception. Here, we'll manually create Events with the Adobe Organizer.

1   Click Events (**Events**) to enter Event view. Make sure Events is selected in the top toolbar, not Smart Events.

2   On the Organizer's bottom toolbar, click Add Event (**Add Event**). The Add New Event dialog box appears on the right.

3   Complete the information in the Add New Event dialog box:

   •   In the Name field, type **Trip to New Orleans**.

   •   Use the calendar controls to input a Start Date of 12/30/2012 and an End Date of 1/12/2013. It's easiest if you choose the year first and then the date.

   •   In the Description field, type **New Year's Celebration in New Orleans**.

4 Assuming that you still have Lesson04 selected in the panel on the left, all content in the Media Browser should relate to this trip. Click anywhere in the media window to select that window, and then press Ctrl+A (Windows) or Command+A (Mac OS) to select all the content in the Media browser, drag it into the window beneath the description, and release your pointer. The Organizer adds this content to the event.

5 At the bottom right of the Add New Event dialog box, click Done. The Organizer creates the event.

To find your content later on, in the Organizer's top toolbar, click Media (**Media**) to exit Events view, and then click Events (**Events**) to return to that view. You should see the Trip to New Orleans event in the Media browser window. If you double-click it, the clips that you associated with the event will appear in the Media Browser. If you hover your pointer over the calendar icon for a particular clip in the Media browser, you'll see the event with which it has been associated.

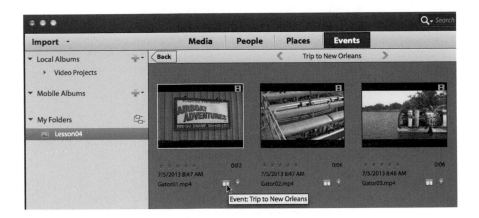

Working with star ratings

As mentioned earlier, star ratings allow you to manually rate your clips on a scale from 1 to 5 (left to right) and then search for clips based on those ratings.

1 Click Media to return to Media view. If you don't see the star ratings for your clips, choose View > Details from the Organizer main menu bar.

2 Hover your pointer over the star ratings beneath any clip, and click the star that corresponds to the desired rating for that clip. Go ahead and rate a few clips. These are all five-star clips as far as I'm concerned, but go ahead and rate some across the board.

3 To change a rating, use the same procedure, and choose a different rating.

4 To delete the star rating, click the last selected star on the right (e.g., the fourth star in a clip rated four stars).

5   To find clips based on their assigned ratings, click the number of target stars in the Ratings bar on the top right, and in the pull-down menu beneath the ratings, choose how to apply the rating. For example, in the figure below, we elected to show all clips with a four-star rating or higher.

6   To stop sorting by star rating and show all clips in the Organizer, delete the star rating on the upper right by clicking the last selected star.

Working with keyword tags

Adobe Premiere Elements includes general categories of keyword tags that you can apply as is or customize with your own categories or subcategories. You can also supplement your entries in the People, Places, and Events tagging structure with manual keywords following this same procedure.

In this exercise, you'll create and apply a custom keyword in the Organizer, and then search for clips based on that keyword. To ensure that you're looking at the same content as appears in this book, make sure you've selected the Lesson04 folder in the My Folders section of the Albums And Folders panel on the left of the Organizer. See the first few steps of the earlier section "Tagging in the Organizer" to accomplish this.

1   On the bottom right of the Organizer, click Tags/Info (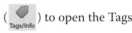) to open the Tags/ Information panel.

2   Below Keywords, click Other.

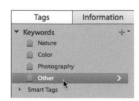

3 Next to Keywords, click the Create New button (),
and choose New Sub-Category.

4 In the Create Sub-Category dialog box, type
Boat Rides in the Sub-Category Name field.
Then click OK.

Adobe Premiere Elements creates the new subcategory.

5 Click the blue tag next to Boat Rides, and drag it onto any of the videos in the
Media browser. In this example, I've already applied the tag to Gator01.mp4 and
Gator02.mp4 and am applying it to Gator03.mp4.

● **Note:** The screen
on your computer may
differ slightly from
what's shown here,
but the differences
shouldn't interfere with
completing the lesson.

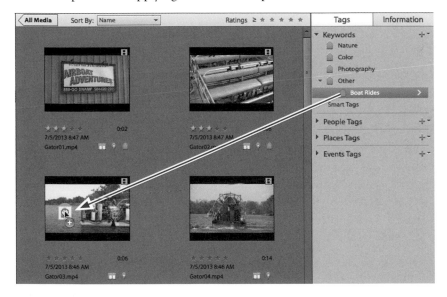

6 To view the clips that you've just tagged, click the greater than icon (>) to the right of Boat Rides, which opens the Tagging Search window that shows Keywords on the upper left and the clips that you just tagged in the Media browser (you may have to click the Tags/Info toggle to expose those fields). This window shows all tags created via keywords as well as the People, Places, and Events that you've set up. You can select any options in any of these categories or combination of categories to include content from these sources in the Media Browser. You can even apply star ratings to further refine your search.

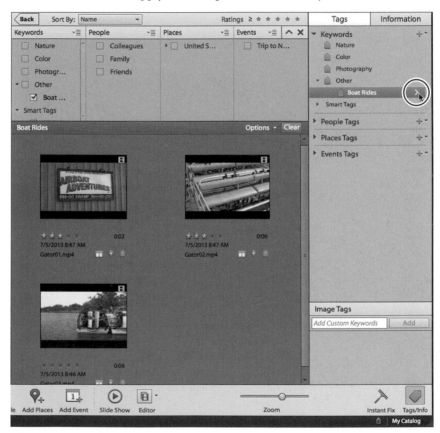

7 In the upper left toolbar in the Tagging Search window, click the Back button (Back) to close that search window.

About the Auto-Analyzer

As mentioned earlier, the Auto-Analyzer evaluates your video clips for content and quality, and is integral to a number of functions, including Smart Tagging, Smart Trimming, and creating InstantMovies (which you'll learn to do later in this lesson). You can run the Auto-Analyzer manually or run it automatically as a background process. In fact, by default, any time your system is running and idle, the Auto-Analyzer will run on clips that you import, so when you're ready to edit, you won't have to wait for the Auto-Analyzer to run.

To control the Auto-Analyzer behavior, in the Organizer, choose Edit > Preferences > Media-Analysis (Windows) or Elements Organizer > Preferences > Media Analysis (Mac OS).

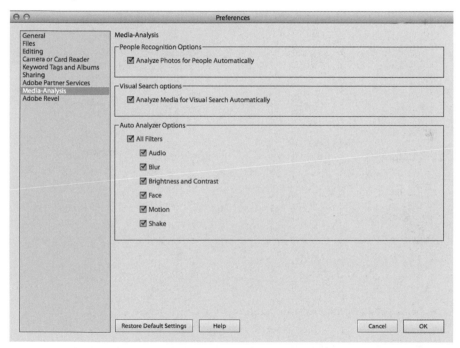

In most instances on most computers, background operation should work just fine. On older, less powerful computers, and those configured with the minimum RAM, background operation may cause a noticeable drag on foreground operations, particularly when you're working with H.264-based, high-definition formats like AVCHD and video shot by DSLRs. If you notice any sluggishness in your foreground operations after importing footage or experience any system instability, try disabling the Auto-Analyzer as a background operation by deselecting Analyze Media For Smart Tags Automatically.

Running the Auto-Analyzer manually

We'll manually run the Auto-Analyzer and apply Smart Tags to the project clips. Again, to ensure that you're looking at the same content that appears in the book, make sure you've selected the Lesson04 folder in the My Folders section of the Albums And Folders panel on the left of the Organizer. See the first few steps of the earlier section "Tagging in the Organizer" to accomplish this.

1 If the Organizer isn't open, click the Organizer icon (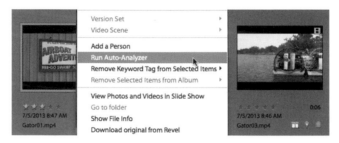) on the Action bar. If it's already open, press Alt+Tab (Windows) or Command+Tab to switch to the Organizer.

2 Press Ctrl+A (Windows) or Command+A (Mac OS) to select all clips, and then right-click and choose Run Auto-Analyzer. This can take a while, so you might want to try one or two clips first.

3 The Organizer starts analyzing the clips and displays a progress bar. The duration of the process will vary by clip length, clip format, and the speed of your computer. After completion, Adobe Premiere Elements will display a status message letting you know that the analysis is complete.

4 In the Organizer, if necessary, press Ctrl+D (Windows) or Command+D (Mac OS) to display file details. A purple tag beneath the clip's thumbnail indicates that Smart Tagging has been applied; hover your pointer over the tag to see which quality-related tags were applied.

5 To remove a tag, right-click the tag in the Organizer, and choose Remove. Repeat as necessary for other tags.

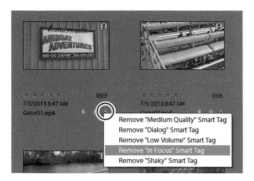

Working with clips after Smart Tagging

Let's take a moment to understand what happens to clips after Smart Tagging has occurred. To review, during Smart Tagging, Adobe Premiere Elements breaks the clip into different scenes based on content changes (as opposed to timecode, like DV files); finds different types of content, such as faces; and rates the quality of each clip based on factors like exposure, focus, and stability.

In the Organizer, you'll know that the clip has been split into multiple scenes if there is a Step Forward icon (■) to the right of the clip. Click that icon, and Adobe Premiere Elements displays all scenes separately in the Organizer, surrounded by a border that's a different shade of gray from the rest of the Organizer. This lets you know that all the scenes are part of a single clip.

You should see separate scenes in the Gator12.mp4 clip, where the Organizer separated sections where the alligator was on land and then in the water. In the Organizer, you can treat each scene as a separate clip—for example, double-clicking it to play it in the preview window. You can consolidate all scenes back into a single frame by clicking the Step Backward icon to the right of the final scene (■).

From the Organizer to Adobe Premiere Elements

After you've collected the clips you want to use in the Organizer, you have several options for transferring them to Adobe Premiere Elements:

- Send them all to Adobe Premiere Elements to start a new project or for insertion at the end of the timeline in an open project. Briefly, you select the desired clips, right-click, and choose Edit With Premiere Elements Editor. Note that you can select complete clips or segments of clips identified by the Auto-Analyzer. The full procedure is documented in "Working in the Organizer" in Lesson 1. This option works well for simple projects, because it adds all content to the timeline quickly.

- Drag the clips into the Project Assets panel. (Remember, you must be in Expert view to see the Project Assets panel.) This option gives you the most flexibility, because you can add the content to the timeline in any order and at any time.

- Create an InstantMovie from the content by selecting it in the Organizer and sending it to Adobe Premiere Elements. This is the option explored in the next exercise.

Creating an InstantMovie

In this exercise, you'll create an InstantMovie from the bayou boatride clips that you tagged previously. Again, an InstantMovie is a professional-looking edited movie complete with titles, soundtrack, effects, and transitions that you create by following a simple wizard.

> ● **Note:** You can create InstantMovies from within Adobe Premiere Elements by adding the desired clips to the timeline in either Quick or Expert view and clicking the Instant Movie button on the Action bar. From there, the procedure is virtually identical to what's described here. When creating an InstantMovie, Adobe Premiere Elements removes all effects, transitions, and titles that you've added to the project, so trim the excess content from your clips, but don't add these elements because they will all be eliminated.

You'll start in the Organizer, using the video clips from the Lesson04 folder. Make sure these clips are the only ones present in the Media browser. In addition, close Adobe Premiere Elements to start with a clean slate in that program. Do not overwrite the file Lesson04_Start_Win.prel (Windows) or Lesson04_Start_Mac.prel (Mac OS): If you want to save your work, save it under a different name.

1   Remove audio and photos from display in the browser: Choose View > Media Types > Photos, and then choose View > Media Types > Audio to remove these media types from the Media browser.

2   Press Ctrl+A (Windows) or Command+A (Mac OS) to select all clips in the Media browser, click the Create button (**Create**) in the upper right corner of the Organizer, and choose InstantMovie ().

Adobe Premiere Elements launches. If the Format Mismatch dialog box opens, click Yes to change the project preset to match the clips.

3   If a Save Project dialog box opens, name the file **Lesson04_InstantMovie.prel**, and save it in the Lesson04 folder.

4   If a dialog box opens asking if you want to fix problems in the clips, click No.

5   In the Choose A Movie Theme dialog box, select Extreme Sports, and click Next. (If this theme is not available, choose another theme.)

● **Note:** The Apply To options become active only when you apply a theme to clips already inserted into the timeline, not when you create an InstantMovie from the Organizer.

6 Customize the theme as desired. Accept the options as is, or do any or all of the following:

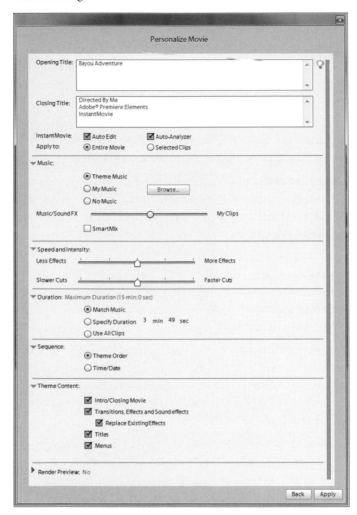

- Customize the opening and closing titles.
- Select the Auto Edit option to have Adobe Premiere Elements analyze your clips and edit them to fit the selected theme. It's recommended you do this; if you don't select Auto Edit, Adobe Premiere Elements uses the clips as is. Also, choose whether or not to apply the Auto-Analyzer to clips that you haven't previously analyzed.

- Click the triangle next to Music to show the Music options. There, select Theme Music to use the background music from the chosen theme, or select No Music. To use your own background music, click My Music, and then click the Browse button to choose the song you want. Then drag the Music/Sound FX slider to the desired setting—to the right to prioritize audio captured with the video clips and to the left to prioritize the selected background music. If you have dialogue in your project that you want to retain (which these clips don't), select the SmartMix option; Adobe Premiere Elements will reduce the volume of the music track when it detects dialogue.

- Click the triangle next to Speed And Intensity to show the Speed And Intensity options. Adjust the Effects and Cuts sliders as desired.

- Click the triangle next to Duration and then choose the desired option. Match Music produces a movie that matches the duration of the selected music and is recommended. Or, you can specify a duration or choose Use All Clips, which uses all clips at their original duration with no background music.

- Click the triangle next to Sequence to show the Sequence options. Choose Theme Order (recommended), which allows Adobe Premiere Elements to use clips as they best match the theme, or Time/Date, which uses the clips in the order in which they were shot.

- Click the triangle next to Theme Content to show the Theme Content options. Choose the content to incorporate into the InstantMovie and whether to replace any existing content with theme-based content. If a content type is grayed out (like the Intro/Closing Movie for the Pan and Zoom theme), it is not included in that theme.

- Click the triangle next to Render Preview, and then click Yes to render a preview of the InstantMovie after completion or No to preview it in real time from the Timeline (recommended).

7 After selecting your options, click Apply to create the InstantMovie and then do the following:

- Click No if asked if you want to select more clips.

- Click Yes if asked whether you want to replace user-applied effects.

- Click No when Adobe Premiere Elements asks if you want to render the movie.

Adobe Premiere Elements creates the InstantMovie and inserts it into the timeline in consolidated form.

8 To separate the InstantMovie into its components to edit them, click to select the new InstantMovie in the timeline, right-click, and choose Break Apart InstantMovie.

9 Use the playback controls in the Monitor panel to preview the InstantMovie. If Adobe Premiere Elements asks if you'd like to render effects before playing the movie, click Yes if you'd like to see a perfect rendition, although this may take a good bit of time, depending on your system. Click No if you have a fast system and/or just want to get a quick idea of how the movie looks.

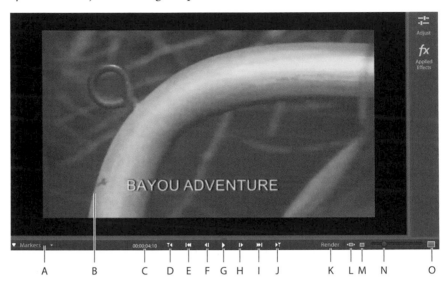

A. Preview area

B. Add Marker

C. Current time

D. Go to Previous Edit Point (Page Up)

E. Rewind

F. Step Back (left)

G. Play/Pause toggle (spacebar)

H. Step Forward (right)

I. Fast-Forward

J. Go to Next Edit Point (Page Down)

K. Render Timeline

L. Fit to Visible Timeline (\)

M. Zoom Out (−)

N. Zoom control

O. Zoom In (=)

Review questions

1   What view must you be in to see the Project Assets panel?

2   What's the difference between the Organizer that ships with Adobe Premiere Elements and the Organizer that ships with Adobe Photoshop Elements?

3   What are the three main content categories in the Organizer?

4   What is Smart Tagging? Are there any situations in which you wouldn't want to apply Smart Tagging?

5   After creating an InstantMovie, how do you break up the movie to edit it further?

Review answers

1   You must be in Expert view. The Project Assets panel does not appear in Quick view.

2   This is a trick question; there is no difference. If you have Adobe Premiere Elements and Adobe Photoshop Elements installed, both programs can insert content into the same shared database and sort through and retrieve data from that database.

3   The main content categories in the Organizer are People, Places, and Events.

4   When you apply Smart Tagging to a clip, Adobe Premiere Elements analyzes the clip to detect scenes based on content; searches for specific content types, like faces; and ranks the quality of your clips. Other than processing time, there's very little downside to applying Smart Tagging. Your video clips will be divided into useful scenes, and you can find high-quality clips much faster than you could manually.

5   Click the clip with your pointer to select it, and then right-click and choose Break Apart InstantMovie.

5 EDITING VIDEO

Lesson overview

In Lesson 4, you learned to organize your video in the Organizer and in the Project Assets panel. In this lesson, you'll learn how to shape that footage into a cohesive video. You'll apply these basic editing techniques:

- Insert, delete, and rearrange clips in Quick view and Expert view

- Trim and split clips in both views

- Create a slide show with transitions

- Use Smart Trim mode to quickly remove lower-quality segments from your videos

Over the course of this lesson, you'll piece together a short video showing an airboat trip through a Louisiana bayou. You'll work with video and audio clips provided for this book.

 This lesson will take approximately two hours. Download the project files for this lesson from the Lesson & Update Files tab on your Account page at www.peachpit.com and store them on your computer in a convenient location, as described in the Getting Started section of this book. Your Account page is also where you'll find any updates to the chapters or to the lesson files. Look on the Lesson & Update Files tab to access the most current content.

Most of the edits will require some trimming of your
imported clips, as shown here in Quick view.

Getting started

● **Note:** If you have not already downloaded the project files for this lesson to your computer from your Account page, make sure to do so now. See "Getting Started" at the beginning of the book.

To begin, launch Adobe Premiere Elements, open the Lesson05 project, and review a final version of the movie you'll be creating. Make sure that you have correctly copied the Lesson05 folder from your Account page onto your computer's hard drive. See "Copying the Classroom in a Book files" in the Getting Started section at the beginning of this book.

1   Launch Adobe Premiere Elements. If it is already open, choose Help > Welcome Screen in the Adobe Premiere Elements menu to return to the Welcome screen.

2   In the Welcome screen, click Video Editor, select Existing Project, and click the Open folder.

3   In the Open Project dialog box, navigate to the Lesson05 folder you copied to your hard drive. Within that folder, select Lesson05_Start_Win.prel (Windows) or Lesson05_Start_Mac.prel (Mac OS), and then click Open. If a dialog box appears asking for the location of rendered files, click the Skip Previews button.

Your project file opens.

4   Choose Window > Restore Workspace to ensure that you start the lesson with the default panel layout.

Watching the guided edit

The first guided edit in Adobe Premiere Elements walks you through the various steps in editing and outputting video in Premiere Elements. Now would be a good time to work through the guided edit. To do so, choose the Editing mode that you'd like to use (either Quick or Expert), and then press the Guided button at the top the Adobe Premiere Elements window.

Choose the first guided edit, Getting Started With Premiere Elements, and work through the various steps. This will introduce you to some of the concepts covered in more detail in this chapter.

Viewing the completed movie before you start

To see what you'll be creating in this lesson, take a look at the completed movie. You must be in Expert view to open the Project Assets panel to view the movie; if you're not, click Expert (Expert) to enter that view.

1   At the upper left side of the Adobe Premiere Elements window, click the Project Assets button (**Project Assets ▾**) to open that panel. Locate the file Lesson05_Movie.mov, and then double-click it to open the video in the preview window.

2   Click the Play button (▶) to watch the video about boating in the bayou that you'll build in this lesson.

3   When you're done, close the preview window.

Working in the Monitor panel

When you open the project for this lesson, you'll see multiple clips in the timeline in either Expert view or Quick view. Regardless of which view you choose, you'll preview your work in the Monitor panel, which you'll explore in this exercise. Although the timeline shows your entire project, the Monitor panel shows one frame of the project, and one frame only. The displayed frame is at the location of the current-time indicator (▼), which is sometimes called the CTI or playhead.

After getting familiar with the tracks in Quick view, you'll explore the functions of the Monitor panel. This lesson starts in Quick view, so click Quick (Quick) at the top of the Adobe Premiere Elements interface (if necessary) to shift into that view. Monitor panel functionality is very similar in both Quick and Expert views, so even if you plan on working in Expert view, you should read this section.

1   Select the first clip in Quick view, and note how the current-time indicator shifts to that frame and the Monitor panel displays that frame. If you click different frames in the first clip, or any clip in the Quick view timeline, the Monitor panel displays this clip. Quick view has four tracks:

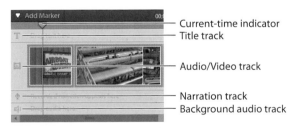

Current-time indicator
Title track

Audio/Video track

Narration track
Background audio track

- **Title:** All text titles go here.

- **Audio/Video:** This single track contains a video file and any audio in that file.

- **Narration:** Recorded narration is inserted on this track. Alternatively, you can drag any audio file to this track.

- **Background audio:** Any audio file can be added to this track.

2 If you moved the current-time indicator, return to the first clip, and click a spot close to the start of the clip. Then click the Play button (▶) in the Monitor panel to begin playback. As the movie is playing, notice that the timecode in the lower left corner of the Monitor panel is advancing. To pause playback, press the spacebar, or once again click the Play button, which becomes the Pause button (⏸) during playback.

A. Add Marker
B. Current-time indicator
C. Preview area
D. Current time (also called timecode)
E. Go to Previous Edit Point (Page Up)
F. Rewind
G. Step back (left)
H. Play/Pause toggle (spacebar)
I. Step forward (right)
J. Fast-forward
K. Go to next edit point (Page Down)
L. Render timeline
M. Fit to visible timeline (\)
N. Zoom out (–)
O. Zoom control
P. Zoom in (=)

3 You can locate a specific frame in your movie by changing your position in time. Place your pointer over the timecode in the lower left corner of the Monitor panel; the Selection tool (↖) changes to a hand with two arrows (☝).

4 Drag the hand with two arrows icon to the right, advancing your video. The pointer will disappear while you're dragging and reappear when you stop and release the mouse button. As long as you keep holding down the mouse button, you can move backward and forward through the video. This is known as *scrubbing* through your video.

5 You can move to a specific point in your movie by entering the time directly in the timecode field. Click the timecode in the lower left corner of the Monitor panel; it changes to an editable text field. Type **915**, and then press Enter (Windows) or Return (Mac OS) to move to a point 9 seconds and 15 frames into the project. Note that you don't have to enter the colons, just the raw numbers.

6 Click the Step Forward button (⏸️) repeatedly to advance your video one frame at a time. Video is simply a series of frames shown at a rate of approximately 30 frames per second. Using the Step Forward (⏸️) or Step Back (⏮️) button enables you to locate moments in time precisely. You also can use the Right and Left Arrow keys on the keyboard to accomplish the same functions.

7 Click the Go To Next Edit Point button (▶️) to jump to the first frame of the next clip. Notice in the timeline that the current-time indicator (🔽) jumps to the beginning of the next clip representation. Click Go To Previous Edit Point button (◀️) to jump to the first frame of the previous clip. Or, you can use the Page Up and Page Down keys on the keyboard to accomplish the same functions.

8 Reposition the current-time indicator (🔽) by clicking and dragging it to the left or to the right.

9 While editing your project, you will spend lots of time zooming in to individual clips for trimming and effect application, and then zooming out to view larger portions of the project. The four controls on the extreme right of the Monitor panel help you accomplish this:

- Click the **Zoom In** button (■) (=) to the right of the Zoom slider (━━━●━) to zoom in to the project. Each video clip becomes larger until it completely fills the timeline. In the diagram on the next page, note the scroll bar that appears beneath the Quick view timeline that you can click and drag to navigate around the project.

- Click the **Fit To Visible Timeline** button (▣) (\) to make all the content in the project fit within the timeline—no scrolling necessary. This is a great way to reset your project after some zoomed-in work.

- Click the **Zoom Out** button (■) (-) to the left of the Zoom slider (━━━●━) to zoom out of the project, making each component smaller.

- Click and drag the **Zoom slider** (━━━●━) (-) to customize the content viewable in the Quick view timeline.

10 To move around the timeline quickly, click and drag the slider bar on the bottom of the timeline in either direction.

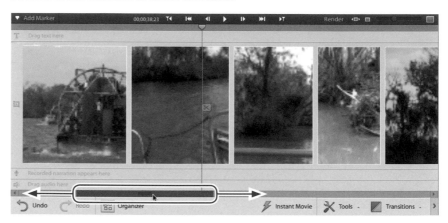

11 Press the Home key on your keyboard to position the current-time indicator at the beginning of the movie. Press the End key to position the current-time indicator at the end of the movie. This is useful when you want to add content to the existing sections of your movie.

Previewing in Adobe Premiere Elements

Adobe Premiere Elements attempts to preview all movies at full frame rate, and typically can do so when you're simply splitting, trimming, and moving clips around. However, once you start to apply effects (as discussed in Lesson 6), the display rate of the preview may slow down. If this occurs, and you need to preview at full frame rate, you can render and play the entire project by clicking the Render button (Render) in the Monitor panel or by pressing Enter (Windows) or Return (Mac OS) on your keyboard, or render a work area using a procedure defined in "Rendering a Work Area" in Lesson 6.

About timecode

Timecode represents the location of the frames in a video. Cameras record timecode onto the video. The timecode is based on the number of frames per second (fps) that the camera records and the number of frames per second that the video displays upon playback. Digital video has a standard frame rate of either 29.97 fps for NTSC video (the North American broadcast video standard) or 25 fps for PAL (the European broadcast video standard). Timecode describes location in the format of hours;minutes;seconds;frames. For example, 01;20;15;10 specifies that the displayed frame is located 1 hour, 20 minutes, 15 seconds, and 10 frames into the scene.

—From Adobe Premiere Elements Help

Editing in Quick view

As mentioned, Adobe Premiere Elements has two editing views: Quick view for basic movie editing and Expert view for more advanced techniques. You can switch between the two views by clicking Quick (Quick) or Expert (Expert) in the bar above the Monitor panel.

Adding clips in Quick view

In Quick view, each clip is a standalone block, which makes it easy to arrange clips into coherent sequences, which is called *storyboard-style* editing. In Quick view, you add clips to the project via controls in the Add Media panel; all content that you add is appended to the end of the project. (You learned these techniques in Lesson 3.) Or, you can drag and drop clips from Windows Explorer (Windows) or Finder (Mac OS). When you drag and drop, you can add a clip to any position in the project. In this exercise, you'll use this second approach.

This project contains 16 video clips, numbered in order from Gator01.mp4 to Gator16.mp4. Gator07.mp4 is not currently in the project, so you'll add that clip in the desired location.

Everyone uses drag and drop a little differently, but here we'll use a popular technique in which you reduce the size of the target window (in this case, Adobe Premiere Elements) and the source window (in either Windows Explorer or the Mac OS Finder), place the target window above the source window with the file you want to add visible in the source window, and then simply drag and drop. You can set up your windows whichever way works for you; the drag-and-drop instructions follow in the exercise.

1 If Adobe Premiere Elements is not already in Quick view, click the Quick view button.

2 Click the Fit To Visible Timeline button (▣) or press the Backslash (\) key so that you're looking at the same setup as is shown below.

3 Press the Home key to move the current-time indicator to the start of the project. Then press the Page Down key or click the Go To Next Edit Point icon in the Monitor panel six times to move to the start of the seventh clip. This is where you want to drag Gator07.mp4. Note that this step isn't absolutely necessary; the current-time indicator doesn't have to be where you add the clip, although it does simplify the operation.

4 In Windows Explorer (Windows) or Finder (Mac OS), navigate to the Lesson05 folder you copied to your hard drive. Within that folder, select Gator07.mp4.

● **Note:** To see the names of the files on the timeline in Quick view, either switch over to Expert view for a moment, or choose Window > Info, which opens the Information window. Then click any clip in the timeline to view the filename and other information about the clip.

5 Drag Gator07.mp4 to the current-time indicator between the sixth and seventh clips in the timeline. Until you release the pointer, Adobe Premiere Elements displays Trim view in the Monitor panel, which shows the last frame of the clip immediately preceding where you're about to drop the file and the first frame of the clip immediately after where you're about to drop the file. This makes it easy to see if you're dropping the clip in the right location; if your Monitor panel shows the same frames as you see below, then you are, so release the clip.

Adobe Premiere Elements adds the clip at the selected location and moves all subsequent clips to the right.

6 Choose File > Save As, and save the project as **Lesson05_working.prel**.

Moving clips in Quick view

Working in Quick view makes it easy to move clips in your movie. If you hover the pointer over the clips at the start of the project, you see that the current order is Gator01.mp4, Gator02.mp4, Gator04.mp4, Gator05.mp4, and Gator03.mp4. You have two options for placing the clips in the proper order: moving Gator03.mp4 two clips to the left or moving Gator04.mp4 and Gator05.mp4 one clip to the right. Let's use both approaches.

1 Hover your pointer over Gator03.mp4 to confirm that it is the fifth clip in the project. Then click to select it, and drag it to the intersection of the second and third clips. Release the mouse when the green vertical line appears at the target location. Note: Trim view in the Monitor panel shows the last frame of the clip immediately preceding where you're about to drop the file and the first frame of the clip immediately after where you're about to drop the file. When you release the pointer, Adobe Premiere Elements inserts the clip at the selected location and moves all subsequent clips to the right.

2 At the bottom left of the window, click Undo (↺ Undo) to undo that operation. Alternatively, you can choose Edit > Undo from the Adobe Premiere Elements menu, or press the old standbys Ctrl+Z (Windows) or Command+Z (Mac OS).

We said we'd use two approaches to moving clips. Now we'll fix the problem the other way.

Note: Although not shown in this exercise, a transition following a scene moves with the scene.

3 Move the third and fourth clips in the project, Gator04.mp4 and Gator05.mp4, one position to the right. To select multiple adjacent clips, press the Shift key and click the clips, release the Shift key, and drag them one position to the right, which is the intersection between Gator03.mp4 and Gator06.mp4. Release the pointer when the vertical line at the back end of the two clips appears at the desired position.

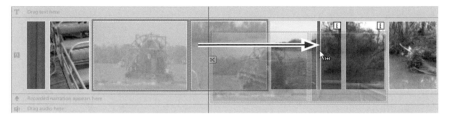

Deleting clips in Quick view

Note: When a clip is deleted from Quick view, any transitions associated with the clip, either before or after, are also deleted.

As your project develops, you may find that you want to delete clips that you've added to your project.

To delete a clip, right-click it in Quick view, and then choose one of the following from the context menu:

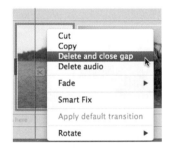

- **Cut** to delete the clip and move all clips following the deleted clip to the left to close the gap. This is the default behavior when deleting clips in Adobe Premiere Elements and is called a *ripple deletion*.

- **Delete And Close Gap** to delete the clip and move all clips following the deleted clip to the left to close the gap.

- **Delete Audio** to delete the audio in the clip but leave the video in place.

Trimming clips in Quick view

In addition to moving clips around, you may also want to shorten your clips by trimming frames from the beginning and end. In this section, you'll accomplish this task.

In editing terminology, the beginning of each clip is called the *In point* and the end of a clip the *Out point*. When you adjust the In and Out points, you don't actually delete frames from the file on your hard drive; you simply point to different frames to start and end playback of that clip on the timeline. When you trim a clip in Adobe Premiere Elements, you are simply changing the In and Out points.

It's a rare project that doesn't have some frames that could use trimming, and this one is no exception. Let's trim three clips: Gator02.mp4, Gator03.mp4, and Gator14.mp4. You'll begin by zooming into the project, making it much easier to see what you're doing.

1 Click the Fit To Visible Timeline icon (⊡) at the lower right of the Monitor panel, or press the Backslash key (\). Then press the Zoom In (▣) icon (or the = key) three times.

2 Drag the current-time indicator to the right edge of Gator02.png, right around 8:20 in the timeline. Then drag the current-time indicator to the end of the clip. Notice how the camera dropped toward the end of the clip? You'll trim that out.

3 Move the current-time indicator back to 8:20.

4 Hover the pointer over the right edge of Gator02.mp4. The pointer will convert to the drag pointer (✛).

5 Click and drag the right edge of Gator02.mp4 to the left until it snaps to the current-time indicator at 00;00;08;20, and then release the mouse button.

You've just trimmed the last few frames from the edge of the clip.

Notice that while you drag the edge, the Monitor panel changes to Trim view, showing the clip you're trimming on the left and the next clip in the timeline on the right. As you drag the right edge to the left, Trim view updates the frame on the left, making it easy to see the edge of the clip that you're trimming.

Also notice the trim icon (▣) that appears on the top right of the clip. This lets you know that the clip has been trimmed.

6 The same kind of camera drop occurred in the next clip, starting at about 00;00;15;10, so move the current-time indicator to 00;00;15;10.

7 Hover the pointer over the right edge of Gator03.mp4. The pointer converts to the drag pointer (⊕).

8 Click and drag the right edge of Gator03.mp4 to the left until it snaps to the current-time indicator at 00;00;15;10, and then release the mouse button.

You've just trimmed the last few frames from the edge of the clip.

9 Grab the slider on the bottom of the timeline, and drag it to the right until Gator14.mp4 appears in full.

This is the clip with the girl in a green shirt, holding the baby alligator in the prescribed manner that's safe for her and won't hurt the baby alligator in any way. Let's trim some frames from the start of the clip.

10 Move the current-time indicator to the point in the clip where the girl is just starting to open her mouth, which should be around 00;01;43;15.

11 Hover the pointer over the left edge of Gator14.mp4. The pointer converts to the drag pointer pointing in the other direction (⊕).

● **Note:** You don't need to place the current-time indicator at the trim point. You can simply click and drag the edge to the new location. Placing the current-time indicator at that location and then snapping to it as demonstrated is just a bit more precise, and helps make sure that you reproduce the results as you see them.

12 Click and drag the left edge of Gator14.mp4 to the right until it snaps to the current-time indicator, and then release the pointer. Adobe Premiere Elements trims the first few frames from the start of Gator14.mp4.

● **Note:** You may not see Trim view on all computers, particularly Mac notebooks. If you don't, make sure you've got the latest graphics card driver for your computer.

13 Drag the current-time indicator slowly to the end of Gator14.mp4. Towards the end, around 1:49:20, is a near perfect specimen of the impatient teenage eye roll, American edition, 2013. Pretty impressive, right? While it's tempting to leave this in for posterity, let's remove it by dragging the current-time indicator to around 00;01;48;00, hovering over the right edge and then clicking and dragging the edge to the left until it snaps to the current-time indicator.

Using the Split Clip tool in Quick view

The Split Clip tool allows you to divide single clips into multiple clips. You can use this tool to split a clip into sections so you can delete one of them, which sometimes is more convenient than trimming. You can also use the tool to split a long clip into separate clips to edit them individually, which is what you'll do in this exercise.

1   Move the current-time indicator to around timecode 00;01;30;00, which should be in the clip Gator12.mp4, one of the few clips with an actual wild alligator in it (apparently, January isn't prime alligator viewing season). As you drag the current-time indicator to the right, you'll notice that the alligator drifts out of view around 00;01;30;26, and then back into view until it submerges later in the shot. Let's split this clip and turn it into two clips that you can edit separately.

2   Position the current-time indicator at 00;01;30;26. You may need to click the Zoom Out button (■) once to see the whole clip in the timeline.

3   Click the file Gator12.mp4 to select it. Clicking the file is important, because if you don't, Adobe Premiere Elements will split all content at that location, which isn't important here, but may not be what you want at other times.

4   Hover the pointer over the scissors icon (■) attached to the current-time indicator until it turns white, and then click the icon, or press Ctrl+K (Windows) or Command+K (Mac). Adobe Premiere Elements splits the clip at that location.

You now have two Gator12.mp4 clips in the timeline.

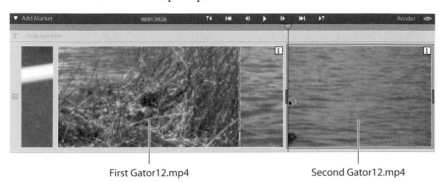

First Gator12.mp4   Second Gator12.mp4

5 When you're finished reviewing the movie, choose File > Save As.

6 In the Save Project dialog box, name the file **Lesson05_working.prel**, and save it in your Lesson05 folder. If the Confirm Save As dialog box appears, click Yes.

Working in Expert view

Although you can perform most basic editing tasks in Quick view, you'll use Expert view for many advanced editing tasks, especially those that involve *layering*, which means having multiple clips in the project at the same location. Before you begin working with Expert view, follow the instructions at the start of this lesson to load Lesson05_Start_Win.prel (Windows) or Lesson05_Start_Mac.prel (Mac OS) if it's not loaded already.

1 To enter Expert view, click the Expert button (Expert) at the top of the Monitor panel.

2 If necessary, click the Collapse-Expand Track triangles on Video 1 and Audio 1 to show the content in those tracks.

● **Note:** For information on zooming in to and out of the timeline and resizing content within the timeline, see "Working in the Monitor panel" earlier in this lesson.

3 If necessary, click the Zoom In button (▣) on the extreme right of the Monitor panel once to approximate what you see here.

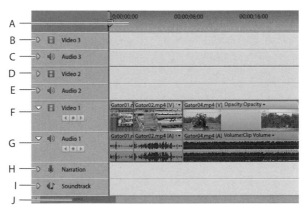

A. Time ruler	F. Collapse-Expand video track
B. Video track 3	G. Collapse-Expand audio track
C. Audio track 3	H. Narration track
D. Video track 2	I. Soundtrack
E. Audio track 2	J. Timeline slider

● **Note:** If you're going back and forth between Quick and Expert views, keep in mind that the Video 1/Audio 1 track corresponds with the audio/video track in Quick view, whereas Video 3 corresponds with the Title track in Quick view. If audio or video is placed on any other tracks in Expert view, it won't appear in Quick view. If non-title content is placed on Video 3, it will appear in Quick view, but you won't have a track left for titles.

Adding and deleting tracks

The timeline consists of vertically stacked tracks in which you arrange media clips. Tracks let you layer video or audio and add compositing effects, picture-in-picture effects, overlay titles, soundtracks, and more.

You perform most of your editing in the Video 1 and the Audio 1 tracks. Directly above these are the Video 2 and Audio 2 tracks. Note that the stacking order of video tracks is important. The Monitor panel displays (and Adobe Premiere Elements produces) the tracks from the top down. Accordingly, any opaque areas of the clip in the Video 2 track will cover the view of the clip in the Video 1 track.

Conversely, the clip in the Video 1 track will show through any transparent areas of the clip in the Video 2 track. Below the Video 1 and Audio 1 tracks are two more audio tracks, Narration and Soundtrack. Audio tracks are combined in playback, and their stacking order is not relevant.

Adobe Premiere Elements starts with three open video tracks (Video 1, Video 2, and Video 3) and five open audio tracks (Soundtrack, Narration, Audio 1, Audio 2, and Audio 3), which should be sufficient for most projects. Should you need additional video or audio tracks, you can add them by choosing Timeline > Add Tracks. You can delete any empty tracks by choosing Timeline > Delete Empty Tracks.

Changing the height of tracks

You can change the height of each track in the timeline for better viewing and easier editing of your projects. As a track enlarges, it displays more information. Let's adjust the height of the Video 1 track.

1 If necessary, scroll down in the timeline to see the Video 1 track.

2 Right-click on any open area in the timeline, and choose Track Size > Small, Track Size > Medium, or Track Size > Large to change the track size for all tracks in the timeline.

3 To customize a specific track, at the left side of the timeline, click the disclosure triangle to the left of the Video 1 track icon. Then place the pointer between the Audio 2 and Video 1 tracks. Your pointer should change to two parallel lines with two arrows ($\updownarrow$). Drag up to expand the height of Video 1.

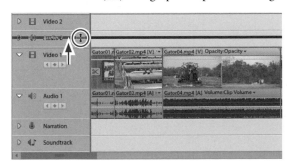

Customizing track views

You can display clips in the timeline in different ways, depending on your preference or the task at hand. You can display a thumbnail image at just the beginning of a clip, at the head and tail of a clip, or along the entire duration of a clip, as shown above. For an audio track, you can display or hide the audio waveform. Toggle through the various views of the video and audio tracks until you find the one that best suits your eye and working style.

To get a good look at the various styles, it's best to click the Zoom In button (■) on the right of the Monitor panel until only three or four clips are showing on the timeline.

By default, Adobe Premiere Elements displays the first frame and the last frame of the clip, or the head and tail, with a blue region in between.

1   To change the default display, click the Set Video Track Display Style button (▤) to the left of the Video 1 track. Click the button four times to see all four styles. Choose the style that you like best.

2   To change the audio view, click the Set Audio Track Display Style button (◀) to the left of the Audio 1 track twice.

Editing in Expert view

One of the most significant differences between Expert and Quick views is that the Project Assets panel exists in Expert view, but not in Quick view. When you're working in Quick view, all content imported via the Add Media controls is immediately placed at the end of the project in the Quick view timeline. In Expert view, all content imported via the Add Media controls is placed in the Project Assets panel, where you can add the content to your project at any location. So you'll start there, adding content from the Project Assets panel to the project.

Adding clips in Expert view

If you worked through the exercises in Quick view, recall that the initial project was missing the clip Gator07.mp4. For your first exercise in Expert view, you'll add that to the project, between Gator06.mp4 and Gator08.mp4. Keep in mind that the

Project Assets panel is available only in Expert view, so if you're not in Expert view, click the Expert button at the top of the Monitor panel.

1 At the lower right of the Monitor panel, click the Fit To Visible Timeline button () or press the Backslash (\) key to fit the project in the timeline.

2 At the upper left of the Adobe Premiere Elements window, click Project Assets (**Project Assets ▾**) to open that panel.

3 Click Gator07.mp4, and drag it to the intersection of the files Gator06.mp4 and Gator08.mp4. Hold the clip for a moment, and notice how Adobe Premiere Elements moves Gator08.mp4 and all subsequent clips to the right to make space for Gator07.mp4.

Also, note how the Monitor panel changes to Trim view to show the last frame of Gator06.mp4 on the left and the first frame of Gator08.mp4 on the right. Before releasing the mouse, drag Gator07.mp4 a bit further to the right, into Gator08.mp4, to see how this is reflected in the Monitor panel. This view makes it simple to tell when you're not dropping the clip in the right place. When you're ready, release the mouse button to complete the edit.

Now you'll learn a different technique for adding clips to the timeline.

4 At the bottom left of the Adobe Premiere Elements window, click the Undo button (↺ Undo), or otherwise undo the edit.

5 Move the current-time indicator between Gator06.mp4 and Gator08.mp4, which should be around 00;00;51;09.

6 In the Project Assets folder, click Gator07.mp4 to select it. Then, while watching the timeline, press the comma key (,) on your keyboard. Adobe Premiere Elements adds Gator07.mp4 to the timeline at the current-time indicator.

Moving clips in Expert view

Now you'll fix the order of clips in Expert view. If you hover your mouse over the clips at the start of the project, you'll see that the current order is Gator01.mp4, Gator02.mp4, Gator04.mp4, Gator05.mp4, and Gator03.mp4. As before, you have two options for placing the clips in the proper order: moving Gator03.mp4 two clips to the left or moving Gator04.mp4 and Gator05.mp4 one clip to the right. Let's try both approaches.

1   Click and hold to select Gator03.mp4, and then press the Alt (Windows) or Option (Mac OS) key. You'll see the rearrange pointer (). Drag Gator03.mp4 until the front edge of the clip touches the intersection between Gator02.mp4 and Gator04.mp4. Watch the Trim view in the Monitor panel to make sure that the front of Gator03.mp4 is at the intersection between the two clips. Wait a moment for Adobe Premiere Elements to move all the clips to the right to make a space for Gator03.mp4. Then release the pointer.

● **Note:** Using the rearrange pointer is not supposed to leave a gap in the timeline, but did so during the writing of this book. Adobe says it will address this issue in the short term, so we've documented the way it's supposed to work, and caution you that the gap may appear.

2   If Adobe Premiere Elements leaves a gap where Gator03.mp4 used to be, right-click the gap, and choose Delete And Close Gap.

3   At the bottom left of the Adobe Premiere Elements window, click Undo (↶ Undo) twice to undo those operations.

Now you'll try the other approach: moving Gator04.mp4 and Gator05.mp4 to the right.

4   To select multiple adjacent clips, press the Shift key and click the clips, in this case Gator04.mp4 and Gator05.mp4, and without releasing the Shift key, press the Alt (Windows) or Option (Mac OS) key. Then you can release the Shift key and drag the selected clips (pay attention here) until the left edge of the two clips is in the intersection between Gator03.mp4 and Gator06.mp4.

5 Watch the Trim view in the Monitor panel to make sure that you're dropping the two clips at the desired location. Wait a moment for Adobe Premiere Elements to move all the clips to the right to make a space for the two clips. Then release the mouse button.

Note: Although not shown in this exercise, in Expert view, any transitions before or after a single clip are deleted during a move. Transitions between multiple adjacent clips that were moved survive the move.

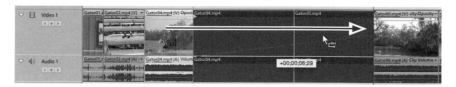

6 If Adobe Premiere Elements leaves a gap where Gator04.mp4 and Gator05.mp4 were previously located, right-click the gap, and choose Delete And Close Gap.

Deleting clips in Expert view

When you're deleting clips in Expert view, you have a lot more control over the results than you do in Quick view. This section describes the various options.

To delete a scene, right-click it in the Expert view, and then choose one of the following from the context menu:

Note: When a clip is deleted in Expert view, any transitions associated with the clip, either before or after, are also deleted.

- **Cut** deletes the clip and moves all clips following the deleted clip to the left to close the gap. This is the default behavior when deleting clips in Adobe Premiere Elements and is called a *ripple deletion*.

- **Copy** copies the clip and any effects or other adjustments made to the clip.

- **Paste Effects And Adjustments** pastes any effects or other adjustments from the source clip to the target clip. This operation can be exceptionally useful when you're applying an effect like an exposure correction to a number of clips from the same scene, and you'll explore it further in Lesson 6.

- **Delete** deletes the clip but leaves a gap at the clip's former location.

- **Delete And Close Gap** does the same thing as Cut; it deletes the clip and moves all clips following the deleted clip to the left to close the gap.

- **Delete Audio** deletes the audio in the clip but leaves the video in place.

- **Delete Video** deletes the video in the clip but leaves the audio in place.

- **Replace Clip From Project Assets** replaces a selected clip on the timeline with a clip selected in the Project Assets panel.

Trimming clips in Expert view

As discussed in the "Editing in Quick view" section, every clip in the timeline has a beginning and an end. In addition to moving clips around, you may also want to shorten clips by trimming frames from the beginning and end. Here's how you'll accomplish this task.

In editing terminology, the beginning of each clip is called the *In point* and the end of a clip the *Out point*. When you adjust the In and Out points, you don't actually delete frames from the file on your hard drive; you simply point to different frames to start and end playback of that clip on the timeline. When you trim a clip in Adobe Premiere Elements, you're simply changing the In and Out points.

It's a rare project that doesn't have some frames that could use some trimming, and this one is no exception. In this exercise you'll trim three clips: Gator02.mp4, Gator03.mp4, and Gator14.mp4. You'll begin by zooming in to the project.

1 Click the Fit To Visible Timeline icon (▣) at the lower right of the Monitor panel, or press the Backslash key (\). Then press the Zoom in icon (■) (or the = key) three times.

2 Drag the current-time indicator to the right edge of Gator02.png, right around 8:20 in the timeline (or click the timecode on the bottom left of the Monitor panel, type **820**, and press Enter or Return). Then drag the current-time indicator to the end of the clip. Notice how the camera dropped towards the end of the clip? You'll trim that out.

3 Move the current-time indicator back to 8:20.

4 Hover the pointer over the right edge of Gator02.mp4. The pointer will convert to the drag pointer (✥).

5 Click and drag the right edge of Gator02.mp4 to the left until it snaps to the current-time indicator at 00;00;08;20, and then release the mouse button. You've just trimmed the last few frames from the edge of the clip.

  Notice that while you drag the edge, the Monitor panel changes to Trim view, showing the clip you're trimming on the left and the next clip on the timeline on the right. As you drag the right edge to the left, Trim view updates the frame on the left, making it easy to see the edge of the clip that you're trimming.

6 The same kind of camera drop occurred in the next clip, starting right at about 00;00;15;10, so move the current-time indicator to 00;00;15;10.

7 Hover the pointer over the right edge of Gator03.mp4. The pointer will convert to the drag pointer (⊕).

8 Click and drag the right edge of Gator03.mp4 to the left until it snaps to the current-time indicator at 00;00;15;10, and then release the mouse button.

   You've just trimmed the last few frames from the edge of the clip.

9 Grab the slider on the bottom of the timeline, and drag it to the right until clip Gator14.mp4 appears in full.

   This is the clip with the girl in a green shirt, holding the baby alligator in the prescribed manner that's safe for her and won't hurt the baby alligator in any way. Let's trim some frames from the start of the clip.

10 Move the current-time indicator to the point in the clip where the girl is just starting to open her mouth, which should be around 00;01;43;15.

11 Hover the pointer over the left edge of Gator14.mp4. The pointer becomes the drag pointer pointing in the other direction (⊕).

Note: You may not
see the Trim view on all
computers, particularly
Mac notebooks. If you
don't, make sure you've
got the latest graphics
card driver for your
computer.

12 Click and drag the left edge of Gator14.mp4 to the right until it snaps to the
current-time indicator, and then release the pointer. Adobe Premiere Elements
trims the first few frames from the start of Gator14.mp4.

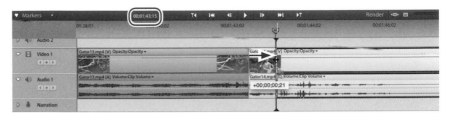

13 Drag the current-time indicator slowly to the end of Gator14.mp4. Towards the
end, around 1:49:20, you'll see that patented teenage eyeroll. To remove it, drag
the current-time indicator to around 00;01;48;00, hover over the right edge, and
then click and drag the edge to the left until it snaps to the current-time indicator.

Note: You don't need to place the current-time indicator at the trim point. You can simply click
and drag the edge to the new location. Placing the current-time indicator at that location and then
snapping to it as demonstrated is just a bit more precise, and in this case helps make sure that you
reproduce the result as you see them.

Using the Split Clip tool in Expert view

The Split Clip tool allows you to divide single clips into multiple clips. You can use
this tool to split a clip into sections so you can delete one of them, which sometimes
is more convenient than trimming. You can also use the tool to split a long clip into
separate clips to edit them individually, which is what we'll do in this exercise.

1 Move the current-time indicator to around timecode 00;01;30;00, which should
be in the clip Gator12.mp4, one of the few clips with an actual wild alligator
in it (apparently, January isn't prime alligator viewing season). As you drag the
current-time indicator to the right, you'll notice that the alligator drifts out of
view around 00;01;30;26, and then back into view until it submerges later in the
shot. Let's split this clip and turn it into two clips that you can edit separately.

2 Move the current-time indicator back to 00;01;30;26. You may need to click the
Zoom Out button (■) once to see the whole clip in the timeline.

3 Click the file Gator12.mp4 to select it.

Clicking the file is important, because if you don't, Adobe Premiere Elements
will split all content at that location, which isn't important here, but may be not
be what you want at other times.

4 Hover the pointer over the scissors icon () attached to the current-time indicator until it turns white, and then click the icon, or press Ctrl+K (Windows) or Command+K (Mac). Adobe Premiere Elements splits the clip at that location.

You now have two Gator12.mp4 clips in the timeline.

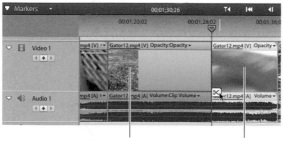

First Gator12.mp4   Second Gator12.mp4

5 When you're finished reviewing the movie, choose File > Save As.

6 In the Save Project dialog box, name the file **Lesson05_working.prel** and save it in your Lesson05 folder. Overwrite the previous file if it exists.

Creating a slide show in Expert view

Video enthusiasts often like to integrate video and slide shows, particularly because we tend to shoot so many photos with our smartphones, tablets, and DSLRs. Adobe Premiere Elements makes this very simple with a Create Slideshow function, which has convenient features like automatic insertion of transitions between images. Because you'll be working with pictures in the Project Assets panel, you must be in Expert view to run this exercise.

● **Note:** The slide show function always inserts the slide show at the end of the Video 1 track.

1 In the upper left corner of the Adobe Premiere Elements window, click Project Assets (**Project Assets ▾**) to open that panel.

2 To make the photos easier to select in the proper order, you can customize the view:

- On the upper left side of the Project Assets panel toolbar, click the Hide Video and Hide Audio icons so that only the still images in the panel are displayed.

- Click the panel menu in the upper right corner of the Project Assets panel, and choose View > List View.

- In List view, sort by any column by clicking the column head. Click the Name column head until the photos are displayed in ascending order, as shown below.

3 Click Picture 1.jpg, press the Shift key, and then click Picture 8.jpg to select all of the pictures. Scroll down to Picture 8.jpg if necessary. Note that if you press Ctrl+A (Windows) or Command+A (Mac OS) to select all of the photos, you'll select all the content in the Project Assets panel, including video and audio content, not just the photos.

Note: Only the Take Video Only choice will be available here, because you're selecting pictures rather than video files with audio.

4 Right-click any selected image, and choose Create Slideshow. If the Smart Fix dialog box appears, click No. The Create SlideShow dialog box opens, and includes several options:

- Ordering (Sort Order or Selection Order)

- Media (Take Video And Audio, Take Video Only, or Take Audio Only)

- Place Images/Clips At
  Unnumbered Markers
  (grayed out now because the
  project has no markers)

- Image Duration

- Apply Default Transition

- Transition Duration

For this exercise, use the default
settings.

5   Click OK to create the slide show. Adobe Premiere Elements inserts the slide
    show with transitions at the end of the Video 1 track.

Working in Smart Trim mode

The Smart Trim editing mode can help you identify suboptimal regions within
your videos so you can either fix or delete them. Smart Trim relies on information
gathered while Adobe Premiere Elements analyzes your clips, so you must Auto-
Analyze your clips before entering Smart Trim mode. You can operate Smart Trim
either automatically or manually, although we recommend that you use Smart Trim
manually until you understand how it works.

You can work with Smart Trim in Quick and Expert views; this exercise dem-
onstrates how it works in Expert view, so click Expert (Expert) at the top of
the Monitor panel, if necessary, to enter that view. Click the Fit To Visible
Timeline icon (🖳) at the extreme right of the Monitor panel to spread the clips
over the timeline. Then click Tools, and then click Smart Trim. If you haven't run
the Auto-Analyzer, Adobe Premiere Elements will run it now.

As you can see in the figure below, Smart Trim identifies problem areas via a zebra
pattern. If you hover your mouse over the zebra pattern, a tool tip details the

problems with the clip. You have multiple options regarding any clip, or portion of a clip, that Adobe Premiere Elements flags as a problem area. Not surprisingly, since a substantial portion of these videos was shot from a moving airboat, Adobe Premiere Elements found lots of shaky footage.

You can right-click the clip, and choose Trim, Keep, or Select All. Trim will delete the selected portion; Keep will retain it and turn off the zebra striping; Select All will select multiple suboptimal regions within the same clip so you can trim or keep them all. In addition to these options, you can trim away any or all of the suboptimal portions of your clip by clicking and dragging an edge to the desired new starting point, just as you would trim any other clip in the timeline.

Smart Trim options

You can also trim a scene by adjusting the smart trim options (click the Smart Trim Options button in the upper right corner of the Monitor panel). Let's view the available choices.

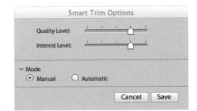

In the Smart Trim Options dialog box, Adobe Premiere Elements uses two variables to identify suboptimal clips: Quality Level and Interest Level. Quality Level is simple to understand: If a clip is shaky or blurry, has poor contrast or lighting, or has other deficits that mar quality, Adobe Premiere Elements identifies the clip in Smart Trim mode as being below the Quality Level threshold, depending on how flawed the clip is and where you positioned the Quality Level slider.

By contrast, Interest Level analyzes qualities, such as the amount of motion in a clip, the presence or absence of dialogue, and other criteria that identify clips that are interesting to watch. If you shot a picture of a blank wall that was sharp, well lit, and completely stable, the Quality Level would be perfect, but Adobe Premiere Elements would flag it as lacking in the Interest Level department. That doesn't do much for those boring conversations with Uncle Harold, because if quality is good, and the audio level sufficient, Smart Trim wouldn't flag the content, so you'll still have to delete those manually.

You can adjust the sliders to set the tolerance levels for either criteria: Moving the slider to the left increases the threshold for suboptimal clips, so that fewer and fewer clips will be flagged. Moving it to the right reduces the threshold so that more clips will be flagged.

For example, if you examine the clips in your project and find that most clips flagged by Adobe Premiere Elements look good to you, move the slider to the left, and Adobe Premiere Elements will set the threshold higher and flag fewer clips. If clips left unflagged in Smart Trim mode look suboptimal to you for either Quality Level or Interest Level reasons, move the slider to the right.

Operating modes

There are two operating modes in the Smart Trim Options dialog box: Manual and Automatic. In Manual mode, which is the default, Adobe Premiere Elements displays all suboptimal regions of a clip via the zebra stripes discussed previously. If you opt for Automatic mode, Adobe Premiere Elements immediately deletes all suboptimal regions present on the timeline. Thereafter, when you drag clips with suboptimal regions to the timeline, Adobe Premiere Elements presents a dialog box asking if it's OK to remove Smart Trim sections.

There's an awful lot of bad video out there, and Smart Trim mode presents a very efficient way to identify it. In a real project, when you've shot 30–60 minutes of footage and want to quickly isolate the best 3–5 minutes to include in your movie, Smart Trim mode can be a godsend. So check it out on your own projects and see how it works for you.

Two final points: First, when Smart Trim flags quality-related problems, you can either delete the offending sections or try to fix them, which you'll practice in Lesson 6. So even if you decide to leave suboptimal clips in the project, Smart Trim helps by identifying sequences you can improve with corrective effects.

Second, to reiterate a comment made earlier, you should *not* use Smart Trim in Automatic mode. Lots of "must have" sequences in your movies—such as your son blowing out the candles on his birthday cake or your daughter accepting her diploma—may not meet Adobe Premiere Elements' quality thresholds, but you still don't want to delete them. In Automatic mode, you don't get that choice.

That's all for this exercise, so you can cancel out of the Smart Trim Options dialog box and exit the project if you'd like, or continue working in the project.

Producing split edits

By default, Adobe Premiere Elements links the audio from a clip to the video from a clip; otherwise, your projects would quickly become an audio synchronization nightmare. But sometimes, you'll want the audio from a clip to precede the video (a J-cut, shown in the figure below) or the video to start before the audio (an L-cut). To produce these types of edits, you must temporarily break the default link between audio and video.

To break the link temporarily, press the Alt (Windows) or Option (Mac OS) key when clicking either the audio or video component of a clip in the timeline. This allows you to drag only the selected media type in either direction, up to the limit of the clip, of course.

To create the J-cut shown in the figure, do the following:

1   Trim about 1 second from the end of Gator03.mp4 and the start of Gator04.mp4.

2   To clear space beneath the Gator03.mp4 video, press the Alt (Windows) or Option (Mac OS) key, click the waveform from Gator03.mp4 on Audio 1, and drag it to the left.

3   Press the Alt (Windows) or Option (Mac OS) key, click the waveform from Gator04.mp4 on Audio 1, and drag it to the left so the audio is beneath the video from Gator03.mp4.

During playback, the viewer will hear the audio from Gator04.mp4 before seeing the video, an interesting way to transition from one clip to another.

When you use the Alt/Option key approach, the audio and video components of the clip are relinked once you finish the edit. For a more permanent solution, click the target clip, right-click, and choose Unlink Audio And Video, which severs the link between the two clips, allowing you to trim or move either as desired. To link the two components back into a single clip, select them both, right-click, and choose Link Audio And Video. For more information, search for "Extend audio before or after linked video" in Adobe Premiere Elements Help.

Wonderful! You've finished another lesson and learned how to cut, trim, split, and arrange your raw video into a cohesive movie. In the next few lessons, you'll polish it into a fine-tuned production.

Review questions

1 What are the key differences between Expert and Quick views from an editing perspective?

2 What are an In point and an Out point, and what can you do with each?

3 What are two methods of shortening your video clips?

4 How does Adobe Premiere Elements combine video tracks at the same position on the timeline?

5 What are the two criteria assessed by Adobe Premiere Elements in Smart Trim mode?

Review answers

1 One of the most significant differences between Expert and Quick views is the ability to see the Project Assets panel. In Quick view, you can add content to the end of projects only via program controls, although you can drag and drop to add content to the middle of a project. In Expert view, you can drag content from the Project Assets panel to anywhere in the project.

2 An In point is the first frame of your clip as shown in Quick or Expert views and the Out point is the last frame. In and Out points can be moved to create a shorter or longer clip.

3 You can shorten your clips by trimming their In points and Out points or by splitting the clip and deleting unwanted portions.

4 Adobe Premiere Elements renders tracks from the top down. Any opaque areas of the clip in the Video 2 track will cover the view on the clip in the Video 1 track. Conversely, the clip in the Video 1 track will show through any transparent (or reduced opacity) areas of the clip in the Video 2 track.

5 Quality Level and Interest Level are the two criteria used in Smart Trim mode. The former assesses picture and audio quality on a technical level; the latter assesses multiple qualities, such as the amount of dialogue and motion, that tend to indicate whether or not a clip is interesting.

6 WORKING WITH EFFECTS

Lesson overview

In this lesson, you'll learn how to apply effects and adjustments to the bayou boat ride clips that you used in previous lessons, as well as several new clips. Specifically, you'll learn how to do the following:

- Apply video effects to single and multiple clips

- Change effects and settings

- Improve the contrast and saturation of your videos

- Copy effects and settings from one clip to another

- Animate a still image using the Pan and Zoom effect

- Render your entire project and a work area within a project

- Control visual effects with keyframes

- Create a picture-in-picture effect

- Composite one video over another with Videomerge

- Track an object and add a graphic with Motion Tracking

 This lesson will take approximately two hours. Download the project files for this lesson from the Lesson & Update Files tab on your Account page at www.peachpit.com and store them on your computer in a convenient location, as described in the Getting Started section of this book. Your Account page is also where you'll find any updates to the chapters or to the lesson files. Look on the Lesson & Update Files tab to access the most current content.

You add a Pan and Zoom effect with the Pan And Zoom tool.

Getting started

● **Note:** If you have not already downloaded the project files for this lesson to your computer from your Account page, make sure to do so now. See "Getting Started" at the beginning of the book.

Before you begin the exercises in this lesson, make sure that you have correctly copied the Lesson06 folder from your Account page onto your computer's hard drive. For more information, see "Copying the Classroom in a Book files" in the Getting Started section at the start of this book.

Now you're ready to begin working with the Lesson06 project file.

1 Launch Adobe Premiere Elements. If it is already open, choose Help > Welcome Screen in the Adobe Premiere Elements menu to return to the Welcome screen.

2 In the Welcome screen, click Video Editor, select Existing Project, and click the Open folder.

3 In the Open Project dialog box, navigate to the Lesson06 folder you copied to your hard drive. Within that folder, select Lesson06_Start_Win.prel (Windows) or Lesson06_Start_Mac.prel (Mac OS), and then click Open. If a dialog box appears asking for the location of rendered files, click the Skip Previews button.

   Your project file opens.

4 Choose Window > Restore Workspace to ensure that you start the lesson with the default panel layout.

Viewing the completed movie before you start

To see what you'll be creating in this lesson, you can take a look at the completed movie. You must be in Expert view to open the Project Assets panel to view the movie, so if you're not, click Expert (Expert) to enter that view.

1 In the upper left side of the Adobe Premiere Elements window, click the Project Assets button (Project Assets ▾) to open that panel. Locate Lesson06_Movie.mov, and then double-click it to open the video into the preview window.

2 Click the Play button (▶) to watch the video about powering the bayou boat ride, which you'll build in this lesson.

3 When you're done, close the preview window.

● **Note:** Adobe Premiere Elements offers a large selection of diversified effects. Check out the gallery of video effects in Adobe Premiere Elements Help to get a quick overview of all those effects actually applied to an image.

Using effects

The tools that you'll work with in this lesson are located in four different panels. All four panels are different in Quick and Expert views. Quick view contains the most widely used tools or effects in each category, and Expert view contains all these plus a broad selection of other tools and effects.

Applied Effects panel   Adjust panel

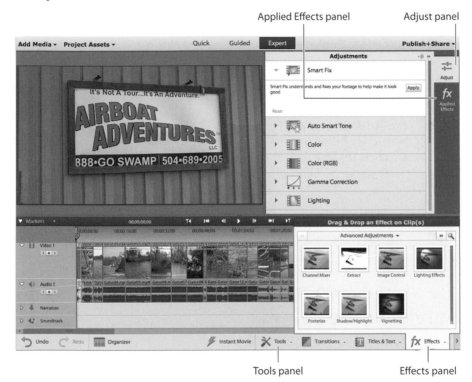

Tools panel   Effects panel

Effects in the Adjust ( ) and Applied Effects ( ) panels are automatically applied to each clip in the timeline. To adjust these, click the clip in the timeline, and then click the respective panel button to open the adjustments.

You'll go through these procedures in various exercises in this chapter. You apply tools by selecting a clip on the timeline, clicking the Tools button (Tools) to open that panel, and clicking the desired tool. Adobe Premiere Elements will apply the tool to that clip and open a customization window unique to the selected tool.

You apply an effect from the Effects panel (Effects) by clicking the Effects panel button to open the panel, finding the desired effect, and then dragging it onto the target clip or clips. You adjust the parameters of the effect that you just applied by clicking the Applied Effects button ( ) to open that panel, which contains all effects that you applied from the Effects panel, plus the Motion and Opacity adjustments.

Now let's take a closer look at the adjustments in each panel.

The Adjust panel

The Adjust panel (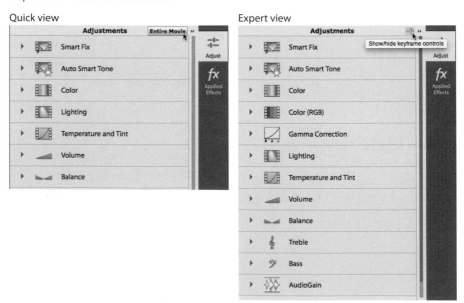) contains the most common adjustments that you'll make to your clips in your projects. In essence, these adjustments are effects, but because they're so commonly used, they're not stored with the other effects that you have to apply manually; instead, Adobe Premiere Elements applies them to every clip automatically, which saves you a step.

When you're working in Quick view, Adobe Premiere Elements provides access to the one-step Smart Fix control, as well as Auto Smart Tone, Color, Lighting, and Temperature and Tint adjustments for video, and Volume and Balance for audio. Note that if you click the Entire Movie button (Entire Movie) at the upper right of the panel, any adjustment that you make to any single clip will be applied to the entire movie. You'll learn more about applying adjustments to the entire movie in "Sharing Adjustments via the Entire Movie Button" later in this lesson.

In Expert view, the adjustments mentioned above are supplemented by Color (RGB) and Gamma Correction for video and Treble, Bass, and Audio Gain for audio. The other major difference between the two views is that Expert view lets you animate effects by adding keyframes, which you accomplish via controls accessed by clicking the Show/Hide Keyframe Controls icon ( ) at the upper right of the Adjustments panel. You'll learn how to use keyframes in "Working with keyframes" later in this lesson.

Quick view   Expert view

The Applied Effects panel

The Applied Effects panel ( ) contains any effects that you've manually applied to the selected clip, plus the very commonly used Motion and Opacity adjustments for video, and Channel Volume, which lets you adjust the volume of each audio channel individually, for audio. The Motion effect, in particular, is one that you'll use in many projects for many different purposes: to customize a picture-in-picture, to zoom in on or out of a video, or to rotate a video. Remember that it's automatically applied for you and always ready for adjustment in the Applied Effects panel.

The Applied Effects panel has the same two differences as the Adjust panel: The Quick view has the Entire Movie button, while the Expert view enables keyframes. In Quick view, the Entire Movie function works only on *applied* effects, not Motion, Opacity, or Channel Volume. To use the function, you must apply an effect to all clips in the movie; then you can customize the effect, and Adobe Premiere Elements will apply your customizations to all clips.

Quick view

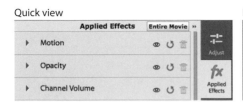

Expert view

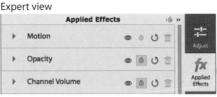

The Tools panel

The Tools panel contains a range of useful tools that you'll use in many projects. To open the panel, click Tools ( ) in the Action bar at the bottom of the Adobe Premiere Elements window. To close the panel, click Tools again. In Quick view, the Tools panel contains the following tools that we'll discuss in this lesson:

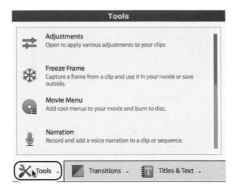

- **Pan & Zoom** is used for adding pan and zoom effects to pictures and videos, which you'll learn to use in "Creating a Pan & Zoom effect" later in this lesson.

- **Time Remapping** is used for fine control of fast and slow motion effects applied to your clips, described later in this lesson in "Working with Time Remapping."

- **Motion Tracking** is used to follow objects in the footage and attach graphics to them, described later in this lesson in "Working with Motion Tracking."

In Expert view, you also have access to the Time Stretch tool, which is covered later in this lesson in "Changing playback speed."

The Effects panel

The Effects panel shows video (in Expert and Quick views) and audio effects (in Expert view only), and FilmLooks you can use in your movie by dragging them onto any clip or clips in the timeline. Quick view offers roughly 40 of the most commonly used effects and FilmLooks, whereas Expert view offers dozens more in well-defined categories. In addition, when you're in Expert view, you can search for an effect by clicking the magnifying lens (🔍) at the upper right of the panel. This opens a search box, where you can type the name of the effect that you're looking for. This search function is not available in Quick view.

Quick view   Expert view

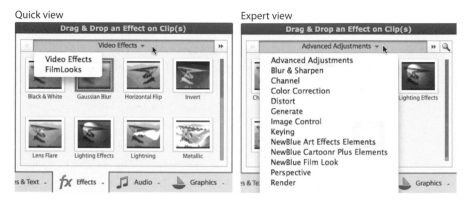

Recommended workflows

From a workflow perspective, it's helpful to think about effects in the following categories. All effects listed are available in Expert view; some are also available in Quick view:

- **Curative effects** correct problems in your video footage, including footage that's too bright or too dark, backlighted video, video that's too shaky because it was shot without a tripod, and even video that's a bit blurry. You should start with the color- and brightness-related curative effects in the Adjustments panel. Beyond these, you can find other curative effects in the Effects panel in the Advanced Adjustments folder, the Color Correction folder, the Blur & Sharpen folder, the Image Control folder, and the Video Stabilizer folder.

- **Overlay effects** allow you to composite one image over another. You can find overlay effects in the Keying and Videomerge folders.

- **The Pan & Zoom effect** enables you to pan around and zoom in on and out of still images and videos, allowing you to animate still images and add additional motion to videos. You can find this tool by clicking the Pan & Zoom icon (⊞) in the Tools panel.

- **Artistic effects** let you create a different look or feel for a clip, or add a Lens Flare (Generate folder) or Vignetting (Advanced Adjustments). Most artistic effects are found in the Effects panel, and they can be quite powerful, like the NewBlue Cartoonr Plus effect that converts your videos to cartoons. Other artistic effects let you add lightning to a clip (Lightning Effects in the Render folder), create an earthquake (Earthquake effect in the NewBlue Art Effects Elements folder), place a spotlight on a subject (Lighting Effects in the Advanced Adjustments folder), or apply a range of other looks and characteristics.

- **The FilmLooks folder** in the Effects panel contains a number of presets that let you quickly and easily add a certain look or feel to your project, like Newsreel, Summer Day, or Vintage.

- **Speed controls** enable you to speed up, slow down, or reverse your clips by using the Time Stretch and Time Remapping tools in the Tools panel.

- **Motion effects** allow you to zoom in on and around your original video clip or still image, and are used to adjust the framing of a video. You adjust these parameters using the Motion controls in the Applied Effects panel.

Although you can apply any and all of these effects at any time during the course of a project, the recommended workflow is to apply curative filters first, then adjust speed and motion, and then add other artistic effects. You can add an effect to any clip and even apply the same effect numerous times to the same clip but with different settings. By default, when you add an effect to a clip, it applies to the entire clip. To apply an effect to only part of a clip, split it first, and then apply the effect to the desired clip segment.

Working with Smart Fix

Unless you disable the Auto-Analyzer application in the Organizer, at some point Adobe Premiere Elements will analyze your clips, either in the background while you're performing other edits or after capture or import. While analyzing the clips, Adobe Premiere Elements looks for problems in the video.

As you saw with Smart Trim in the previous lesson, Adobe Premiere Elements uses some of this information to recommend which clips to trim away. In addition, if your video or still image is too dark, Adobe Premiere Elements will apply the Shadow/Highlight effect, as you'll see in this exercise. If a standard definition (SD) video is too shaky, Adobe Premiere Elements will apply the Stabilizer effect. If you're working with shaky high-definition (HD) video, Adobe Premiere Elements won't apply the Stabilizer effect automatically because it's too processor-intensive, although you can apply the effect manually, as you'll learn in a subsequent exercise.

Note: Applying
Smart Fix to the Gator
videos in this project
won't find anything to
fix. Even though many
are shaky (being shot
on a boat and all), the
clips are HD, so Smart
Fix won't automatically
stabilize them.

Since all the videos in this project were shot outside, Adobe Premiere Elements didn't find any that were too dark, so here we'll use a clip from a previous project.

1 If necessary, click the Expert button (Expert) to enter Expert view.

2 At the bottom right of the Monitor panel, just to the right of the Render button (Render), click the Fit To Visible Timeline button (▭), or press the Backslash key (\).

3 In the upper left of the Adobe Premiere Elements window, click the Project Assets button to open that panel.

4 Right-click Video 4.mp4, and choose Run Auto Analyzer. Note that this is a file from a previous book, courtesy of NASA.

5 Click and drag Video 4.mp4 into the Video 1 track on the timeline, about an inch after the last picture on that track. Adobe Premiere Elements opens the Smart Fix window. If Smart Fix doesn't run automatically, click Adjust in the Monitor panel, select Smart Fix in the Adjustments panel, and click Apply.

6 In the Smart Fix dialog box, click Yes to fix the quality problem in the clip.

7 Click the Project Assets button to close that panel.

▶ **Tip:** Toggling the
effect off (👁) and on
(👁) is a great way to
see how the effect is
modifying your clip.
You'll use this toggle
frequently with most
curative effects.

8 In the timeline, click the copy of Video 4.mp4 you just added to the timeline to select it (if it's not already selected), and then click the Applied Effects button to open that panel. You'll see that Adobe Premiere Elements has applied the Shadow/Highlight effect to the clip.

Drag the current-time indicator over Video 4.mp4. Then click the eye icon (👁) next to the Shadow/Highlight effect (officially called the "Toggle the effect on or off" icon) to turn the effect on and off, and you'll see that the Shadow/Highlight effect does a nice job of brightening the shadows without "blowing out" the lighter regions. Although the clip looks a bit pixelated once brightened, this is a function of the compression applied to the clip so that it would fit on the DVD, not a result of applying the effect.

9   Delete the Video 4.mp4 video you added to the end of the timeline by right-clicking the clip and choosing Delete.

▶ **Tip:** To apply Smart Fix to a clip on the timeline, click the clip to select it, click Adjust in the Monitor panel, select Smart Fix in the Adjustments panel, and click Apply.

▶ **Tip:** If you're shooting in HD, the only clips that Adobe Premiere Elements will fix are those that are too dark (since it won't automatically apply the Stabilizer effect to SD clips). The more I use Adobe Premiere Elements, the more I prefer the Gamma Correction effect to the Shadow/Highlight effect, because they accomplish the same function (boosting the brightness of pixels in the middle of the brightness spectrum, without boosting the lightest or darkest pixels), and Shadow/Highlight can cause pulsing in the edited video. So while Smart Fix is good for a quick fix, it may not be the best fix. You'll learn about Gamma Correction in the next section.

Perfecting your clips

If you're serious about perfecting your clips, you should work in Expert view, which provides the most options. Of course, more options can cause confusion, particularly when controls are fairly similar, like Color and Color (RGB). Dig a bit deeper, however, and you'll see that all controls have one or two unique features that make them invaluable for a very specific problem (or two). We'll run

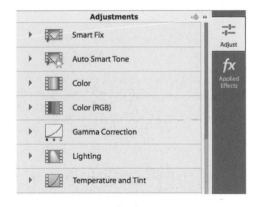

through exercises with all effects but Temperature and Tint, so if the purpose isn't obvious from the brief description below, it will be once you finish the exercises.

*   **Auto Smart Tone** addresses brightness and contrast issues in your clips, and learns from how you've adjusted clips previously. This should be the first effect you try for addressing these issues.

*   **Color** provides separate adjustments for hue, lightness, saturation, and vibrance, but not separate controls for red, green, and blue. The most typical use for this function is to adjust saturation or vibrance.

*   **Color (RGB)** provides specific controls for red, green, and blue. Use this to fix clips where one color is dominating.

- **Gamma Correction** differs from Brightness and Contrast in that it lets you adjust just those pixels in the middle of the brightness spectrum instead of all those in the frame. This is useful for fixing backlighting or similar problems.

- **Lighting** provides separate controls for brightness, contrast, exposure, black, and white. The adjustments are similar to those in Auto Smart Tone, but more useful to those who want individual control over these options. Unlike Auto Smart Tone, the Lighting adjustment does not "learn," so you'll start from scratch each time you apply it.

- **Temperature And Tint** provides separate adjustments for temperature and tint. Use these to give your footage a distinct look or feel, or to fix white balance issues that you can't quite fix with Color (RGB).

In terms of workflow, it's almost always best to address brightness and contrast first, and then color. Accordingly, over the next few exercises, we'll take a look at the brightness and contrast adjustments, and then the color adjustments. Pay close attention to the workflow presented in the Auto Tone section, because much of the workflow will be identical for the other adjustments.

Working with Auto Smart Tone

Auto Smart Tone is an effect that corrects brightness and contrast issues in your clips. It's also a smart adjustment that learns as you customize the controls for your various clips. For example, if you demonstrate a tendency to boost the contrast and brightness to the max on your clips, when you apply Auto Smart Tone to new clips, Adobe Premiere Elements will anticipate your customization proclivities and automatically boost brightness and contrast. If your next project demands a more muted and understated look, you can reset the learning process to start anew. You'll learn how below.

Once you apply the effect, Adobe Premiere Elements divides the clip into scenes with similar footage. If you choose to customize the effect, you can move through the video clip, scene by scene, and make your adjustments.

Applying the Auto Smart Tone effect

We don't have a lot of problem clips in this project, and most are so short that they contain only one scene. So we'll work through this effect with one of the few clips where Auto Smart Tone finds multiple scenes, even though the benefit isn't very dramatic.

1   Click to select Gator04.mp4, and position the current-time indicator over that clip.

2 Click the Adjust button to open that panel.

3 Click the triangle to the left of the Auto Smart Tone adjustment to reveal its controls. Click Apply to apply the effect. You'll see the Applying Auto Smart Tone dialog box, with a progress bar, open momentarily and then close. Premiere Elements adjusts the brightness and contrast of your clip.

4 Click Custom to open the Auto Smart Tone dialog box.

Joystick controll

Go to Previous Edit Point (Page Up)

Render

Step Back (Left Arrow key)

Go to Next Edit Point (Page Down)

Play/Pause Toggle (spacebar)

Step Forward (Right Arrow key)

5 Keeping in mind that the four corners represent different extremes in brightness and contrast, click the joystick controller in the middle of the image, and drag it around the box to achieve the desired look. Note that you can use the playback controls beneath the clip to move through the clip. Leave the controller in approximately the same position that you see in the figure to achieve the same look.

6 In the control panel beneath the preview window, click the Next Scene (Next Scene ▶) and Previous Scene (◀ Previous Scene) buttons to move from scene to scene *within* the clip. Gator04.mp4 contains two scenes, so you should be able to click ahead and adjust both.

7 To check your work against the original clip, click the Effect Visible option on the bottom left of the Auto Smart Tone window to toggle the effect on and off.

8 If you don't want Adobe Premiere Elements to learn from this adjustment (if the clip has unique problems), deselect the Learn From This Correction option on the bottom left of the window.

9 When your adjustments are complete, click Done at the bottom right of the Auto Smart Tone window to complete the edit.

The next time you apply Auto Smart Tone, it will apply the lesson "learned" from this and previous edits to the selected clip. For example, we brightened Gator04.mp4 significantly. Follow the steps outlined above to apply Auto Smart Tone to Gator05.mp4. If this was the first time you've used Auto Smart Tone, and there are no other "lessons" influencing the behavior of this effect, Adobe Premiere Elements will brighten that clip as well. Then click Undo to undo that adjustment.

You can "unlearn" all previous lessons in the Preferences dialog box. Choose Edit > Preferences > General (Windows) or Adobe Premiere Elements 12 > Preferences > General (Mac OS) to open the Preferences dialog box to the General tab. Click Clean Auto Smart Tone Learning to reset the "learned" effect.

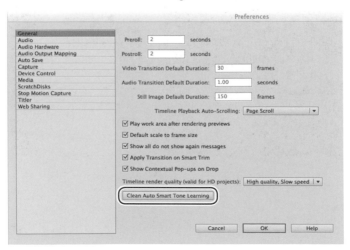

Adjusting brightness and contrast with Lighting Effects

Auto Smart Tone is great for quick adjustments, particularly when you need to make similar changes to multiple clips. However, some editors prefer more precise control over specific adjustments like brightness and contrast or the black and white pixels in a clip—and these are some of the controls available in the Lighting Effects found in the Adjustments panel.

Briefly, when you adjust brightness, you adjust the brightness of all pixels in a frame by an even amount. This is useful when the entire frame is just too dark.

When you adjust contrast, you increase the difference between the brightest and darkest pixels in a frame, making the brightest pixels even brighter, and the darkest pixels even darker. As you'll see, this is useful when the video looks slightly dingy.

When you adjust black, you increase the number of black pixels in the video by converting an increasing number of pixels that are close to black to absolute black, which usually cures fading. The white adjustment works the same way for white pixels. Let's see how these adjustments can work together to make a video "pop" visually.

1   In Expert view, click to select Gator10.mp4, and position the current-time indicator over that clip.

2. Click the Adjust button to open that panel.

3   Click the disclosure triangle to the left of the Lighting effect to reveal its controls. At the bottom right of the panel, click More to expose all the individual controls shown in the figure.

4   Adjust the controls to the values shown in the figure.

Tip: Truth be told, it's a very rare clip that can't use some contrast improvement. Try this on your own clips and you'll see what I mean.

5 At the top right of the Adjust dialog box, next to the Auto Fix checkbox, click the eye icon (👁). Do you see how these adjustments seem to remove a layer of gray from over the clip? That's the dinginess mentioned above. You removed this by increasing the brightness of all the pixels in the video, increasing the contrast between the brightest and darkest pixels, and then slightly increasing the number of black pixels in the frame.

Tip: You probably noticed the Auto Fix checkbox to the right of the Lighting control. Sometimes this works really well, sometimes not. To try it, just click the checkbox. If it doesn't improve the video, click it again to disable it.

Tip: If you push contrast too far, you can lose details in the darkest and lightest regions of the video. For example, watch the heron closely as you enable and disable the effect. Note the loss of some fine detail along the neck and body. Watch the brightest and darkest regions for loss of detail when adjusting contrast.

What about the exposure control? I knew you were going to ask. Basically, exposure is very similar to brightness, but slightly different; I would adjust one, but not both. For more information, check out Lightroom Adjustments: Exposure vs Brightness, at bit.ly/exposure_brightness.

Adjusting the midtones with Gamma Correction

Move your current-time indicator over Gator08.mp4 in the timeline, and drag through the entire clip. The sky is certainly bright enough, but the shadows beneath the fabulous Spanish moss are just too dark, particularly around 00;00;48;20. Here, you want an effect that will boost just these shadows while not affecting the brightest or darkest pixels. That's precisely what Gamma Correction is designed to do.

The classic use for the Gamma Correction effect is a backlighting situation, when the light behind the subject is brighter than the subject itself, resulting in a face that's too dark in footage shot with automatic exposure. In essence, that's what we have in Gator08.mp4. I was trying to capture the Spanish moss, but my Canon Vixia, shooting in automatic mode, darkened the video because the sky behind the Spanish moss was so bright. Let's fix that.

1 If necessary, click the Expert button (Expert) to enter Expert view.

2 Click to select Gator08.mp4, and position the current-time indicator over that clip.

3 Click the Adjust button to open that panel.

4 Click the disclosure triangle to the left of the Gamma Correction effect to reveal its controls. At the bottom right of the panel, click More to expose the numeric slider.

5 Adjust the controls to the values shown in the figure.

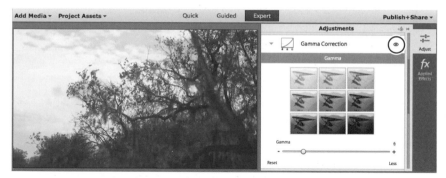

6 At the top right of the Adjust dialog box, click the eye icon (👁). Do you see how the effect boosts the brightness in the shadowed regions without totally blowing out the whites in the sky? That's the desired effect.

▶ **Tip:** If you prefer, you can use the tic-tac-toe-like presets board to choose values for each of these configurations, choosing a different item to configure by clicking the various tabs across the top.

OK, we've looked at three ways to address brightness and contrast issues in our clips; let's move on to color-related issues.

Boosting saturation with the Color Effect

As much as I would have wished that our bayou boat trip occurred on a sunny, breezy day, the fact of the matter was that the weather was cloudy and slightly dreary, and the water was gray and unappealing. Move your current-time indicator over Gator03.mp4 and you'll see what I mean.

We could accept and share this reality with all who watch our video, or we could fix it in post (as they say). Let's explore one effect you can use to do the latter— specifically, the Color adjustment. This effect lets you modify the Hue, Lightness, Saturation, and Vibrance values of a clip.

The hue adjustment modifies the intrinsic colors in the clip. I almost never use this adjustment, preferring the Red/Green/Blue controls discussed in the next section. Lightness modifies the brightness of a clip; I prefer to use the Brightness, Contrast, and Gamma controls to address these issues. Saturation adjusts the strength of the colors within a clip, and is the Color adjustment I use most frequently. Vibrance is similar to saturation, but protects skin tones, which can quickly become too neon-ish when you push saturation too far. So, use saturation when there are no faces in the video, and vibrance where there are faces. Let's see how boosting saturation can make the weather for our boat ride look better than it actually was.

1 In Expert view, click to select Gator03.mp4, and position the current-time indicator over that clip.

2 Click the Adjust button to open that panel.

3 Click the disclosure triangle to the left of the Color effect to reveal its controls. At the bottom right of the panel, click More to expose the numeric sliders.

4 Adjust the controls to the values shown in the figure.

▶ **Tip:** If you apply too much saturation, colors can bleed from one object to another, which is close to happening in the red bars in the propeller cage in this clip. You can also see something funky going on at the distant shoreline. In real life, I probably would have adjusted saturation to about 20 and left it at that.

5 At the top right of the Adjust dialog box, click the eye icon (👁). Now, the water in the harbor looks blue, the boat looks freshly painted, and everything else looks brighter and more interesting.

Adjusting a single color with the Color (RBG) effect

Sometimes you want to adjust only a single color, which you can't do with the Color effect. For example, move your current-time indicator over Gator09.mp4, which is predominantly comprised of water that I wish were blue. If you boost saturation as demonstrated in the previous exercise, you very quickly see distortion at the shoreline. As you'll learn in this exercise, you can avoid that problem by using the Color RGB effect, which lets you separately adjust red, green, and blue values.

Separate adjustments are also useful when correcting white-balance issues, which often manifest as overly blue tones caused by white balancing for incandescent bulbs for indoor shooting and shooting outside. In these cases, you can use the Color (RGB) effect to eliminate the blue tone. Here's how. Note that you have to be in Expert view to access the Color (RGB) effect.

1 Click to select Gator09.mp4, and position the current-time indicator over that clip.

2 Click the Adjust button to open that panel.

3 Click the disclosure triangle to the left of the Color (RGB) effect to reveal its controls. At the bottom right of the panel, click More to expose the numeric sliders.

4   Adjust the controls to the values shown in the figure.

5   At the top right of the Adjust dialog box, click the eye icon (👁). Now, the water in the harbor looks blue, with minimal effect on the other colors in the frame.

6   Choose File > Save As, and save your project as **Lesson06_Work.prel**.

Stabilizing shaky footage

One common problem with vacation video footage is excessive shakiness, which can occur any time you don't use a tripod (or when you're shooting from a speeding airboat). Via the Smart Fix function, Adobe Premiere Elements stabilizes the worst of the SD clips, but for HD clips like those we're using in this project, you'll have to do it manually. The worst of the clips in this project is Gator05.mp4, which was shot while we were moving at full speed across the harbor.

Note that the Stabilizer effect is available in the Effect panel in both Quick and Expert views. In Quick view it's in the Video Effects folder; in Expert view it's in the Video Stabilizer folder.

1   In the Action bar at the bottom of the main window, click the Effects button (*fx* Effects) to open the Effects panel.

2   From the pull-down menu at the top of the panel, choose the Video Effects folder (Quick view) or Video Stabilizer folder (Expert view). In Quick view, use the slider on the right of the panel to scroll down to the Stabilizer effect on the fourth row.

3   Drag the Stabilizer effect from the Effects panel onto the fifth clip in the timeline, and drag the current-time indicator over the fifth clip.

4   Click the Applied Effects button (*fx*) at the top right of the Monitor panel to open the Applied Effects panel.

▶ **Tip:** For serious white balance issues, try the Three-Way Color Corrector effect, which you can access in Expert mode. See Adobe Premiere Elements Help for assistance with this effect.

5 In the Applied Effects panel, click the disclosure triangle to the left of the Stabilizer effect to open the parameter settings.

6 Click the eye icon (👁) next to the Stabilizer effect to toggle it off and on (👁). Note how Adobe Premiere Elements zoomed in on the frame when it stabilized the video.

7 Drag the current-time indicator to 00;00;26;25. Notice the black bar atop the video where the adjustment was too strong and extended beyond the frame's edge. To eliminate this, select Limit To Zoom. Notice how Adobe Premiere Elements zooms further into the clip to eliminate the black bar.

8 Scrub through the other portions of the clip to see if any bars appear.

9 Click the Play button beneath the Monitor panel. Even on a very fast computer, it's likely that you'll see the message shown in the figure below. Let's eliminate that by rendering this effect.

Previewing and rendering effects

When you apply an effect or configure an adjustment, Adobe Premiere Elements will show a very close approximation of the result when you preview in the Monitor panel. In most instances, this is good enough to allow you to perfect your configuration options and move on to the next edit.

If the quality isn't sufficient, right-click the frame in the Monitor panel, and choose Playback Quality > Highest. This tells Adobe Premiere Elements to prioritize frame quality over playback speed. As a result, on slower computers, playback may be jerky, but frame quality should be very good.

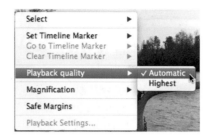

On the other hand, if playback speed isn't sufficient—as it isn't with the Stabilization effect you just applied—right-click in the Monitor panel, and make sure that Automatic is selected. This tells Adobe Premiere Elements to prioritize smoothness over frame quality. With Automatic selected, you might see some blurriness or pixelation in the frame, but playback should be smooth.

If neither setting gives you the preview quality that you need to finalize the edit, you'll have to render the clip.

If you made the adjustments in the previous exercise, you should see an orange line above multiple clips in the timeline, including Gator05.mp4. In general, the orange line indicates that some adjustment has been made to the clip that must be rendered before final production. For example, if you apply a title above a clip, you'll see the orange line. If you insert a clip into a project that doesn't match the Project Setting—like the JPEG images inserted into the slide show at the end of the project—you'll see the orange line as well. You don't have to render to preview your work; however, rendering will show you exactly how the final video will look. Unless you're running on a very slow computer, the rendered video will also play back at full speed.

To render the entire project, click Enter (Windows) or Return (Mac OS), or press the Render button (Render) at the bottom right of the Monitor panel. Adobe Premiere Elements opens the Rendering dialog box, which tells you how many previews need to be rendered and how long it will take. After rendering, Adobe Premiere Elements turns the orange bar to green, and you can start previewing your clips from the beginning.

Rendering a work area

In most instances, it's not necessary to render every edit, and sooner or later you'll have lots of orange lines over your timeline. At some point, you'll apply an effect that you do want to render, again, particularly with CPU-intensive effects like the Stabilizer. If you press Enter (Windows) or Return (Mac OS) to render, you render the *entire* timeline, which can be time-consuming. As an alternative, you can simply render the work area that you're interested in.

The work area is a region of the project defined by two vertical markers ( ) that live in the time scale above the timeline. By default, the work area starts at the beginning of the project and ends with the last content on the timeline, and expands with your project as you add more content. However, you can drag the work area bars to define any region in the timeline, so that you can render only that region. In this exercise, you'll learn how.

1 Choose Timeline > Delete Rendered Files. If that option isn't available, choose Delete Rendered Files For All Projects. Click OK in the Confirm Delete dialog. This deletes the files that you previously rendered, and should turn the green bars above the timeline to orange.

2 Press the Backslash key (\) to show the entire project in the timeline.

3 Drag the left work area marker ( ) from the very front of the timeline to the start of Gator05.mp4.

4 Drag the right work area marker ( ) from the very end of the timeline to the end of Gator05.mp4.

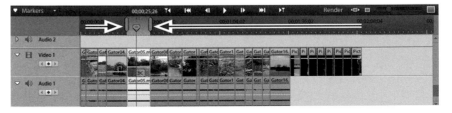

5 Press Enter (Windows) or Return (Mac OS) to render the work area. When it's done rendering, Adobe Premiere Elements will start previewing at the start of Gator05.mp4. When ready, press the spacebar to stop video playback.

6 Choose File > Save As, and save your project as **Lesson06_Work.prel**. Replace file as needed.

A few more notes on the work area

Sometimes it may not be convenient to zoom out to see the entire clip and the edges of the work area bar. As an alternative to dragging the edges, you can place the current-time indicator at the start of the work area you want to create, and press Alt+[(Windows) or Option+[(Mac OS) to set the start of the work area. Then drag the current-time indicator to the end of the work area, and press Alt+] (Windows) or Option+] (Mac OS) to set the end point. Then press Enter (Windows) or Return (Mac OS) to render the work area.

To reset the work area bar to the entire project, double-click the very top of the time scale area. If you click too low in the timeline, the current-time indicator will move to that location. Click higher, and the work area bar will reset.

If you're zoomed in on the project, you can use the same technique to set the work area bars at the visible edges of the project. Just double-click the very top of the time scale, and the work area bars will move to the edges of the visible portion of the timeline.

Working with Time Remapping

Time Remapping lets you adjust the speed of a clip—forward or backward—and then return to the original speed of the clip. This can produce very elegant, TV- and movie-like results. We'll return to the bayou boat ride project to apply a global speed change to several clips; in this exercise, you'll use Time Remapping to analyze the author's golf swing. After you've done this, you'll reframe the clip using Motion controls to center the video.

Loading the project

1   Launch Adobe Premiere Elements, if it isn't already running.

2   Choose File > Open Project. If you haven't saved the previous project, do so as **Lesson06_Work.prel** now.

3   In the Open Project dialog box, navigate to the Lesson06 folder you downloaded to your hard drive. Within that folder, select Lesson06_Driver_Win.prel (Windows) or Lesson06_Driver_Mac.prel (Mac OS), and then click Open (Windows) or Choose (Mac OS). If a dialog box appears asking for the location of rendered files, click the Skip Previews button.

    The project opens.

4 Choose Window > Restore Workspace to ensure that you start the lesson with the default panel layout.

Time Remapping is available in Quick and Expert views, so you can work in either view.

Time-Remapping your clips

The original clip is a little less than eight seconds long; the first four seconds are the setup, and then the swing and transition. In this exercise, you'll use reverse motion to create an instant replay, and then slow down the swing to painful slow motion to analyze the flaws.

As with many Adobe Premiere Elements tools, Time Remapping has a dedicated workspace for configuring and resetting the effect. In fact, it resembles Quick view to a great degree because it has a very similar Monitor panel and timeline. However, instead of the Action bar, you'll find configuration options for the Time Remapping function.

Operationally, you'll create one or more TimeZones, which produce the desired speed changes. You don't have the option to slow or accelerate audio, so you can either keep the original audio, which obviously won't match the video, or remove the audio, which seems like the right decision in most applications.

Note that there are many variables affecting the timecode and duration field in this exercise, and you can drive yourself nuts trying to reproduce the precise times in the figures. Instead, focus on the high-level task, which is adding two time zones: one at 50% speed and the other at 25% speed. If the times on your screen are within a half second or two of those shown in the figures, you will accomplish that task.

1 Click to select driver.mp4 in the timeline.

2 In the Action bar at the bottom of the window, click the Tools button (✕ Tools) to open the Tools panel.

3 Use the slider on the right of the panel to scroll down to the Time Remapping tool, which is at or near the bottom in both Quick and Expert views. Then click Time Remapping in the Tools panel to apply the tool to the selected clip and to open the Time Remapping panel.

4 Drag the current-time indicator to about 00;00;04;05 in the Monitor panel, and then click the plus sign (◼) next to the current-time indicator to create a TimeZone. By default, Adobe Premiere Elements creates a 17-frame TimeZone.

5   Click and drag the right edge of the TimeZone to about 00;00;07;00. This applies the effect to the selected 2.8 seconds in the clip. If you know the duration to which you want to apply the effect, you can enter the desired time in the Duration field on the lower right rather than dragging the edge of the TimeZone.

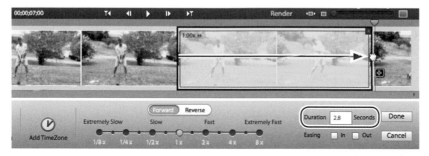

6   Note the Forward/Reverse toggle in the Action bar area. Select Reverse, and then click the 8x button on the Time Control slider to move the speed selector to 8 times faster than real time. You could also click and drag the speed selector to that location.

7 Press the Home key to return the current-time indicator to the start of the clip, and then press the spacebar to play the clip. The video will play at normal speed until it reaches the end of the TimeZone, return at 8x speed to the 4:05 mark, and then play the swing again at full speed.

Creating variable-speed, slow-motion effects

OK, let's focus on forward action and really analyze that swing. You'll slow down the takeaway to 50% speed, and then, at the top of the backswing, slow the speed to 25% during the critical downswing. At the end, you'll return the clip to 100% speed.

1 To start, click the Reset button ( ) on the lower left, and click Yes to remove all TimeZones.

2 Drag the current-time indicator to about 00;00;04;05 in the Monitor panel, or click the monitor timecode, enter **405**, and then press Enter (Windows) or Return (Mac OS). Then click the plus sign ( ) next to the current-time indicator to create a TimeZone.

3 Click and drag the right edge of the TimeZone to about 00;00;05;00, just before the downswing begins. In the prerelease versions used to create the files for this lesson, I had to drag the edge to 00;00;05;02 to make the current-time indicator stay at 00;00;05;00 once I released the edge.

4 Make sure that Forward is selected in the Forward/Reverse toggle. Then click the 1/2x button on the Time Control slider. You could also click and drag the speed selector to that location. This slows the clip to half speed.

5 On the bottom right of the Time Remapping panel, select the Easing In check box, which smooths the shift from 1x to 1/2x speed at the start of the effect. Because you want to transition directly from 1/2x speed to 1/4x speed in the next TimeZone, you don't want to select Easing Out, which will ease out to the original 1x speed.

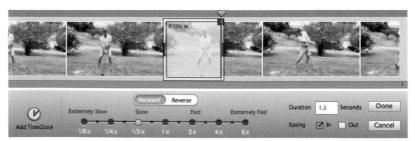

6 Click and drag the current-time indicator as close to the right edge of the previous TimeZone as possible while still seeing the plus sign ( ), which should be around 00;00;05;16. If you drag it so that it touches the right edge of the first TimeZone, the plus sign will disappear.

7 Click the plus sign to create another TimeZone, and drag the right edge to about 00;00;06;18. Again, you may have to drag a bit past this timecode to make the timecode stop at 00;00;06;18 when you release the TimeZone edge.

Make sure that Forward is selected in the Forward/Reverse toggle. Then click the 1/4x button on the Time Control slider to move the speed selector to that value, and select the Easing In and Easing Out options. These will smooth the transition from 1/2x to 1/4x speed at the start of the effect and then transition from 1/4x to 1x at the very end.

● **Note:** When not selected, TimeZones with forward motion are light green; TimeZones with reverse motion are light orange. All TimeZone speed and direction indicators are on the upper right.

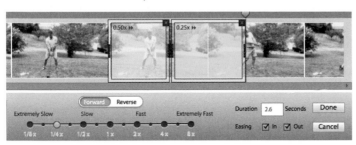

8 Press the Home key to return the current-time indicator to the start of the clip, and then press the spacebar to play the clip. The video will play at normal speed to the 4:05 mark, ease to 1/2 speed, then ease into 1/4 speed, and then ease back to full speed at the very end.

9 At the bottom left of the Time Remapping panel, click the Remove Audio button ( ) to remove audio from the clip. Click Yes to confirm that you do want to remove the audio.

● **Note:** When you apply Time Remapping to a clip in the timeline, Adobe Premiere Elements adjusts all subsequent clips on the timeline accordingly. If you slow down the clip, all subsequent clips will be pushed to the right. If you accelerate the clip, Adobe Premiere Elements will shift subsequent clips to the left to close any gap.

10 At the bottom left of the Time Remapping panel, click the Frame Blending button ( ) to apply frame blending to the slow motion effect. Frame blending can smooth the appearance of slow motion but sometimes can introduce blurriness in the clip. Click the Render button (Render) on the bottom right of the Monitor panel in the Time Remapping tool to render the effect; then play back the clip with and without Frame Blending, and choose the option that you prefer.

11 At the bottom right of the Time Remapping panel, click Done to apply Time Remapping, close the panel, and return to the main interface.

▶ **Tip:** To change any Time Remapping options or to remove Time Remapping from a clip, follow steps 1–3 of the previous exercise to open the Time Remapping panel, and click Reset ( ) on the bottom left. When you close the panel, Adobe Premiere Elements removes the effect.

Reframing content with Motion controls

Time Remapping is working, but the framing of the shot is off; there's too much space over the subject's head, and he needs to be more centered in the frame. You can improve both problems using the Motion controls. In this exercise, you'll learn how to use Motion controls to reframe a video; later in the lesson, you'll learn how to use these controls to reframe still images.

Motion controls are available in Quick and Expert views; you can work in the view in which you feel most comfortable.

Reframing video with Motion controls

Let's start by reframing some video.

1 Click driver.mp4 to select the clip in the timeline.

2 Click the Applied Effects button () on the top right of the Monitor panel to open the Applied Effects panel.

3 In the Applied Effects panel, click the disclosure triangle to the left of the Motion effect to open the parameter settings.

● **Note:** If you zoom too far into a clip, you can create blurriness or softness in the clip. If blurriness results from your reframing efforts, you can minimize it to some degree by applying the Sharpen effect.

4 Zoom in on the video and make it larger. Do any of the following:

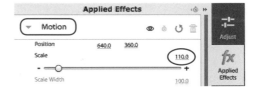

- Drag the Scale slider to the right to a value of 110.

- Click the numeric entry to make it active, type **110**, and then press Enter (Windows) or Return (Mac OS).

- Hold the pointer over the numeric value until it becomes the pointer with arrows (). Click and drag to the right to 110.

Now you'll reframe the image.

5 In the Monitor panel, right-click the frame, and choose Magnification > 50%. If you're working on a notebook computer or very small monitor, choose Magnification > 25%.

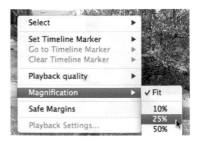

6 Click the frame in the Monitor panel to make the center crosshair active. You should see a white box outside the visible frame in the Monitor panel. (If you can't see the top and bottom outlines of the box, expand the entire Adobe Premiere Elements window, or if you don't have room on your screen, decrease the magnification following the instructions in step 5.)

As you've probably guessed, this is an outline of the entire video, which you can drag around to optimize positioning within the preview area in the Monitor panel. As you drag the frame, note that the numeric Position parameters on the right update as you move it. You can position the frame either by dragging it directly, as you just did, or by typing in new numeric parameters. I typed in 700 and 328, which shifted the video to the right and up a bit.

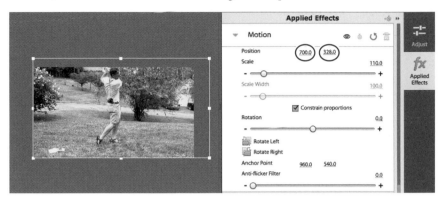

7   In the Monitor panel, right-click the frame, and choose Magnification > Fit. This sets your preview to the largest possible size while showing all the pixels in the video, which is helpful when you're previewing Motion control adjustments.

8   Click the eye icon next to the Motion effect to toggle it off (☜) and on (☜). You'll see that you've increased the size of the subject of the video and moved him toward the center. It's not a huge difference, but even a small improvement is welcome.

9   Press the Home key to return the current-time indicator to the start of the clip, and then press the spacebar and watch the entire clip.

Whenever you adjust the size or positioning of a video, as you've done here, you might push other critical content located elsewhere in the clip out of the viewing window. Either preview the entire clip that you've adjusted or, for longer clips, drag the current-time indicator through the clip slowly to identify any problem areas.

10 Let's review some of the other options and controls in the Motion effect:

• **Constrain proportions:** By default, Adobe Premiere Elements constrains the proportions of your size adjustments, adjusting horizontally and vertically to preserve the aspect ratio of your video. That's why the Scale Width slider and numeric entry are grayed out. If you deselect Constrain Proportions, the Scale Width slider will become active, and the Scale slider will convert to a Scale Height slider. You can then adjust the two controls separately. This can distort your video or still images, so be careful if this isn't the look you're seeking.

- **Rotation:** These controls allow you to level out videos shot a bit off-kilter and easily shift still images shot in portrait mode to landscape, and vice versa.

- **Anchor Point:** This is the point around which all Motion controls, including positioning and rotation controls, operate. By default, it's set to the center of the image or video.

- **Anti-flicker Filter:** This filter reduces flicker in pan-and-zoom effects created using the Motion controls. If you're using the Motion controls to create a pan-and-zoom effect and see flicker in the result, try dragging the Anti-flicker Filter slider to the right. Always render and gauge the results before applying the filter, because it can cause blurriness.

11 If you want to save your work, now would be a good time, although you won't be returning to this project.

Reframing an image with Motion controls

Although we're sure that you'd love to work on that golf swing for a few more exercises, it's time to add some finishing touches to the bayou boat ride clip.

1 Launch Adobe Premiere Elements, if it isn't already running.

2 Choose File > Open Project. If asked, click No, and don't save any changes to the existing project.

Note: Motion controls operate identically in Quick and Expert views, but we'll be working in the latter, so you should work there too if you want your screen to match what you see in the book.

3 In the Open Project dialog box, navigate to the Lesson06 folder you copied to your hard drive. Within that folder, select the file Lesson06_Work.prel, and then click Open (Windows) or Choose (Mac OS). If a dialog box appears asking for the location of rendered files, click the Skip Previews button.

The project opens.

4 Move the current-time indicator over the first picture in the slide show at the end of the videos, which should be Picture 1.jpg. Notice in the Monitor panel that the picture has black vertical bars, or letterboxes, on the sides. This often happens when you add images shot using a 4:3 aspect ratio to 16:9 projects.

5 Click Picture 1.jpg to select it.

6 Click the Applied Effects button (🔳) at the top right of the Monitor panel to open the Applied Effects panel.

7 In the Applied Effects panel, click the disclosure triangle to the left of the Motion effect to open the parameter settings.

8 Zoom in to the picture to make it larger. Do any of the following:

- Drag the Scale slider to the right to a value of 125.

- Click the numeric entry to make it active, type **125**, and then press Enter (Windows) or Return (Mac OS).

- Hold the pointer over the numeric value until it becomes the pointer with arrows (🖐). Press your left mouse button, and drag to the right to 125.

9 Choose File > Save to save your project.

Changing playback speed

Time Remapping is an awesome feature, but sometimes you just want to quickly change the speed of a clip, and there's a simpler way to get that done. In this project, for example, Gator01.mp4 and Gator09.mp4 are just too short, and there's a turtle in Gator11.mp4 that you can see only if you slow the video way down. We'll use Time Stretch to get more out of those shots.

1 In Expert view, right-click Gator01.mp4, and choose Time Stretch. Adobe Premiere Elements opens the Time Stretch dialog box. (Time Stretch is also available in the Tools panel.)

2 Type **50** in the Speed box (where it will appear as 50%), and select Maintain Audio Pitch.

3 Click OK to close the dialog box. Adobe Premiere Elements extends the clip to its new duration and pushes back all subsequent files.

● **Note:** As you can probably guess, the Reverse Speed option, when selected, will reverse the clip, making the video play backward.

4 Right-click Gator09.mp4, and choose Time Stretch. Hover your pointer over the Duration field until it becomes the pointer with arrows (⟨⟩). Drag to the right until the duration is 00;00;04;00. Or click the duration field to make it active, and type **400**. Adobe Premiere Elements changes the duration to 4:00. Select Maintain Audio Pitch, and click OK to close the dialog box.

5 Right-click Gator11.mp4, and choose Time Stretch. Type **10** in the Speed box (where it will appear as 10%), and select Maintain Audio Pitch. Click OK to close the dialog box. Preview the clip.

Now we have a better view of the turtle, but the clip is way too long, and it also takes too long to first see the turtle. Let's fix that.

6 Hover your pointer over the left edge of the Gator11.mp4 until it becomes the drag pointer (⊕). Click and drag the edge to the right to remove about 3:28 from the start of the clip.

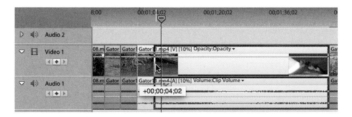

7 Hover your pointer over the right edge of the Gator11.mp4 until it becomes the drag pointer (⊕). Click and drag the edge to the left to remove about 35:24 from the end of the clip.

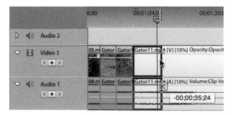

8 Choose File > Save to save your project.

Creating a Pan & Zoom effect

If you use a lot of still images in your productions, you've probably wanted to add motion to those images. The Adobe Premiere Elements Pan & Zoom tool is great for doing just that.

The basic unit of operation of the Pan & Zoom tool is the *focus frame*, and the tool creates motion by moving from focus frame to focus frame. You control three basic variables: the size and location of each focus frame, its duration (how long the frame stays at that location), and how long it takes to move from focus frame to focus frame.

Any timing changes made in the Pan & Zoom tool are reflected in the timeline, with all subsequent content on that track adjusted accordingly. For example, in the customization exercise below, you'll increase the duration of the image from 4 seconds to 12 seconds, and the pictures on the timeline after Picture 4.jpg will be pushed back.

For pictures with faces, there's a Face Frames option ([📷 Face Frames]) that tells Adobe Premiere Elements to create a project that inserts a focus frame on each face and pans to all faces in the project. If there are no faces, Adobe Premiere Elements starts with a wide shot, and then zooms into the center of the image for a close-up.

The focus frames in an image are presented in the thumbnail view at the bottom of the tool's dialog box. To choose a focus frame and edit any parameters, click the focus frame in the thumbnail view. When you hover your pointer over the focus frame, as the pointer is hovering over the first focus frame in the figure on the next page, its parameters will appear.

You can change the order of focus frames by dragging the thumbnails into the desired order. Click Play Output to preview the Pan & Zoom effect at any time, after which you must click Exit Preview ([✖ Exit Preview]) to exit the effect.

In the timeline above the thumbnail view, the green area is hold time and the blue area is pan time. The duration of each is shown in seconds.

Let's apply the Pan & Zoom tool to Picture 4.jpg and have a look at the interface; in the next exercise you'll customize the Pan & Zoom effect. You can be in either Quick or Expert view for the following exercises.

Applying the Pan & Zoom effect

1   Click Picture 4.jpg to select it.

2   In the Action bar at the bottom of the window, click the Tools button ([✖ Tools]) to open the Tools panel.

3 Use the slider on the right of the panel to scroll down to the Pan & Zoom tool (⊞), which is near the middle in both Quick and Expert views. Then click Pan & Zoom in the Tools panel to apply the tool to Picture 4.jpg and open the Pan & Zoom tool.

4 At the bottom of the Pan & Zoom tool window, click Play Output (Play Output ▸) to watch the effect.

5 In the upper right corner of the tool window, click Exit Preview (⌘ Exit Preview). Then, in the thumbnail view across the bottom of the Pan & Zoom tool, click the second thumbnail.

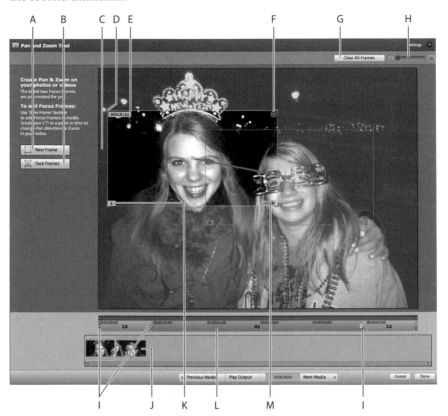

A. New frame	H. Zoom controls for focus frame
B. Face frames	I. Focus frame markers
C. Preview area	J. Focus frame thumbnails
D. Resize handle for focus frame	K. Focus frame number
E. Hold time	L. Pan & Zoom timeline
F. Delete frame	M. Focus frame size controls
G. Clear all frames	

Customizing the Pan & Zoom effect

Now that you have a bit of background, let's create our own Pan & Zoom effect. While you can try to work around the faces found by the program, it's often easier to start fresh and create the effect from scratch. Adobe Premiere Elements does a great job finding faces, but hey, we humans are pretty good at that too, particularly when it's our daughters in the picture.

In this festive picture, I want to create an effect that starts with the full wide shot for two seconds, takes one second to transition to a two-second close-up of the girl on the left, one second to transition to a two-second close-up of the girl on the right, then one second to transition to a two-second wide shot similar to the starting point.

1 If you're still in Preview mode, click the Exit Preview button at the top of the preview window (or press Esc on your keyboard) to exit Preview mode. At the top right of the Pan & Zoom tool, click Clear All Frames (Clear All Frames).

2 Drag the current-time indicator to the start of the clip.

3 On the left toolbar, click New Frame (New Frame). The Pan & Zoom tool creates a new focus frame at the start of the clip.

4 Hover your pointer over the lower right corner of the focus frame; it becomes a drag pointer ( ). Click and drag the edge until it's as large as possible. You can click and drag the frame to the upper-left corner to make room to expand the frame.

5 To set the hold time to 2 seconds, hover your pointer over the focus frame until HOLD: 1s appears at the upper left. Click that to open the Hold Time dialog box.

6 Increase the duration to 2 seconds. As with most Adobe Premiere Elements controls, you can either click and drag the time to the right, or click the time to make the field active and type **200**. Click OK to close the dialog box.

7 Set the second focus frame. To create a pan time of 1 second, you'll need to create it one second after the end of the first focus frame. To do this, while watching the timecode located immediately to the right of the Play Output button ( Play Output ⊙), drag the current-time indicator to 00;00;03;00.

8 On the left toolbar, click New Frame (⬚ New Frame). The Pan & Zoom tool creates a new focus frame at the 3-second mark.

9 Use the resize handles on the focus frame to frame the face of the girl on the left. To move the frame, click the pointer within the frame. A hand symbol (✋) will appear. Click and drag the frame to the desired location.

● **Note:** The time over the blue line linking the center of the two frames is the pan time. We're setting pan time by dragging the current-time indicator to the desired position before creating a new frame. If you were editing an existing set of focus frames, you would reset pan time by clicking the pan time number, which would open a Pan Time dialog box. We'll experiment with that below.

10 Set the hold time to 2 seconds. Hover your pointer over the focus frame until HOLD: 1s appears at the upper left. Click that to open the Hold Time dialog box, and then set the time to 2 seconds.

11 Set the third focus frame, again with a one-second pan time. Watching the timecode located immediately to the right of the Play Output button (Play Output ⏵), drag the current-time indicator to 00;00;06;00.

12 On the left toolbar, click New Frame (⬚ New Frame). The Pan & Zoom tool creates a new focus frame at the 6-second mark.

13 Use the resize handles to frame the face of the girl on the right.

14 Set the hold time to 2 seconds. Hover your pointer over the focus frame until HOLD: 1s appears on the upper left. Click that to open the Hold Time dialog box, and then set the time to 2 seconds.

15 Set the fourth focus frame, this time with a two-second pan time. Watching the timecode located immediately to the right of the Play Output button (Play Output ⏵), drag the current-time indicator to 00;00;10;00.

16 On the left toolbar, click New Frame (⬚ New Frame). The Pan & Zoom tool creates a new focus frame at the 10-second mark.

17 Use the resize handles and the grab control to make the frame as large as possible and position it at the top of the frame.

18 Set the hold time to 2 seconds. Hover your pointer over the focus frame until the HOLD: 1s hold time appears on the upper left. Click that to open the Hold Time dialog box, and then set the time to 2 seconds.

19 Click the 2 second (2s) pan time between the two images to open the Pan Time dialog box. Set the pan time to 1 second, and click OK to close the dialog box.

● **Note:** The Pan & Zoom tool doesn't currently support the Face Frames option in video.

20 Drag the current-time indicator to the start of the timeline, and then, at the bottom of the Pan & Zoom tool, click Play Output (Play Output ⏵) to watch the effect. Then click Done on the bottom right to close the Pan & Zoom tool dialog box. If necessary for smooth preview, click the Render button (Render) at the lower right of the Monitor panel.

● **Note:** If the Pan & Zoom tool creates extra frames at the end of the clip, you can just trim them off as you normally would on the timeline.

21 Choose File > Save to save your project.

Working with keyframes

Every clip in the timeline, and most effects and adjustments that you apply to them, can be modified over time. This involves a concept called *keyframing*. A keyframe is essentially a location in the timeline where you specify a value for a specific property. When you set two keyframes, Adobe Premiere Elements interpolates the value of that property over all frames between the two keyframes, effecting a progressive change over the given time range and basically creating an animated effect.

Keyframes give you significant flexibility and creativity in your projects. Although they sound challenging at first, if you work through the next few exercises, you'll quickly grasp their operation and utility.

Using keyframes to animate effects

● **Note:** Keyframing is available only in Expert view.

Animating an effect using keyframes is a very powerful capability: Essentially, it lets you create custom transitions using any Adobe Premiere Elements effect. In this exercise, you'll use keyframes to animate the appearance of an effect.

Note that this section is more advanced than some users of Adobe Premiere Elements may need. You may choose to skip this lesson—but before you do, you should know that keyframing unlocks an immense well of creativity in Adobe Premiere Elements, and a few minutes of focused time here could quickly pay dividends in more creative projects. Of course, if you do choose to skip it now, you can always revisit it later.

In this exercise, you'll animate the Vignetting effect to add a unique visual transition to the start of the project. The Vignetting effect is a great tool for focusing the viewer's attention on a specific portion of the video; think of a soft hazy circle surrounding the happy bride or graduate in portraits you've seen. Our use here isn't quite so classic a case, but it should serve to illustrate the effect.

▶ **Tip:** On the Mac, in the Applied Effects panel, the Show/ Hide Keyframe toggle works only when the disclosure triangle for a particular effect has been clicked and those parameters are displayed. If it seems like nothing is happening when you click this button, check to make sure you've completed step 5.

1   If the Lesson06_Work.prel project is not open, open it by choosing File > Open Recent Project and choosing it from the menu that appears.

2   In the Action bar on the bottom of the Adobe Premiere Elements window, click the Effects button (*fx* Effects) to open the Effects panel.

3   From the pull-down menu at the top of the panel, choose the Advanced Adjustments folder. If necessary, use the slider on the right of the panel to scroll down to the Vignetting effect, which is the last one in the folder.

4   Drag the Vignetting effect from the Effects panel onto the first clip in the timeline (Gator01.mp4).

5   Click the Applied Effects button (*fx*) on the top right to open the Applied Effects panel.

6 In the Applied Effects panel, click the disclosure triangle to the left of the Vignetting effect to open the parameter settings.

7 In the upper right corner of the Applied Effects panel, click the Show/Hide Keyframe Controls icon ( ).

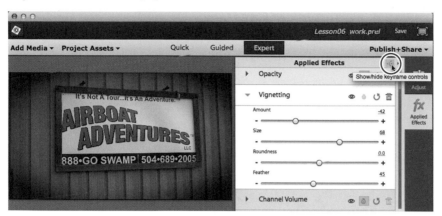

8 Note the mini-timeline at the top of the Vignetting effect, which has the same values as the main timeline for the selected clip and has a matching current-time indicator. Move the current-time indicator to the start of the clip, and click the small stopwatch icon ( ) to the left of the Amount control to animate this property.

After you click the stopwatch, a small diamond appears in the mini-timeline within the Applied Effects panel to the right of the configurable properties in the Amount control. This is the initial keyframe for the Amount value for this effect.

9 Drag the Amount slider all the way to the left to a value of −100.

Next we'll configure two other properties in the effect.

10 Click the stopwatch to the left of the Size option, and drag the slider to the left to the 0 value.

11 Click the stopwatch to the left of the Roundness option, and drag the slider to the right to 100. You should now have a focused, round vignette around the Airboat Adventures sign.

▶ **Tip:** Keyframes allow you to apply specific values to specific regions of the clip; when you have no keyframes, the selected values apply to the entire clip. Because we didn't create a keyframe for the Feather option, the default 45 configuration is applied universally over the entire clip. If you changed from 45 to 100, the new value would be applied universally.

Now you'll set the second keyframe.

12 In the mini-timeline in the Applied Effects panel, drag the current-time indicator to the right, about two seconds into the clip.

Note: Be sure to click the stopwatch icon only once when you're animating a property. If you accidentally click it twice, a dialog box will appear asking you if you want to delete existing keyframes for the clip. Click Cancel, and continue with the exercise.

13 Drag the Amount slider to the middle to a value of 0, which essentially turns off the effect.

Changing the value automatically adds a second keyframe, which is represented as a second diamond in the mini-timeline in the Applied Effects panel. After you turn on the animation, Adobe Premiere Elements automatically animates the effect between the two values. Note that Adobe Premiere Elements didn't create a new keyframe for the Size or Roundness parameters, because you did not adjust either option.

▶ **Tip:** With many (if not most) effects, you'll have to adjust all the options that you initially keyframed to completely remove the effect. Just repeat step 12 for each option, finding the value that zeroes out the effect.

▶ **Tip:** Clicking the universal toggle animation button for an effect creates a keyframe at the location of the current-time indicator for every keyframable value in the effect. This becomes a hassle if you want to adjust any particular value universally for the entire clip. It's usually simpler to click the stopwatches next to the configuration options that you want to keyframe, as you did in the exercise.

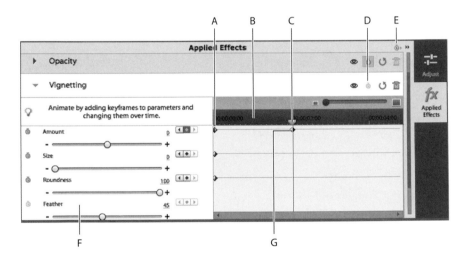

A. Initial keyframes

B. Mini-timeline

C. Current-time indicator

D. Universal toggle animation button (enables keyframes for all options in effect)

E. Show/Hide keyframes

F. Keyframable configuration options in the Vignetting effect

G. Second keyframe

14 Drag the current-time indicator to the start of the timeline, and then press the spacebar to play the clip. The clip starts out with the vignette in full effect and returns to a normal appearance at the 00;00;04;00 mark. Press the spacebar again to stop playback.

15 Choose File > Save As, and save your project as **Lesson06_Work.prel**. Replace if necessary.

● **Note:** If you hadn't set the second set of keyframes, the Vignetting effect would have continued without change through the end of the clip, but wouldn't continue on to subsequent clips.

Effect controls

Note the icons to the right of the Shadow/Highlight effect in the Applied Effects panel. We've discussed the "Toggle the effect on or off" icon; let's quickly cover the others.

- The stopwatch icon (officially, "Toggle Animation") lets you animate the effect with keyframes—covered later in this lesson in "Working with keyframes."
- The Reset icon resets the effect to its default parameters.
- The trash can icon deletes the effect.

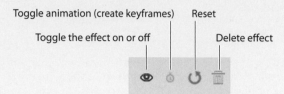

Toggle animation (create keyframes)   Reset

Toggle the effect on or off   Delete effect

Note that you can't delete any adjustments in the Adjustments panel or delete the Motion or Opacity effects in the Applied Effects panel.

Creating a fade-out using keyframes

Fading to black is one of the most common effects producers use at the end of their projects. Adobe Premiere Elements makes this simple to do with a control in the Applied Effects panel, although often you'll want to customize the effect. In this exercise, you'll learn how to fade to black and how to control keyframes in two locations in Adobe Premiere Elements: the Applied Effects panel and the timeline.

1 Click to select the Picture 8.jpg image, which is the last image in the timeline. You may need to scroll to the right in the timeline to fully see the image.

   Let's make the video tracks as large as possible to provide some working space.

2 To the right of the Picture 8.jpg clip, right-click a blank area on the timeline, and choose Track Size > Large. You may have to adjust the scroll bars on the right of the timeline to see the clip after adjusting the track size.

3 Drag the current-time indicator to about two seconds from the end of the project.

4 If necessary, click the Zoom In tool (■) in the Monitor panel to increase your view of the clip.

The orange line spanning horizontally across the clip is the connector line (or graph) between keyframes. As you'll see, you can access any keyframable value for any applied effect via this graph, although by default, the graph controls the Opacity property. You can tell because the text right after the name Picture 8 in the Video 1 track says Opacity: Opacity. This means that the orange line represents the Opacity value in the Opacity effect, which has only that one value.

5 To the right of the Monitor panel, click the Applied Effects button to open that panel, and then click the disclosure triangle next to the Motion effect.

6 Back in the timeline, click the Opacity: Opacity disclosure triangle above Picture 8.jpg to open the menu. Choose Motion > Position, and hold your pointer there. Notice that the parameters that you can choose on the timeline are identical to those in the Applied Effects panel. In essence, although you can apply and adjust keyframes to only one parameter at a time on the timeline, you can access any parameter available in the Applied Effects panel. Most of the time, it's most convenient to adjust these options in the Applied Effects panel. One notable exception is the Opacity value, which is used to fade to black.

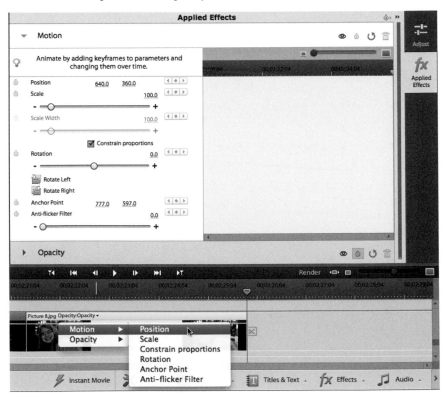

7 In the timeline, in the menu next to the Picture 8.jpg title, choose Opacity > Opacity. Now the orange keyframe graph controls Opacity, or the transparency values of the picture. To fade to black, you'll adjust from 100% opacity to 0%.

8 Working with the Picture 8.jpg file, place your pointer over the orange connector line. The pointer now includes a double-arrow icon (⬍).

9 Click and drag the connector line down toward the bottom of the clip. As you drag, you'll see a small window with changing numbers that represent the Opacity values. Drag the Opacity value to 0%; the Monitor panel fades to black. When you finish experimenting, drag the connector line back up toward the top of the clip to restore the clip's opacity to 100%.

Now you'll add keyframes to help Adobe Premiere Elements create a fade to black at the end of the movie.

At this point, the current-time indicator should be positioned about two seconds from the end of the clip.

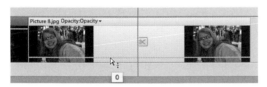

10 Press the Ctrl key (Windows) or Command key (Mac OS), and position your pointer on the orange connector line where it intersects with the current-time indicator line. Your pointer will change to a small cross icon (⬍₊), which is the Create Keyframe pointer.

11 Click the connector line once, right at the current-time indicator. You should see a small yellow diamond added to the orange connector line, representing your first keyframe.

12 Press the Page Down key to move the current-time indicator to the end of the movie. Repeat step 11 to create a keyframe at that location.

13 Click the keyframe at the end of the movie clip, and drag it down to the bottom of the track. The number on the right of the yellow box next to the pointer is the Opacity value; drag it until that value equals 0.00.

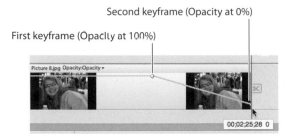

Second keyframe (Opacity at 0%)

First keyframe (Opacity at 100%)

14 To view the Opacity fade-out, move your current-time indicator to the beginning of the Picture 8.jpg clip, and then press the spacebar.

15 Save your project as **Lesson06_Work.prel**.

In Lesson 7, you'll learn how to create a similar effect using the Dip To Black transition. Although the visual effect is similar, working with keyframes lets you customize the effect to a much greater degree.

● **Note:** Sometimes when you use this technique to fade to black at the end of a clip, the clip doesn't seem to fade completely to black by the end. To fix this, using the technique described above, create another keyframe about one quarter of a second before the end of the clip, and drag that down to 0 opacity. Or, if you prefer, you can click and drag the keyframe at the end of the clip about one quarter of a second to the left. This will ensure that the clip fades completely to black by the end of the video.

Adjusting keyframes

After you've set a keyframe, you can modify it by dragging it to a new location or value. To delete a keyframe, right-click it, and choose Delete.

As mentioned earlier, you can access all keyframes inserted on the timeline in the Applied Effects panel. For example, try selecting Picture 8.jpg, and then clicking the Applied Effects button to open the Applied Effects panel (if it's not already open). If keyframes are not displayed, click the disclosure triangle to the left of the Opacity effect to open the parameter settings, and then click the Show/Hide Keyframe Controls icon (⊚) at the top right in the Applied Effects panel to view the keyframes.

You can set and modify opacity-related keyframes in either or both the timeline or the Applied Effects panel. In general, the timeline is best for fast and simple adjustments, like the fade-out that you just applied, whereas the Applied Effects panel is a better choice for complicated, more precise adjustments.

The other keyframe-related controls shown in the context menu in the figure below are advanced options that control the rate and smoothness of change applied by Adobe Premiere Elements. For more on those options, search for "Controlling change between keyframes" in Adobe Premiere Elements Help.

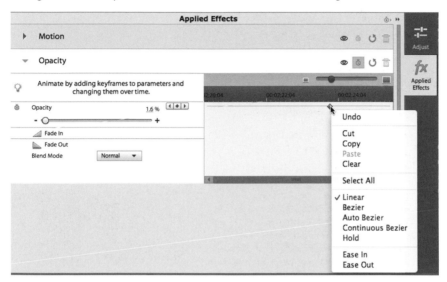

Applying effects to multiple clips

You may often find that you would like to apply adjustments made to a single clip to multiple clips. For example, if you shot 100 clips under identical lighting conditions, you may want to apply all color and brightness adjustments to all of those clips. If you've applied and configured a cool effect like NewBlue Cartoonr Plus (available only in Expert view) to a clip, you may want to apply the same effect in the same way to another clip, or to multiple clips. If you plan to use a FilmLook, you might want to apply the same one to all clips in your project.

Adobe Premiere Elements offers many options for applying a single effect to multiple clips:

• **Sharing applied effects by copying and pasting:** In both Quick and Expert views, you can copy and paste an Applied Effect from one clip to another in the Applied Effects panel.

- **Sharing applied effects by creating presets:** In Expert view, you can save an Applied Effect to a preset that you can apply to additional clips like any other effect.

- **Copying and pasting all effects and adjustments:** In both Quick and Expert views, you can copy and paste all effects and adjustments applied to a clip to another clip in the timeline.

- **Sharing adjustments via the Entire Movie button:** Although you can't save adjustments as presets, or copy and paste them individually, in Quick view you can apply adjustments made to any single clip to the entire movie via the Entire Movie button (**Entire Movie**).

- **Sharing Applied Effects via the Entire Movie button:** You can use the Entire Movie button to apply adjustments made to any Applied Effect to all clips, as long as that effect has been applied to all clips.

- **Applying an effect to multiple clips**: If you select one or more clips on the timeline, you can apply any effect to all selected clips by dragging the effect onto any of the selected clips. Once you've applied the effect, however, if you need to modify or delete it, you'll have to do so individually for each clip.

- **Applying an effect to multiple clips via an adjustment layer:** In Expert view, you can create an adjustment layer over the target clips. Then you can apply an effect to the adjustment layer, and Adobe Premiere Elements will apply that effect to all clips under the layer. If you need to customize or delete the effect, you can customize the settings on the adjustment layer, or delete the effect on the adjustment layer, or delete the adjustment layer itself.

Sharing Applied Effects via copy and paste

We've already applied and customized the Vignetting effect to the start of the production. Let's copy and paste that effect to the first picture in the slide show so the slide show opens with that same effect.

1   Click Gator01.mp4 in the timeline to select it.

2   If necessary, click the Applied Effects button to open that panel.

3   Right-click the Vignetting effect, and choose Copy.

Note: You can also click to select the effect and choose Edit > Copy, or press Ctrl+C (Windows) or Command+C (Mac OS) to copy the selected effects.

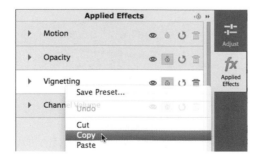

4 In the timeline, navigate to Picture 1.jpg. If necessary, click the Applied Effects button to open that panel.

5 Right-click in the blank area beneath the Opacity effect in the Applied Effects panel, and then choose Paste. Adobe Premiere Elements applies the Vignetting effect to this clip with the same properties, including the keyframes.

6 Grab the current-time indicator, and scroll through Picture 1.jpg on the timeline. You'll see the Vignetting effect at the start of the image, disappearing in two seconds.

● **Note:** This copy-and-paste function works well because we wanted the same effect to operate identically on the new clip. When pasting an applied effect with keyframes from one clip to another, the keyframes transfer as well. The next exercise addresses keyframes in the context of presets.

Saving a preset

Suppose you wanted to reuse the Vignetting intro again—not only within this project, but also for future projects. Because it's an Applied Effect (as opposed to an adjustment), you can save the effect, including all configuration options and keyframes, as a preset. Once saved, you apply it by dragging the preset onto any clip, just like any effect.

1 Click Gator01.mp4 in the timeline to select it. If necessary, click the Applied Effects button to open that panel.

2 In the Applied Effects panel, right-click the Vignetting effect, and choose Save Preset. The Save Preset dialog box opens.

3 Type **Vignetting transition-in preset** in the Name field.

4 Select Anchor To In Point as the Type.

The Type option controls how keyframes are handled when you apply the new preset to a clip with a duration different from the original clip. Scale scales the keyframes proportionally to the length of the target clip, and deletes existing keyframes on the target clip. Anchor To In Point positions the preset's first keyframe at the same distance from the target clip's In point as it was from the original clip's In point. This is the option to select with all "transition in" type effects like the Vignetting effect. Anchor To Out Point positions the preset's last keyframe at the same distance from the target clip's Out point as it was from the original clip's Out point. This is the option to select with all "transition out" type effects.

5 If desired, enter a description for your preset.

6 Click OK to save the preset.

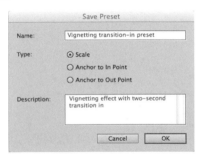

7 To view a custom preset, choose the My Presets folder from the pull-down menu in the Effects panel, which is visible only in Expert view. From there, you apply a preset by dragging the effect onto a clip or clips, just like any other effect.

Copying and pasting all effects and adjustments

The benefit of the above two techniques is precision: You can copy and paste a single effect or create a preset from a single effect. However, you can use these techniques only with *effects*, not with adjustments. In this exercise, you'll learn how to share adjustments.

As you'll see, however, it's a tradeoff; you must copy and paste *all* adjustments and effects, not any single adjustment—so you lose the precision of the previously discussed techniques. That's OK if the adjustment you're trying to copy to one or more other clips is the only adjustment made to the source clip, or, of course, if you wanted to copy all adjustments and effects to one or more other clips anyway. But if there are multiple adjustments and effects applied to the source clip—some that you want and some that you don't—they all will be transferred to the target clip or clips.

Let's copy the lighting effects that we applied to the heron in Gator10.mp4 to the alligator in both Gator12.mp4 clips.

1 Click Gator10.mp4 in the timeline to select it.

2 Right-click, and then choose Copy.

3 Click the first Gator12.mp4 clip in the timeline, and then press and hold the Shift key and click the second Gator12.mp4 clip. Right-click either clip, and choose Paste Effects And Adjustments.

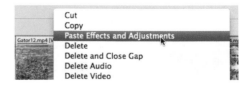

Premiere Elements applies the Lighting Adjustment to both clips, which you can verify in the Adjust panel.

4 Save your project as **Lesson06_End.prel**. We'll do some additional work in this project, but this completes the edits that will make their way into the next chapter.

Sharing adjustments via the Entire Movie button

In Quick view, you can share adjustments to all clips in the movie using the technique described below. Note that when I say all clips, I mean *all clips*; there's no way to exclude any clips. Typically, this makes this technique most useful when adjusting multiple clips from the same source.

1 Click Gator01.mp4 in the timeline to select it.

You can use any clip, but this was first, so it's the clip that I selected.

2 Click the Adjust button to open the Adjustments panel.

3 At the top right of the Adjustments panel, click the Entire Movie button (Entire Movie). If you don't see the Entire Movie button, it's because you're not in Quick view.

4 Click the disclosure triangle next to Color to reveal those controls.

5 Click More to reveal the discrete slider-based controls for the Color adjustment.

6 Drag the Saturation value all the way to the right to 100. We're not looking for subtlety here—just trying to illustrate how this control works.

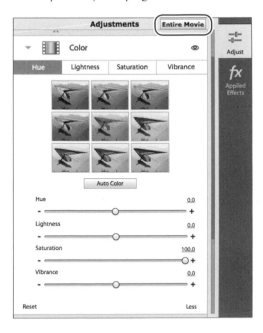

7 Drag the current-time indicator through the movie; you'll see that Adobe Premiere Elements applied the adjustment to all clips and pictures in the movie.

8 At the bottom left of the window, click Undo to undo the adjustment.

Sharing Applied Effects via the Entire Movie button

You can use the same technique to share adjustments made to all Applied Effects that are applied to all clips in the movie. Without applying any effects, for example, you can adjust the Motion and Opacity controls of all clips in the movie by clicking the Entire Movie button (Entire Movie) and then making your adjustments as described in the previous exercise.

If you wanted to adjust any other effect using this technique, you'd have to first apply it to every clip in the movie, still images and all, which you'll do in the next exercise. Then you can use the technique previously described to adjust the parameters for that effect for all clips in the movie.

Applying an effect to multiple clips

Adobe Premiere Elements makes it easy to apply an effect to one clip, a selected group of clips, or all clips in the project, as you'll learn now. In the next exercise, you'll learn how to use an adjustment layer to apply an effect to multiple clips, which is faster, more flexible, and easier to customize. In both exercises, we'll work with FilmLooks.

Briefly, FilmLooks are configured effects or collections of configured effects that give your video a certain look or feel. They're available in both Quick and Expert views, and are very easy to apply. Because FilmLooks remove all applied effects and reset all adjustments, they're best used early in the project design process, or via adjustment layers. Let's apply a FilmLook to the entire project.

1   Click the timeline to select it, and press Ctrl+A (Windows) or Command+A (Mac OS) to select all content in the timeline.

2   In the Action bar at the bottom of the timeline window, click the Effects button (ƒx Effects) to open the Effects panel.

3   From the pull-down menu at the top of the panel, choose the FilmLooks folder.

4   Drag the Summer Day effect from the Effects panel onto any clip in the timeline.

5   Click Yes when Adobe Premiere Elements asks if you want to remove all applied effects and adjustments.

When you click Yes, all applied effects will be removed and all adjustments reset. If you click No, the FilmLook won't be applied.

6   Press the Home key to move the current-time indicator to the start of the project, and then press the spacebar to preview the project. If playback isn't smooth enough to gauge the quality of the FilmLook, render the project by pressing Enter (Windows) or Return (Mac OS) or by clicking the Render button (Render) on the bottom right of the Monitor panel.

7   Click the Applied Effects button (fx) on the top right to open the Applied Effects panel. Click any clip in the timeline to select it.

8   In the Applied Effects panel, click the disclosure triangle to the left of the Split Tone effect to open the parameter settings.

The Summer Day FilmLook is a preconfigured version of the Split Tone effect, plus some customized parameters for the Color, Lighting, and Temperature and Tint adjustments, which you can see by opening the Adjustments panel. Beyond removing your applied effects and adjustments, applying a FilmLook directly to multiple clips makes it very time-consuming to customize, since you have to modify each clip individually. That's why using an adjustment layer is a better option.

9   Click Undo to remove the FilmLook effect from the project.

Using adjustment layers

Adjustment layers are project elements that you add to a project like any other clip. However, when you apply effects or adjustments to an adjustment layer, these are applied to all clips below the adjustment layer. We'll create one now.

1   If necessary, click the Expert button (Expert) to enter that view.

2   Click the Project Assets button (Project Assets ▾) to open that panel. In the panel menu on the top right, choose New Item > Adjustment Layer. Adobe Premiere Elements creates the adjustment layer and inserts it in the Project Assets panel.

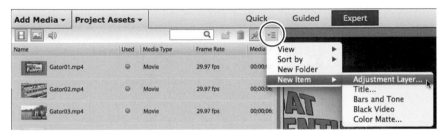

3   Drag the new adjustment layer onto the Video 2 track.

4 Click the Project Assets button to close that panel.

5 Click and drag the adjustment layer until it covers all the content on the Video 1 track.

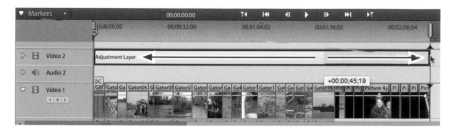

6 Drag the Summer Day effect from the Effects panel onto the adjustment layer.

7 Drag the current-time indicator through the movie. Adobe Premiere Elements has applied the FilmLook to all clips in the project without removing all applied effects or adjustments.

8 Click the adjustment layer to select it, and then click the Applied Effects button ( ) on the top right to open the Applied Effects panel. Click the disclosure triangle to the left of the Split Tone effect to open the parameter settings.

As you learned in the previous exercise, the Summer Day FilmLook is a precon-figured version of the Split Tone effect, plus some customized parameters for the Color, Lighting, and Temperature and Tint adjustments, which you can see by opening the Adjustments panel. However, since you applied the FilmLook to an adjustment layer, you can customize the FilmLook for the entire project by modify-ing the adjustments and Applied Effects in the adjustment layer. Plus, you don't lose all the other effects and adjustments that you previously made to your clips.

Creating a Picture-in-Picture overlay

● **Note:** Picture-in-Picture overlay is accessible only in Expert view.

Adobe Premiere Elements can superimpose multiple tracks of video over other tracks. In this exercise, you'll superimpose one video clip in a small frame over a preexisting background clip that covers the entire screen. This effect is called a Picture-in-Picture (PiP) overlay.

This project was derived from a French report prepared by my eldest daughter. I couldn't use the images that she originally used, because I didn't know their origin, and didn't want to trigger any copyright issues. So I grabbed some images from the CIA website that were copyright-free and in the public domain. If the images don't precisely match the description, you'll know why. Of course, as you'll discover, you'll have to speak French to tell.

1 To load the project file containing the new content, choose File > Open Project, and then navigate to the Lesson06 folder you copied to your hard drive.

2 Within that folder, select the file Lesson06_Videomerge_Win.prel (Windows) or Lesson06_Videomerge_Mac.prel (Mac OS), and then click Open (Windows) or Open (Mac OS). If you want to save the project you were working on, you know the drill. If a dialog box appears asking for the location of rendered files, click the Skip Previews button.

3 Choose Window > Restore Workspace to ensure that you start the lesson with the default panel layout.

4 If necessary, press the Home key to move the current-time indicator to the start of the project. Then drag the current-time indicator about one second to the right so that the Preview monitor looks like the figure below.

5 Click the Project Assets button to open that panel, and locate Greenscreen.mp4. Click once to select the clip, hold down the Shift key, and drag the clip toward the lower left corner of the clip in the Monitor panel.

6 Release the pointer, and choose Picture In Picture from the menu that appears.

7 Click No in the Videomerge panel (if it appears).

The superimposed clip will have handles on the edges, indicating that the clip is active.

8 Click anywhere in the clip, and drag it to a position that approximates that shown in the figure below.

● **Note:** If you need room in the Monitor panel, grab the bottom right edge of the Project Assets panel, and drag it upward and to the left to minimize the panel as much as possible, as you see in the figure.

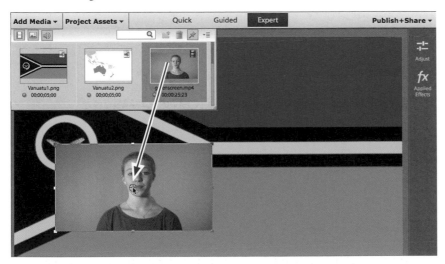

9 Click the Applied Effects button to open the Applied Effects panel.

10 In the Applied Effects panel, click the disclosure triangle to the left of Motion to reveal its properties. Make sure Constrain Proportions is selected.

11 Place your pointer over the Scale value, and drag the value to 45. As you change the scale, the Greenscreen.mp4 clip scales to 45% of its original size.

If necessary, you can reposition the clip using the Position controls, or simply drag the clip to the desired position in the Monitor panel.

12 With Greenscreen.mp4 still selected, click the disclosure triangle to the left of the Opacity effect to reveal those properties. Click the Fade Out icon to fade the Greenscreen.mp4 clip at the end.

13 We want to fade out the background image as well. In the Video 1 track in the timeline, select the Vanuatu6.gif clip. In the Applied Effects panel, click the disclosure triangle to the left of the Opacity effect to reveal those properties. Click the Fade Out icon to fade the Vanuatu6.gif clip at the end.

14 Press the Home key to go to the start of your project, and then click the Play button or press the spacebar to review your work.

15 Save your project as **Lesson06_pip.prel**.

Compositing two clips using Videomerge

Compositing is the process of merging two clips together, one on top of the other, while removing the background color of the top clip to reveal the second. This process allows you to place your subject in a variety of environments, both real and simulated.

The Adobe Premiere Elements Videomerge effect makes compositing as easy as dragging and dropping. Videomerge automatically determines the background of the top clip and makes it transparent. Video or image clips on the tracks below it become visible through the transparent areas. You'll get the best results with Videomerge if you shoot the clip to be composited using the following rules:

- Create a strong (preferably dark or saturated) solid, uniform-color background to shoot against.

- Make sure the background is brightly and uniformly lit to avoid shadows.

- In choosing a background color, avoid skin tones and colors that are similar to the subject's clothing or hair color. (Otherwise, the skin, clothes, or hair will become transparent, too.) Bright green and blue are the best choices.

With this information in mind, reload the Lesson06_Videomerge_Win.prel (Windows) or Lesson06_Videomerge_Mac.prel (Mac OS) project file (you should have already saved the first project as Lesson06_pip.prel); we're going to take this feature for a spin.

1 In the timeline, press the Home key to make sure that the current-time indicator is at the beginning of the video.

2 Click the Project Assets button to open that panel, and locate Greenscreen.mp4. Click once to select the clip, hold down the Shift key, and drag the clip toward the center of the Monitor panel.

3 Release the pointer, and choose Place On Top And Apply Videomerge from the menu that appears.

   Adobe Premiere Elements inserts Greenscreen.mp4 in the Video 2 track over Video 1, automatically detects the green background, and makes it transparent. The results are good, but this is a good opportunity to look at Videomerge's configuration options in case any of your projects ever need a bit of tweaking.

4 In the timeline, click Greenscreen.mp4 to select it, and then click the Applied Effects button to open that panel. If necessary, click Project Assets to close the Project Assets panel to make the entire Monitor panel visible.

5 In the Applied Effects panel, click the disclosure triangle to the left of the Videomerge effect to display the configuration options.

6 If you're not achieving a clean effect and you see residue of greenscreen in the background video or the background video showing through the subject, try any or all of the following:

- Reselect the background color. Make sure the Select Color option is enabled, and then click the eyedropper (✐) to select it. The background behind the subject will reappear. Press Ctrl (Windows) or Command (Mac OS), and then click the background close to the subject's head. This tells Videomerge which color to eliminate, and pressing Ctrl (Windows) or Command (Mac OS) averages a 5x5-pixel block surrounding the pixel that you clicked to achieve a smoother result. If you're having problems around the edges, try clicking there, but the middle region of the clip is typically the most important.

Note: If you need room in the Monitor panel, grab the bottom right edge of the Project Assets panel, and drag it upward and to the left to minimize the panel as much as possible.

- Cycle through the Presets, which are Soft, Normal, and Detailed.

- Adjust the Tolerance slider in both directions.

7 If you're having trouble getting clean edges, try experimenting with one of the Garbage Mattes in the Keying folder in the Effects panel. Search for Garbage Matte in Adobe Premiere Elements Help for more information.

Note: If you're uncomfortable with the subject obscuring some of the content behind her, you could always use Motion controls to scale the frame to about 45% of its original size, and move it to the bottom left or right.

8 Repeat steps 12 and 13 from the previous exercise to apply a Fade Out effect to both clips.

9 Press the Home key to go to the start of your project, and then click the Play button to review your work. If the video doesn't play smoothly, click the Render button (Render) on the bottom right of the Monitor panel to render the clip.

10 If you want, save your project as **Videomerge_end.prel**.

Working with Motion Tracking

Motion Tracking gives you the ability to automatically track moving objects in a project so you can add labels, thought bubbles, or other effects to the moving object. This exercise teaches you how to use this function, which is demonstrated in Expert view.

1 To load the project file containing the new content, click File > Open Project, and then navigate to the Lesson06 folder you copied to your hard disk.

2 Within the Lesson06 folder, select the file Motion_Tracking_Win.prel (Windows) or Motion_Tracking Mac.prel (Mac OS), and then click Open. If a dialog box appears asking for the location of rendered files, click the Skip Previews button.

3 Click to select the clip in the My Project panel, Alfie.mov, and make sure the current-time indicator is at the start of the clip.

4 Click the Tools icon (✕ Tools) to open the Tools panel, and then choose Motion Tracking. The Motion Tracking panel opens.

5 At the left of the Motion Tracking panel, click Select Object (↖ Select Object). A bounding box appears in the preview window.

6 Click and drag the edges of the bounding box around the head of the (always hungry) dog.

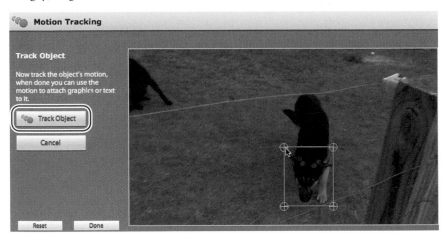

7 At the left of the Motion Tracking panel, click Track Object (Track Object). The Motion Tracking dialog box appears as Adobe Premiere Elements tracks the object.

8 Click the Graphics icon (Graphics), and select the Thought And Speech Bubbles folder on top. Drag the Speech Bubble 05-RIGHT onto the box in the preview window.

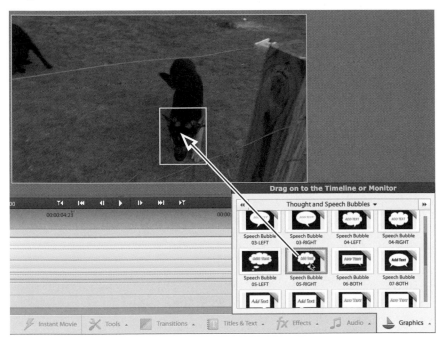

9   In the Change Text dialog box, type **Feed me!** Then click OK to close the dialog box.

10 Drag the Position controls to finalize placement of the thought bubble over Alfie's head.

11 Press the Home key to move to the start of your project, and then click the Play button to review your work. Watch how the thought bubble moves with Alfie.

12 Save your project as **Lesson06_Alfie.prel**.

Exploring on your own

Congratulations! Now you know how to apply video settings, change effects and settings, copy effects from one clip to another, create an image pan, animate an effect with keyframes, create a Picture-in-Picture effect, and composite one video over another with Videomerge. Here are some effects that you can experiment with on your own:

•   Create a PiP effect using two or more clips on the same screen.

•   Get a sense of the different effects available in Adobe Premiere Elements by choosing Help > Premiere Elements Help, or by pressing F1 to access Online Help. The Applying Effects section includes a gallery of video effects.

•   Experiment with the various effects presets located in the Presets folder in the Effects panel, including the Horizontal and Vertical image pans.

Review questions

1 What are curative effects, and when should you apply them?

2 What's the quickest way to apply identical effects and settings to multiple clips?

3 What is a keyframe, and what does it contain?

4 How do you modify keyframes once they've been added to a clip?

5 How do you apply the same effect to multiple clips on the timeline?

6 Why is using an adjustment layer more efficient than applying an effect to multiple clips?

Review answers

1 Curative effects improve one or more aspects of a clip, such as exposure, backlighting, or excessive shakiness. You should apply curative effects to a clip before applying artistic and other effects.

2 There are two ways to copy effects from one clip to another. To copy a single effect from one clip to another, click the source clip in the timeline to select it, open the Applied Effects panel, right-click the effect, and choose Copy. Then click the target clip in the timeline, open the Applied Effects panel, right-click in the gray area beneath other effects, and choose Paste. To copy multiple effects from one clip to another or to multiple clips, right-click the source clip on the timeline, and choose Copy. Then select the target clip or clips, right-click, and choose Paste Effects And Adjustments.

3 A keyframe contains the values for all the controls in an effect and applies those values to the clip at the specific time.

4 Once you've added keyframes to a clip, you can adjust them by clicking and dragging them along the connector line. If there are two keyframes, moving one farther away from the other extends the duration of the effect; moving a keyframe closer to another shortens the effect.

5 Select all target clips in the timeline, and apply the effect to any single clip.

6 The adjustment layer is more efficient because you can modify all clips by making changes to the adjustment layer. Plus, with FilmLooks, you don't delete all existing effects and adjustments.

7 CREATING TRANSITIONS

Lesson overview

If you've followed the lessons in this book in order, you should now feel comfortable adding and deleting footage in your projects and trimming clips to improve the pacing of the movies you're producing. In this lesson, you'll work with a project in which the clips have already been sequenced and trimmed, and add nuance and dimension using transitions between the clips. You'll learn how to do the following:

- Apply video and audio transitions

- Preview transitions

- Customize transition settings

- Replace a transition

- Delete a transition

- Apply the default transition to multiple clips

- Create fade-ins and fade-outs

- Render transitions

 This lesson will take approximately one hour. Download the project files for this lesson from the Lesson & Update Files tab on your Account page at www.peachpit.com and store them on your computer in a convenient location, as described in the Getting Started section of this book. Your Account page is also where you'll find any updates to the chapters or to the lesson files. Look on the Lesson & Update Files tab to access the most current content.

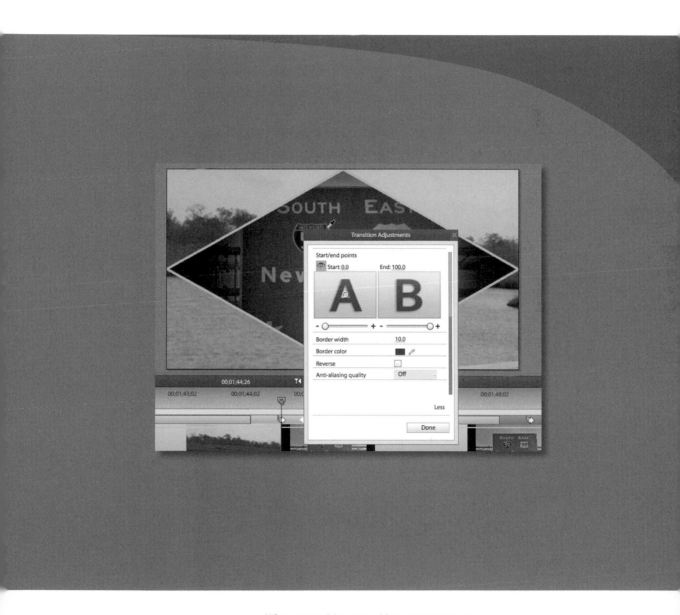

When customizing a transition, you can set start and end points, border width and color, and other parameters.

Getting started

● **Note:** If you have not already downloaded the project files for this lesson to your computer from your Account page, make sure to do so now. See "Getting Started" at the beginning of the book.

You'll modify scenes in this lesson's project by adding transitions in stages. But first you'll open the Lesson07 project and prepare your Adobe Premiere Elements workspace.

1   Make sure that you have correctly copied the Lesson07 folder from your Account page onto your computer's hard drive. See "Copying the Classroom in a Book files" in the Getting Started section at the start of this book.

2   Launch Adobe Premiere Elements. If it's already open, choose Help > Welcome Screen in the Adobe Premiere Elements menu to return to the Welcome screen.

3   In the Welcome screen, click Video Editor, select Existing Project, and click the Open folder.

4   In the Open Project dialog box, navigate to the Lesson07 folder.

5   Within that folder, select the file Lesson07_Start_Win.prel (Windows) or Lesson07_Start_Mac.prel (Mac OS), and then click Open. If a dialog box appears asking for the location of rendered files, click the Skip Previews button.

    Your project file opens.

6   Choose Window > Restore Workspace to ensure that you start the lesson in the default panel layout.

Viewing the completed movie before you start

To see what you'll be creating in this lesson, you can take a look at the completed movie. You'll have to be in Expert view to open the Project Assets panel to view the movie, so if you are not, click Expert (Expert) to enter that view.

1   At the upper left side of the Adobe Premiere Elements window, click the Project Assets button (Project Assets ▾) to open that panel. Locate the file Lesson07_Movie.mov, and then double-click it to open the video into the preview window.

2   Click the Play button (▶) to watch the video about a visit to Airboat Adventures in Lafitte, Louisiana, which you'll build in this lesson.

3   When you're done, close the preview window.

Working with transitions

Transitions phase out one clip while phasing in the next. The simplest form of a transition is the *cut*. A cut occurs when the last frame of one clip is followed by the first frame of the next. The cut is the most frequently used transition in video and film, and the one you, too, will use most often. However, you can also use other types of transitions to achieve effects between scenes.

Transitions

A transition can be as subtle as a cross-dissolve or as emphatic as a page turn or spinning pinwheel. You generally place transitions on a cut between two clips, creating a double-sided transition. However, you can also apply a transition to just the beginning or end of a clip, creating a single-sided transition, such as a fade to black.

When a transition shifts from one clip to the next, it overlaps frames from both clips. The overlapped frames can either be frames previously trimmed from the clips (frames just past the In or Out point at the cut), or existing frames repeated on either side of the cut. It's important to remember that when you trim a clip, you don't delete frames; instead, the resulting In and Out points frame a window over the original clip. A transition uses the trimmed frames to create the transition effect, or, if the clips don't have trimmed frames, the transition repeats frames.

—From Adobe Premiere Elements Help

Viewing available transitions in Quick and Expert views

Adobe Premiere Elements includes a wide range of transitions, such as 3D motion, dissolves, wipes, and zooms. To view the available transitions in the Transitions panel, click the Transitions button (Transitions) on the Action bar on the bottom of the Adobe Premiere Elements window.

As you've seen with other collections of tools and effects, Quick view contains a smaller collection of the most commonly used transitions, whereas Expert view contains the entire collection, organized by folders. Expert view also includes audio transitions, but Quick view doesn't. In Expert view, you can search for transitions by clicking the magnifying lens (🔍) at the upper right.

In both views, you can see an animated preview of the transition by clicking the transition in the Transitions panel. Applying, replacing, deleting, and opening the customization window are slightly different in the two views, so we'll cover those differences first, and then circle back and look at the customization controls, which are identical in both views.

Quick view   Expert view

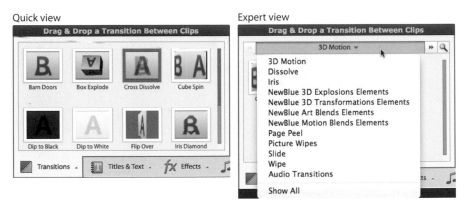

In both of the following exercises, you'll insert a transition between the last video before the slide show, Gator16.mp4, and the first still image, Picture 1.jpg. You'll find it easier to follow along if you zoom in to the timeline so that only the video clip and the first few pictures are showing.

Working with transitions in Quick view

Let's start by reviewing the basics in Quick view.

1   If you are in Expert view, click the Quick button (Quick) at the top of the Monitor panel to enter Quick view.

● **Note:** You don't need to reposition the current-time indicator to place transitions between clips; however, it's often helpful to do so to locate the correct point in your project.

2   Click along the right edge of Gator16.mp4, moving your current-time indicator to that location. Files can be pretty hard to find in Quick view, but Gator16.mp4 is the last video file. If you have to click into Expert view to view the file names and find the clip, please do so.

3   In the Action bar, click Transitions (Transitions) to open the Transitions panel, click the Iris Diamond transition, and drag it to the intersection of Gator16.mp4 and Picture 1.jpg. When you hover the pointer over the intersection, Trim view appears in the Monitor panel, showing that you're at the intersection of those two clips.

Note that the Transitions panel will close when you drag the transition from it; in the figure below, you're seeing the panel and the target.

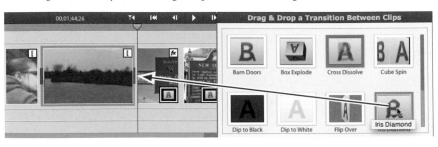

4 Release the pointer. Adobe Premiere Elements opens the Transition Adjustments dialog box.

5 In the Transition Adjustments dialog box, make sure that Duration is set to 1, and that the Alignment option is set to Between Clips and outlined in blue. Then click Done. We'll explain these options and discuss additional configuration options in the "Viewing transition properties" section later in this lesson. Adobe Premiere Elements inserts the transition and an icon between the clips, showing its location.

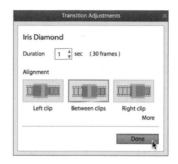

● **Note:** The prerelease version of Premiere Elements 12 displayed the transition icon even when a transition wasn't inserted. For example, there was no transition inserted between Gator15.mp4 and Gator16.mp4, though the immediately preceding figure shows one. If there are transition icons showing where they shouldn't be in your project, don't sweat; it may be distracting, but it won't impact your work.

6 Click the Render button (Render) to render the transition. Playback will start at the beginning of the clip, so you'll have to move toward the end of the project to see the transition you just added.

7 Press the spacebar to preview the transition. After the transition ends, press the spacebar to stop playback.

8 To replace a transition, repeat steps 3–5 with a different transition. That is, drag a different transition to the intersection between the two clips, release your pointer, and click Done in the Transition Adjustments dialog box, as described in step 5. Adobe Premiere Elements will replace the first transition with the second. When you're done experimenting, make sure the Iris Diamond transition is in place between the two clips.

9 To access the Transition Adjustments dialog box and reconfigure the transition settings, double-click the transition icon in the clip on the timeline.

10 To delete the transition, click the transition icon in the clip, making sure that it's outlined in blue and that neither clip involved in the transition is also outlined in blue. Press the Delete key; Adobe Premiere Elements deletes the transition.

Working with transitions in Expert view

Let's move on to our transition exploration in Expert view. To restore the project to its original pristine condition, either click Undo at the left end of the Action bar until the icon grays out, or choose File > Revert, and click Yes to discard your changes. Then click the Expert button (Expert) at the top of the Monitor panel to enter that view.

Again, you'll start by inserting a transition between the Gator16.mp4 video clip and the Picture 1.jpg still image. And in addition to inserting, replacing, configuring, and replacing a transition, you'll learn how to copy and paste a transition.

1   In the timeline, position the current-time indicator between Gator16.mp4 and Picture 1.jpg.

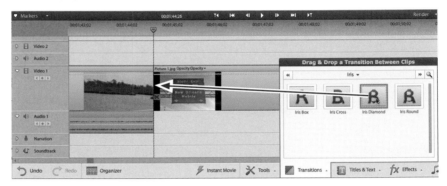

2   In the Action bar, click Transitions (Transitions) to open the Transitions panel, and then click to open the Iris folder. Click the Iris Diamond transition, and drag it to the intersection between Gator16.mp4 and Picture 1.jpg. Don't release the pointer.

Drag the pointer so that the transition box is only on Gator16.mp4; then center the box between the two clips, and then only over Picture 1.jpg. Notice how the icon changes from Between Clips (⊹) to Left Clip and Right Clip. This relates to the alignment options in the Transition Adjustments dialog box, explained later in this lesson.

● **Note:** In the test software used while writing this lesson, the spot where you dropped the transition did not affect the alignment shown in the Transition Adjustments dialog box. For example, if you dropped the transition over Gator16.mp4 with the Left Clip icon showing, the Transition Adjustments dialog box might still default to the Between Clips alignment option. This may be changed in the final version, but if it still functions this way, don't sweat it; just choose the preferred location in the Transition Adjustments dialog box.

3 Release the pointer when it's centered between the two clips. Adobe Premiere Elements opens the Transition Adjustments dialog box.

4 In the Transition Adjustments dialog box, make sure that the Duration value is set to 1 and the Between Clips alignment option is selected and outlined in blue. Then click Done. We'll explain these options and discuss additional configuration options in the "Viewing transition properties" section later in this lesson.

Adobe Premiere Elements inserts the transition and an icon between the clips, showing its location.

5 Click the Render button (Render) to render the transition. Playback will start at the beginning of the clip, so you'll have to move toward the end of the project to see the transition you just added.

● **Note:** This is the perfect time to render only a specific work area, which you learned about in "Rendering a work area" in Lesson 6. Move the current-time indicator a few seconds before the transition, and press Alt+[(Windows) or Option+[(Mac OS) to set the start of the work area. Then move the current-time indicator a few seconds after the transition, and press Alt+] (Windows) or Option+] (Mac OS) to set the end of the work area. Then click the Render button; only the work area will render.

6 Drag the current-time indicator to a few moments before the transition on the timeline, and then press the spacebar to preview the transition. After the transition ends, press the spacebar to stop playback.

At this point, there are several ways you can change or refine your transition. None of them are necessary to complete the exercise, but I encourage you to try them all to get a feel for each function.

- To replace a transition, repeat steps 2–4 with a different transition. That is, drag a different transition to the intersection between the two clips, release the pointer, and click Done in the Transition Adjustments dialog box identified in step 4 (one second and Between Clips). Adobe Premiere Elements replaces the first transition with the second. After trying this, make sure that the Iris Diamond transition is in place between the two clips.

- To access the Transition Adjustments dialog box and reconfigure the transition settings, double-click the transition icon on the timeline.

● **Note:** To restore the work area to the complete project, double-click the very top of the time scale at the top of the timeline to push the work area brackets to the start and end of the project.

- To delete a transition, click the transition icon in the clip, making sure that it's highlighted and that neither clip involved in the transition is also highlighted. Then right-click, and choose Delete.

- To change the duration of a transition, grab either edge and pull, though at times you may not be able to drag an edge. Adobe Premiere Elements will display a timecode box to let you know how much time you are adding or subtracting. For example, you can add 15 frames to the transition by dragging the left edge 15 frames toward the right.

- To copy a transition, click the transition icon in the clip, making sure that it's highlighted and that neither clip involved in the transition is also highlighted. Then right-click and choose Copy, or press Ctrl+C (Windows) or Command+C (Mac OS).

- To paste the transition, move the current-time indicator between the two target clips, and then choose Edit > Paste or press Ctrl+V (Windows) or Command+V (Mac OS).

Viewing transition properties

When you add a transition to a clip, its default length is determined by your preference settings, although you can change the length of transitions after applying them. Additionally, there are several other attributes of transitions that you can adjust, including the alignment of all transitions and border settings on some transitions.

In this exercise, you'll customize the Iris Diamond transition that you've applied previously. So if you changed or deleted that transition, drag it back between Gator16.mp4 and Picture 1.jpg. We'll do this in Expert view, so click the Expert button (Expert) at the top of the Monitor panel if necessary to switch to that view.

1   Drag the current-time indicator to the intersection of Gator16.mp4 and Picture 1.jpg, so the transition is showing in the Monitor panel.

2 Double-click the transition icon to open the Transition Adjustments dialog box.

The first property that you can modify here is duration. Any change you make in the duration will override the default transition value set in your preferences. There are no hard and fast rules for duration, but here are some general recommendations:

- For projects created for high-bandwidth computer or optical disc playback, one second is a good default.

- For streaming playback, one-second transitions may create noticeable artifacting, so consider cutting the transition to a half second or shorter. Unfortunately, at the time this lesson was written, you couldn't set transition duration to shorter than one second via the control available in the Transition Adjustments dialog box.

  But you can set a transition shorter than one second via Preferences—you can change the default transition duration in the General Preferences dialog box. Note that the Video Transition Default Duration value is expressed in frames, so if you wanted to set the default to half a second, you'd need to specify 15 frames. In Expert view, you can click and drag the edge of the transition to the desired duration. Be advised, however, that if you open the Transition Adjustments dialog box after dragging the transition to a custom length, Adobe Premiere Elements will reset the duration to that selected in the Transition Adjustments dialog box.

- To create a noticeable transition between major sections or scenes in your production, consider a transition of 2–3 seconds.

  To set Duration, type the desired number in the Duration field and press Enter (Windows) or Return (Mac OS), or click the triangles to the right of the Duration field to increase or decrease the duration in whole seconds.

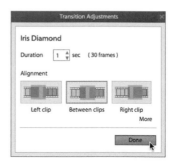

3 Set the transition alignment:

- Left Clip aligns the end of the transition to the end of the first clip.

- Between Clips centers the transition over the cut.

- Right Clip aligns the beginning of the transition to the beginning of the second clip.

I recommend using Between Clips for most transitions.

4 Near the bottom right of the Transition Adjustments dialog box, hover your pointer over the word *More* until it becomes a button (More), and then click the button to see more configuration options. Use the scroll bar on the right to view all the options.

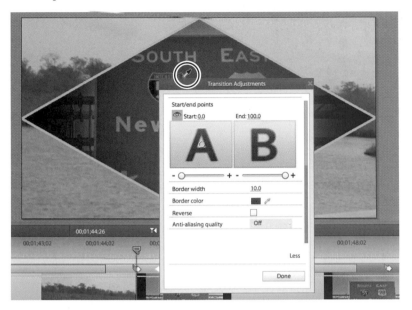

5 Near the top of the dialog box (and not shown in the figure), click Play to play a preview of the transition. Click Stop to stop the preview.

6 To adjust the start or end points of the transition, click and drag the sliders beneath the respective windows to the desired location. In most instances, you're probably best served by using the default values. We'll do that for this exercise.

Not all transitions have border configuration options, the ability to reverse the transition, or anti-aliasing options. This one does, though, so let's create and customize the transition border.

7 Click the value for Border Width, type the number **10**, and then press Enter (Windows) or Return (Mac OS).

This creates a 10-pixel border on the edge of your transition. The default color of the border is black, but you can modify this as well.

8 To modify the border color, you can either use the eyedropper or the Color Picker dialog box. Let's use the former and then take a look at the latter. Click the eyedropper next to the Border color control, and then click the reddish color showing on the Interstate badge just below the word *South* on the road sign in Picture 1.jpg. This changes the border to this color. Not quite red enough. Let's fix that.

9 Click the color swatch that just turned red to open the Color Picker dialog box. Here you can choose a color in multiple ways:

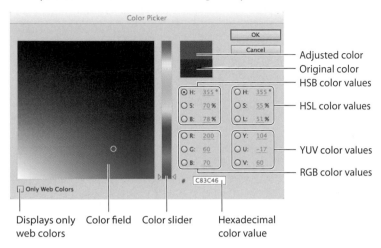

- Click the color slider in the middle to choose a general color, and then click to choose a specific color in the Color field.

- Type specific values in one of the four sets of color-values settings (Hue, Saturation, and Brightness (HSB); Hue, Saturation, and Lightness (HSL); Red, Green, and Blue (RGB); or YUV). As with most numeric controls, you can either drag the numbers to these values or click the field to make it active and type the numbers in.

10 Adjust the color by changing the R, G, and B values to 200, 60, and 70, as shown in the figure. When you're done, click OK to close the Color Picker dialog box.

11 Back in the Transition Adjustments dialog box, if desired, select the Reverse option. This reverses the transition so that rather than starting small and growing in size, the iris diamond starts large and shrinks in size. Typically, the default option (Reverse deselected) works best here.

12 The final option in the Transition Adjustments dialog box reflects Anti-Aliasing Quality (Off, Low, Medium, or High). Typically, if your transition has a border, you should choose High, which will smooth rough edges in some regions of the effect. Do so here.

13 Click Done to close the Transition Adjustments dialog box.

14 Click the Render button (Render) to render the transition.

15 Drag the current-time indicator to a position before the transition, and then press the spacebar to play your modified transition. After the transition ends, press the spacebar to stop playback.

16 Choose File > Save As, name the file **Lesson07_Work.prel** in the Save Project dialog box, and then click Save to save it in your Lesson07 folder.

▶ **Tip:** Jot down the numbers when you choose a color for your transitions so you can easily re-create the same color with your titles.

● **Note:** Using the color-value sets is particularly useful when you want to match colors from other design elements (like titles), because many other Adobe Premiere Elements color dialog boxes offer one or more of these settings.

Adding a single-sided transition to create a fade-in

Transitions do not necessarily need to be located between two clips. For example, you can easily add a fade-in and fade-out to the beginning and end of your movie.

1   In Expert view, press the Home key to position the current-time indicator at the beginning of the first clip.

2   In the Action bar, click Transitions (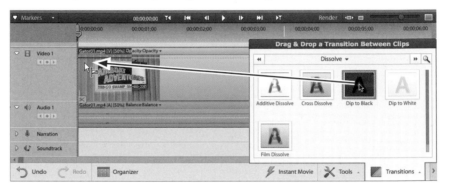 Transitions) to open the Transitions panel, and click open the Dissolve folder. Drag the Dip To Black transition from the Transitions panel to the beginning of Gator01.mp4 on the Video 1 track.

3   In the Transition Adjustments dialog box, make sure that the Duration is set to 1, and that the Right Clip alignment option is selected and outlined in blue. Then click Done.

4   Press the Home key to move the current-time indicator to the start of the project, and then press the spacebar to play the transition. The beginning of the transition starts at black and then fades into the video. After the transition ends, press the spacebar to stop playback.

5   To extend the duration of this transition by a half second, grab the right edge of the transition box in the timeline, and drag it to the right until the text field beneath the drag pointer indicates that you've added 00;00;00;15. Release the pointer.

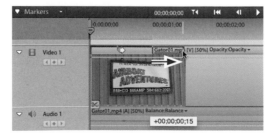

6   Save your project as Lesson07_Work.prel.

Applying the default transition to multiple clips

There's no rule that says you need to use transitions between all clips in your mov-ies. However, rather than using cuts between clips, many producers insert very short cross-dissolve transitions between clips to smooth out any visual jarring between the clips. A feature in Adobe Premiere Elements makes this very simple to do. In this exercise, you'll start by changing the duration of the default video and audio transitions, and then apply them to multiple clips simultaneously. You need to be in Expert view to complete this exercise.

1 Choose Edit > Preferences > General (Windows) or Adobe Premiere Elements Editor > Preferences > General (Mac OS) to open the Preferences panel.

2 Highlight the number in the Video Transition Default Duration box to make it active, and type in **5**.

3 Highlight the number in the Audio Transition Default Duration box to make it active, and type in **.5**. Press Enter (Windows) or Return (Mac OS) to close the Preferences panel.

   Generally, you want audio transitions to be slightly longer than the related video transition, so the progression from one clip to another will sound less abrupt.

   Next, we'll verify that the Cross Dissolve transition is the default video transition.

4 Click the Transitions button in the Action bar to open the Transitions panel, and open the Dissolve folder. The Cross Dissolve transition has a yellow or dark gray box around it, indicating it's the default selection. If it doesn't, or to choose a different transition as the default, right-click the transition, and choose Set Selected As Default Transition.

5 Verify that Constant Power is the default audio transition: Open the Audio Transitions folder and, if Constant Power isn't the default, right-click it and make it so.

6 Click the Fit To Visible Timeline icon (⬚) or press the Backslash key (\) to display the entire contents of the project in the timeline.

● **Note:** In the Preferences dialog box, the Video Transition Default Duration is represented in frames, and the Audio Transition Default Duration is represented in seconds. In a 30-frames-per-second video, that means that you selected a Video Transition Default Duration that's 1/6 of a second and an Audio Transition Default Duration that's 1/2 of a second.

Working with audio transitions

The dominant audio in this project is the narration and the background music that you'll add in Lesson 9. Both run from start to finish with no breaks; other than fading up from the start and fading out at the end, there are no transitions.

With some other projects where the primary audio follows the video, audio transitions can be as important as video. Fortunately, the workflow is almost identical to video transitions in Expert view: Open the Transitions panel, select the Audio Transitions folder, and choose one of the two audio transitions, Constant Gain or Constant Power. Most editors prefer Constant Power because it's smoother, whereas Constant Gain can sound abrupt. For that reason, Constant Power is the default audio transition, as indicated by the dark gray outline you see around it when you open the Audio Transitions folder.

You apply audio transitions the same way as video transitions—by dragging them between two target clips. You'll see the same Transition Adjustments dialog box, but you can adjust only Duration, because the Alignment controls are grayed out. Additionally, you can replace, switch, delete, and stretch audio transitions just as you can with video transitions, and even add them en masse to multiple clips, as you'll do in the "Applying the default transition to multiple clips" section.

7 Drag to select Gator01.mp4 through Gator16.mp4 on the timeline. Don't select any of the photos or the audio on the Narration track.

8 Choose Timeline > Apply Default Transition.

▶ **Tip:** Click OK if the "Insufficient media" error message appears. See "Insufficient media explained" later in this lesson for an explanation of what this means.

9 Adobe Premiere Elements applies the default transitions on the audio and video tracks between all selected clips. If you apply the default transition to clips with existing transitions, Adobe Premiere Elements will replace the transitions, but won't change the duration of the previously inserted transitions.

10 Click the Render button (Render) to render all of the transitions. If you previously selected a work area to render, double-click the very top of the time scale above the timeline to reset the work area to the whole project.

11 Drag the current-time indicator around the project and preview the transitions. This is definitely a subjective selection; if you don't like the look, don't use it.

Making transitions work in your movie

Now that you know the how of transitions, let's talk about the when and why. Although there are few absolutes about the art of transitions, your productions will benefit by incorporating the following two factors into your creative decisions:

First: You don't need to include a transition between every pair of clips in your movies. If you watch a Hollywood movie, for example, you'll see that noticeable transitions (that is, those longer than four or five frames) are seldom used between clips within a scene, but are often used between scenes.

Why? Because a transition lets the viewer know that there's been a change in time or location. For example, if a scene jumped from a dusky kitchen to a sunlit back-yard, that would confuse viewers. You can imagine them saying, "Hey, what happened here? One second they were in the kitchen drinking after-dinner milkshakes, and the next second they were playing dodgeball in the yard." However, if the editor inserts a fade to black between the two scenes or adds some other noticeable transition, the viewer understands that a change of time or location has occurred.

Within the context of the bayou boat ride project, there are two distinct scenes: the videos and the slide show. Between these two scenes is a natural location for a noticeable transition; hence the Iris Diamond. Aesthetically, there are better choices for a movie—for instance, you'll find lots of cool transitions in the NewBlue folders—but Iris Diamond was an instructive choice for this lesson because it has all the available customization options.

You inserted the Dip To Black to fade from black at the start of the video and would have faded to black at the end if you hadn't already done effectively the same thing in Lesson 6 by applying Opacity keyframes. Virtually all edited home videos use these two elements, as do many business videos.

And second: Within scenes, transitions are up for grabs. A very short transition between videos in a sequence works well because it smooths the flow, but many—if not most—producers use straight cuts. In slide shows, you should try more noticeable transitions, because each slide is like a separate scene.

Of course, with family videos, your goal is to produce smiles, not to win an Academy Award. If you want to use transitions as content rather than in their traditional role, feel free to add as many as you like, anywhere you'd like. Just be sure to consider the following convention: When you're using transitions, you should match the tone of the transition to the tone of the movie. In a fun family video, like a trip to the beach or other vacation, you could use any transition that Adobe Premiere Elements offers—in some cases, the zanier the better. On the other hand, when you're shooting a solemn event—say, a wedding or graduation—the tone is usually more serious. In these instances, you'd probably want to use only a Cross Dissolve or the occasional Dip To Black transition to maintain that tone.

Dealing with "Insufficient media" issues

By now, you know enough to deploy transitions artfully in your projects, but you may still have some questions. For example, you may wonder why the "Insufficient media" error message appears at times, or what is the significance of a transition containing "repeated frames."

Imagine two clips next to each other on the timeline—Clip A first, Clip B second. You insert a 1-second cross dissolve between the two. Within this one-second transition are frames from both clips.

If you trimmed frames from the end of Clip A and the beginning of Clip B, Adobe Premiere Elements will use these trimmed frames in the transition. If there's motion within the trimmed frames, this motion will appear in the transition. If there are no trimmed frames in either or both clips, Adobe Premiere Elements will use the last frame in Clip A and/or the first frame in Clip B for the frames in the transition, which can appear a bit unnatural. What to do?

First, understand that this happens only when you don't trim frames from the start and end of your clips, which seldom happens for most producers, since you're trimming like crazy to shorten the overall length of the production. Or at least you should be. So it's not a frequent problem.

Second, if one clip has trimmed frames and the other doesn't, move the transition over the clip *without* the trimmed frames, which will ensure full motion from both clips during the transition. That is, if Clip A doesn't have trimmed frames, align the transition on the left clip, if Clip B doesn't have trimmed frames, locate the transition on the right clip.

Third, recognize that most viewers won't notice the difference, particularly casual viewers. So unless you're a real perfectionist, just let it be. At least now you know the source of the error message.

Exploring on your own

My compliments; that's another lesson well done! You've discovered how transitions can make your projects more professional-looking by adding continuity between clips. You've learned about placing, previewing, modifying, and rendering different transitions, as well as applying them en masse.

As you continue to edit with transitions, you'll get a better idea of how to use them to enhance the tone or style of your project. The best way to develop that style is by trying different transitions and discovering how they affect your movie. So here's your task list for further exploration:

- Experiment with different transitions; preview their animated icons in the Transitions panel. Remember that dragging a transition onto an existing transition will replace it.

- Get comfortable modifying the default parameters of your transitions. One by one, select the transitions you've added, and explore their settings in the Transition Adjustments dialog box.

Review questions

1 Where are Video Transitions located, and what are two ways to locate specific transitions?

2 How do you modify transitions?

3 How can you extend the duration of a transition?

4 How can you apply a transition to multiple clips simultaneously?

Review answers

1 Video Transitions are located in the Transitions panel, which you can access in the Action bar. You can browse for individual transitions, which (in Expert view) are organized in categories and by transition type. Additionally, in Expert view, you can find a specific transition by typing its name or part of its name into the search field in the Transitions panel.

2 Double-click the transition icon in the timeline to open the Transition Adjustments dialog box.

3 In Expert view, you can click and drag the transition to any length. In both views, you can double-click the transition icon in the timeline to open the Transition Adjustments dialog box, and customize the duration there, but only using whole numbers.

4 You can use one of two techniques to apply transitions to multiple clips. One is to select multiple clips on the timeline, and choose Timeline > Apply Default Transition. Adobe Premiere Elements will insert the default transition between all selected clips. The other is to copy a previously applied transition, select multiple clips on the timeline, and then paste the transition onto any selected clip(s).

8 ADDING TITLES AND CREDITS

Lesson overview

In this lesson, you'll learn how to create original titles and rolling credits for the bayou boat ride movie you've been working on. You'll be adding still titles and rolling titles, placing images, and using drawing tools. Specifically, you'll learn how to do the following:

- Add and stylize text

- Superimpose titles and graphics over video

- Use graphics elements like speech bubbles

- Create and customize rolling titles

- Use title templates

This lesson will take approximately two hours. Download the project files for this lesson from the Lesson & Update Files tab on your Account page at www.peachpit.com and store them on your computer in a convenient location, as described in the Getting Started section of this book. Your Account page is also where you'll find any updates to the chapters or to the lesson files. Look on the Lesson & Update Files tab to access the most current content.

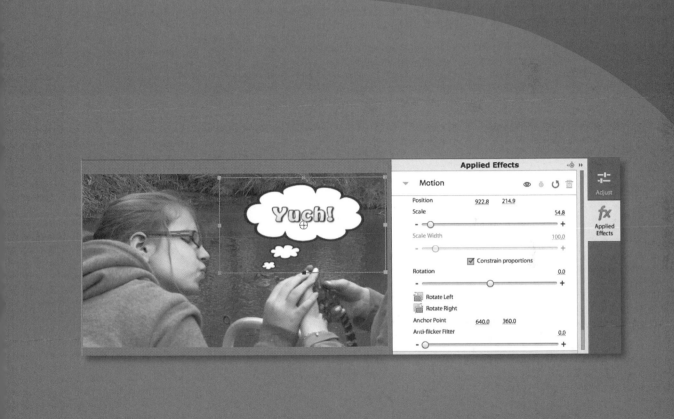

It's easy to create and customize speech bubbles in
Adobe Premiere Elements.

Working with titles and title-editing mode

● **Note:** If you have not already downloaded the project files for this lesson to your computer from your Account page, make sure to do so now. See "Getting Started" at the beginning of the book.

Within Adobe Premiere Elements, you can create custom graphics and titles. When you add a title over one of your video clips, it's also added to the Project Assets panel as a new clip. As such, it's treated much like any other clip in your project—it can be edited, moved, deleted, and have transitions and effects applied to it.

Adobe Premiere Elements allows you to create original titles using text, drawing tools, and imported graphics. However, to help you quickly and easily add high-quality titles to your project, Adobe Premiere Elements also provides a number of templates based on common themes, such as sports, travel, and weddings.

Note that there is a guided edit that describes how to add a title to your video. This chapter will cover everything in that tutorial and more, but if you want a quick overview of the process, go ahead and run through the guided edit.

Getting started

You'll modify scenes in this lesson's project by adding titles and graphics to various clips in the project. But first, you'll open the Lesson08 project and prepare your Adobe Premiere Elements workspace.

1   Make sure that you have correctly copied the Lesson08 folder from your Account page onto your computer's hard drive. See "Copying the Classroom in a Book files" in the Getting Started section at the start of this book.

2   Launch Adobe Premiere Elements. If it is already open, choose Help > Welcome Screen to return to the Welcome screen.

3   In the Welcome screen, click Video Editor, select Existing Project, and click the Open folder.

4   In the Open Project dialog box, navigate to the Lesson08 folder.

5   Within the Lesson08 folder, select the file Lesson08_Start_Win.prel (Windows) or Lesson08_Start_Mac.prel (Mac OS), and then click Open. If a dialog box appears asking for the location of rendered files, click the Skip Previews button.

Your project file opens.

6   Choose Window > Restore Workspace to ensure that you start the lesson in the default panel layout.

Viewing the completed movie before you start

To see what you'll be creating in this lesson, you can take a look at the completed movie. You'll have to be in Expert view to open the Project Assets panel to view the movie, so if you are not, click Expert (Expert) to enter that view.

1   At the upper left side of Adobe Premiere Elements, click the Project Assets button (**Project Assets ▾**) to open the Project Assets panel. Locate the file Lesson08_Movie.mov, and then double-click it to open the video in the preview window.

2   Click the Play button (▶) to watch the bayou boat ride video, which you'll build in this lesson.

3   When you're done, close the preview window and close the Project Assets panel.

Titles and text overview

Adding titles in Quick and Expert views is very similar, but let's discuss titles in general before learning that procedure. Adobe Premiere Elements contains a number of title templates that you can access by clicking the Titles & Text button (🎞 Titles & Text) in the Action bar to open the Titles & Text panel, which contains identical content in both Quick and Expert views. All of the text and title content is separated into themed folders that match the categories that you will use as DVD menus in Lesson 10. Click the folder pull-down menu to view the categories, many of which contain multiple options.

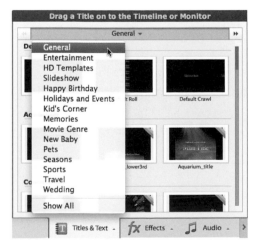

Title templates are a great way to add a nice creative touch to your videos; after all, no one but you will know that you didn't create the professional-looking title from scratch. If you're creating a DVD from your video, you should review the available DVD themes while choosing your title templates, so you can choose the matching title template and theme that you like best. Once you learn how to create your own titles, customizing a title template is a snap, and that's what we'll do here.

Adobe Premiere Elements offers two basic kinds of titles: full screen and overlay. A full-screen title has no video underneath, so it usually takes up the entire frame. In contrast, overlay titles are superimposed over a video or videos. In this lesson you'll learn how to create both kinds of titles and also how to use speech bubbles, which are a graphic element that you complete using Adobe Premiere Elements text tools.

Although you can create a title by choosing File > New > Title, it's simplest to just drag a title template where you want it; if you want a full-screen title, you drag it to the desired location on the video track (Quick view) or Video 1 track (Expert view), making sure that the Insert icon ( ) appears before you release your mouse. This tells Adobe Premiere Elements to push all content on the timeline to the right to fit the content that you just added.

As you'll see in the figure below, I've added the default title to the start of the project, which you'll do in Expert view in a moment. You can see the Insert icon, so all other content will be pushed back by the duration of the title. You set title duration in the Preferences dialog box by choosing Edit > Preferences > General (Windows) or Adobe Premiere Elements Editor > Preferences > General (Mac OS). Titles aren't specifically mentioned in this dialog box, but rest assured, Still Image Default Duration controls the length of titles as well as still images.

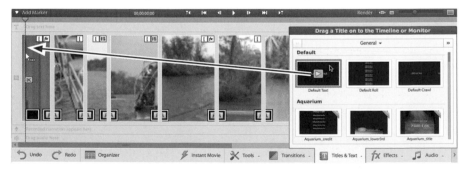

● **Note:** Changing the Still Image Default Duration preference takes effect only after closing Adobe Premiere Elements and reopening it. It also affects only titles you created or images you import after you've changed the preference. It will not change the duration of any images in the project or titles created before you change the preference, whether they are in the Project Assets folder or deployed on the timeline.

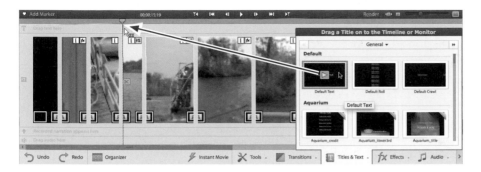

To create an overlay title, drag the title to the Text track in Quick view or any video track over your primary video track in Expert view. If you think you'll be switching between Quick and Expert views, you should place titles inserted in Expert view in the Video 3 track so they'll appear in the Title track in Quick view; otherwise, you won't see them in Quick view. If you use Expert view exclusively, you can place titles in any video track.

If you add an overlay title in Quick view over a clip that's shorter than the default title duration, Adobe Premiere Elements will cut off the title at the right edge of the clip. This is not a big deal, because you can click and drag the edge of the clip to any duration. However, in Expert view, Adobe Premiere Elements will insert the title at its full duration.

Once the title is added to your project, you edit it the same way in either view: Adobe Premiere Elements opens the title you just added in title-editing mode, which uses the Monitor panel as a WYSIWYG editing tool.

To exit title-editing mode, simply click anywhere in the timeline that's not the location of a title. Adobe Premiere Elements saves all changes automatically. To reenter title-editing mode, double-click any title.

Now that you know what to expect in Quick view, we'll look at the rest of the lesson in Expert view.

Creating a simple full-screen title

If you were following along with the previous discussion by making the actual edits, congrats; that's a great way to learn, and much more fun than reading dry words on a page. To return to a clean slate, either click Undo (↶ Undo) until it grays out or reload Lesson08_Start_Win.prel (Windows) or Lesson08_Start_Mac.prel (Mac OS).

In this exercise, you'll add a title clip at the beginning of the movie, and then customize the title. Remember, you'll be working in Expert view, so if you're not in that view, click Expert (Expert) at the top of the Monitor panel.

1 In the Action bar, click Titles & Text (⊞T Titles & Text) to open the Titles & Text panel. Make sure that the General category is selected.

2 Click and drag the Default Text title template to the beginning of the project, and then release the pointer. Adobe Premiere Elements inserts the title at the start of the project and opens the title in title-editing mode with the text active. The text and drawing tools are visible in the Adjustments panel on the right, with tabs for Text, Style, Animation, and Shapes. You will visit all these tabs during your work in this lesson.

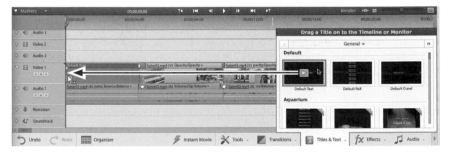

▶ Tip: You can add multiple text entries to a single title, or you can create multiple titles, each containing a unique text string.

3 The Horizontal type tool should be selected by default. If it's not, click the Horizontal type tool button (T) in the Adjustments panel to select it now.

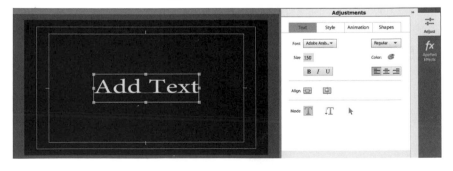

4 Click in the text box, and drag your pointer over the default text to select it. Type the words **Bayou Boat Ride**, and then press the Enter (Windows) or Return (Mac OS) key to create a new line. Next, type the words **New Year's Day, 2013**. The text will disappear to the right, but we'll fix that in a moment.

5 To reposition the text, click the Selection tool ( ), and then click anywhere on the text to select the text block. Drag to reposition the text so it appears centered in the upper third of the Monitor panel. Don't worry about the size or exact position for now; you'll reposition the text later in this lesson.

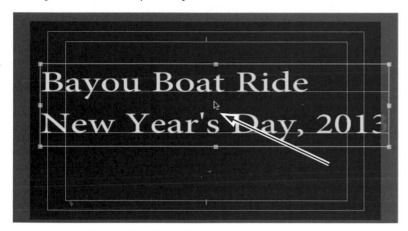

6 Choose File > Save As. Then, in the Save As dialog box, name the file **Lesson08_Work.prel**, and click Save to save it in your Lesson08 folder.

Adobe Premiere Elements treats basic titles, such as the one you just created, like still image files. After you've created a title, the application automatically adds an image file to the Project Assets panel.

Modifying title text

After creating and adding a title to the project, you can change text or its appearance at any time, much as you would in a word processor or page layout program. In this exercise, you'll learn how to adjust the alignment of your type as well as its style, size, and color.

Changing text alignment, style, and size

Let's fine-tune the default title that you just inserted. You should be in the Text view of the Adjustments panel; if not, click the Text tab (Text) on the top of the panel to enter that view.

1   To center the text within the text box, use the Selection tool ( ) to select the title text box, and then click the Center Text button ( ). You don't have to select the actual text, just the box.

2   In the Monitor panel, choose the Horizontal type tool, and drag it in the text box to select the second line of text. From the Font pull-down menu, choose Adobe Garamond Pro; choose Bold from the menu next to it. Choose another font and style if you don't have this font on your system.

3   With the second line of text still selected, to change its font size, do the following:

   •   Place the pointer over the Size value field. The pointer changes to a hand with two black arrows ( ).

   •   Drag to change the Size value to 75. If you have difficulties getting a precise value by dragging, click the size value once, type **75** into the text field, and press Enter (Windows) or Return (Mac OS).

Now that you've changed the size of the first line, you can see that the text is, in fact, centered.

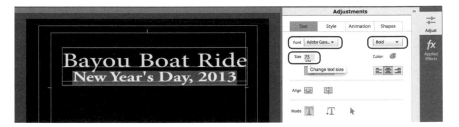

4   At the top of the Adjustments panel, click the Style tab (Style) to enter Style view. Scroll down until you can see the Lithos Gold Strokes 52 style near the bottom. Then select the first line of text—the words "Bayou Boat Ride"—with the Horizontal Type tool, and choose Lithos Gold Strokes 52. This changes the style for the selected text.

5 At the top of the Adjustments panel, click the Text tab (Text) to enter that view. With the words "Bayou Boat Ride" still selected, change the font size to 85, either by dragging the Size value to the right or by clicking the Size value once, typing **85** into the text field, and pressing Enter (Windows) or Return (Mac OS).

6 Choose File > Save to save your work.

Centering elements in the Monitor panel

At this point, your title probably isn't precisely centered horizontally within the frame. You can fix this manually, or you can let Adobe Premiere Elements do the work for you.

1 Using the Selection tool, click the text box to select the title.

2 Choose Text > Position > Horizontal Center. Or right-click the text box, and then choose Position > Horizontal Center. Adobe Premiere Elements centers the text box horizontally within the frame. Depending on how you positioned the box earlier in this lesson, you might see little or no change.

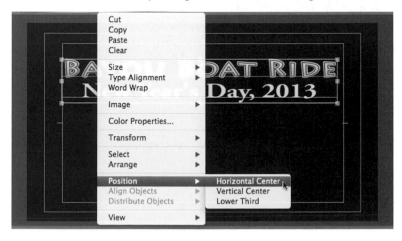

3 Choose File > Save to save your work.

Title-safe and action-safe margins

The title-safe and action-safe margins visible in the Monitor panel when you're in title-editing mode designate a title's visible safe zones. These margins are visible by default, although you can turn them off as detailed here.

Safe zones are useful when you're producing DVDs or other video that will be viewed on a traditional TV set rather than on your computer. The reason is that when displaying video, most consumer TV sets cut off a portion of the outer edges of the picture, which is called *overscan*. The amount of overscan is not consistent across TVs, so to ensure that everything fits within the area that most TVs display, keep text within the title-safe margins, and keep all other important elements within the action-safe margins.

If you're creating content for computer-screen viewing only, title-safe and action-safe margins are irrelevant, because computer screens display the entire image. You can place text as close to the edge as you'd like, and your screen will still display it in full.

To turn title-safe and action-safe margins on or off, right-click inside the Monitor panel, and choose View > Safe Title Margin or View > Safe Action Margin from the Monitor panel menu. The margin is visible if a check mark appears beside its name.

Changing the color of type

As you've seen, changing type style and size is easy. You can change all text within a text box equivalently by first selecting the text box using the Selection tool and then applying the change. Or you can restrict a change to only portions of the text by selecting them using the Horizontal Type tool. Now you'll change the color of the words "New Year's Day, 2013" to match the Bayou Boat Ride text.

You should be in Text view for this exercise, so if you're not, click the Text tab (Text) near the top of the Adjustments panel to enter that view.

1   Select the Horizontal type tool (T), and then drag over the words "New Year's Day, 2013" to highlight the text.

Next, you'll change the gradient and color of the type. Note that any changes you make will apply to only the selected type.

2   Click the Color Properties button ( ) in Text view to open the Color Properties dialog box.

3   In the middle of the dialog box, note the Gradient pull-down menu. Experiment with the different options on that menu, and notice how they change the appearance of the text. Choose 4 Color Gradient (which means that the gradient is composed of the four colors in the boxes at the corners of the rectangle beneath the Gradient menu).

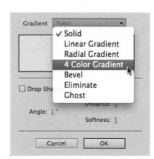

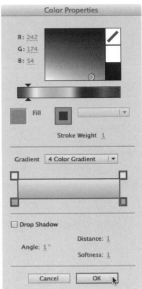
Color Properties

4 Click the box at the top left of the gradient rectangle to select it. Set the RGB values to R: **253**, G: **232**, and B: **73**. Note that after you enter the first value, you can switch to the next values by pressing the Tab key. Then click the box on the upper right, and insert the same values: R: **253**, G: **232**, and B: **73**. One at a time, click the two boxes on the bottom, and set the values for both at R: **242**, G: **174**, and B: **54**.

▶ **Tip:** How did I know that these RGB values would match the colors in the Bayou Boat Ride text? I selected the Bayou Boat Ride text, opened the Color Properties dialog box, and copied down the RGB values used for that style (of course). If you want to maintain consistent colors among the various design elements in your project, isolate a single set of RGB values and use them consistently.

5 Click OK to close the Color Properties dialog box. Using the Selection tool, click outside the text box in the Monitor panel to deselect the text and review your work.

6 Choose File > Save to save your work.

Adding an image to your title files

To add an extra element of depth and fun to your titles, you can import and insert images from any number of sources. For instance, you can use photos from your digital still camera as elements in your title file. In this exercise, you'll place a shot of the baby alligator in the lower half of the title image.

1 With the Monitor panel still in title-editing mode, right-click the Monitor panel, and then choose Image > Add Image.

The Open dialog box appears.

▶ **Tip:** If you have overlapping frames, you can change the stacking order by right-clicking on a selected frame and then choosing one of the Arrange commands from the context menu. To align multiple frames, select the frames you want to align, right-click, and then choose any of the Align Objects commands.

2 In the Open dialog box, navigate to the Lesson08 folder. Within that folder, select the file marquee.psd, and then click Open (Windows) or Open (Mac OS) to import the image into your title.

3 The image appears stacked in front of the text box in your title. Use the Selection tool to drag the placed image downward, making sure that the bottom of the image stays above the action-safe area. (If this were text, you'd have to make sure it was within the title-safe zone.)

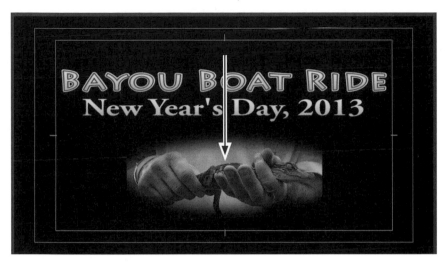

▶ **Tip:** How long should your titles appear onscreen? Long enough for your viewers to read them, of course. Want more specificity? The rule of thumb is that your title should be twice as long as it takes to read the title out loud. So start your timer, read the title twice, stop the timer, and that's your duration.

4 If you're unhappy with the size of the image you've inserted, drag any anchor point to resize the placed image. Hold down the Shift key while dragging to maintain the proportions of the image.

5 To make sure that the image is centered perfectly, right-click the image, and choose Position > Horizontal Center.

6 Choose File > Save to save your work.

Applying fade-in and fade-out effects

Any transition that you use on video clips can also be added to title clips. In this exercise, you'll add a fade-in and fade-out effect to the title clip.

1 With the title selected, click Applied Effects to open the Applied Effects panel.

2 Click the disclosure triangle next to Opacity to view the Opacity controls.

3 Under Opacity, click the Fade In button. The title image seems to disappear from the Monitor panel. Drag the current-time indicator in the timeline to the right to see the image fade in.

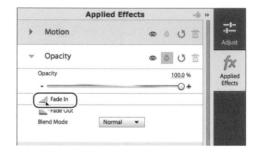

If you adjusted the default transition duration to five frames (as detailed in Lesson 7), after five frames the clip's opacity reaches 100% and becomes fully visible again. Although five frames is an appropriate length for interscene dissolves, fade-ins should be one full second. Let's fix that (if necessary).

4 In the timeline, drag the second keyframe in the Video 1 track to the 00;00;01;00 mark, as shown in the little yellow box beneath the pointer. That extends the fade-in from five frames to one full second. Note that this step is easier if you're zoomed in on the timeline and if the Video 1 track is taller than the default size.

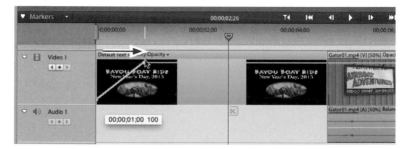

5 Back in the Applied Effects panel, click the Fade Out button to fade out the title. If necessary, drag the third keyframe to the left to the 00;00;04;00 mark to extend the fade out to one second.

6 If the current-time indicator isn't at the start of the project, press Home to move it there. Then press the spacebar to play the title you just created. Press the spacebar to stop playback when you're finished.

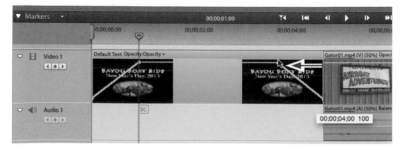

7 Choose File > Save to save your work.

Animate a still title

Text animations are fun effects that are very easy to apply.

To apply an animation, you must be in title-editing mode; the easiest way to enter this mode is to double-click a title in the timeline. Select the text element that you want to animate, and click the Animation tab (Animation) to open that view in the Adjustments panel. Preview any animation by hovering your pointer over the animation until the Play button appears and then clicking Play. Click Apply at the bottom of the Animation view to apply the selected animation to the selected text.

To remove an animation, select the animated text, click the Animation tab to open that view, and click the Remove button at the bottom of the panel.

If you tried this immediately with the title in this project, don't get upset: A text animation can have only one line, so it won't work with our current title. With more than one line, the Apply button in the Animation panel never becomes active.

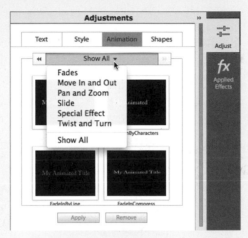

Superimposing a title over video clips

Now you know how to build a full-screen title. Next, you'll create an overlay title. In this exercise, you'll add an overlay title over Gator09.mp4 (which as you'll see isn't a gator at all but a pelican). The fun new skills you'll learn here are how to create a background for your title text so that it's readable over the background video and how to use shapes to highlight critical elements in your video content.

1   Move the current-time indicator to the start of Gator09.mp4, just after the end of the cross-dissolve transition from Gator08.mp4.

2   In the Action bar, click Titles & Text (🎬 Titles & Text) to open the Titles & Text panel. Make sure that the General category is selected.

● **Note:** Because this title is on Video 2, not Video 3, you won't see it if you enter Quick view.

3 Click and drag the Default Text title template to the Video 2 track, right where it intersects with the current-time indicator, and release the pointer. Adobe Premiere Elements inserts the title and opens the title in title-editing mode.

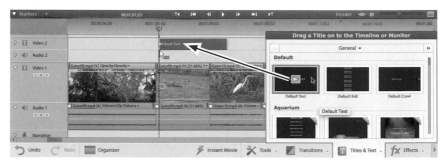

4 Click in the text box, and drag the pointer over the default text to select it. Type the word **Pelican**.

You can see right away that this text will be hard to read without some kind of a background. Let's get the text squared away, and then you'll create the background.

5 Drag the text you just added to select it. In the Text tab, click the Font pull-down menu, choose Adobe Garamond Pro, and change the Size to **100**. Then click the Selection tool, and position the text so it's in the bottom center of the frame.

6 Click elsewhere in the title to deselect the text that you just created.

Now let's add a background.

7 Click the Shapes tab (Shapes) to open that view. Select the Rectangle tool (▮); the cursor changes to a cross-hair. Drag to create a rectangle over the text you just created. Don't worry about obscuring the text; in a moment, you'll position the rectangle behind the text.

8 Click the Color Properties button (●) to open the Color Properties dialog box. Set the color to black by clicking the large black color chip in the upper right of the Color Properties dialog box. Click OK to apply the color to the rectangle you created and to close the Color Properties dialog box.

9 Soften the black color by making the background slightly transparent. Right-click the rectangle, and choose Transform > Opacity. The Opacity panel opens. Type **60** into the Opacity % field, and click OK to close the panel.

10 Now you'll shift the new rectangle behind the text. Right-click the rectangle, and choose Arrange > Send To Back to place the rectangle behind the white type. The white text is now clearly visible over the rectangle. If necessary, you can edit the size of the rectangle by clicking it to make it active and then dragging any edge to a new location. If necessary, you can also trim the right edge of the title so that it doesn't extend over to the next clip.

▶ **Tip:** When you add multiple elements, such as text, squares, or circles, to a title, you create a stacking order. The most recent item added (in this case, the rectangle) is placed at the top of the stacking order. You can control the stacking order—as you did here—using the Arrange commands from the context menu or the Text menu.

11 Let's add a pointer to the pelican. Click elsewhere in the title to deselect the box you just created. Then select the Line tool (✐), and draw a line from the text title to the pelican.

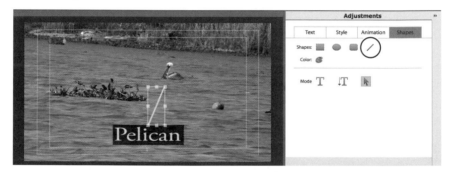

12 You want to match the duration of the title to the length of the pelican clip. The title is five seconds long, while the clip is just under 4 seconds long. Trim the title to the right edge of the Gator09.mp4 clip by grabbing the edge and dragging it just over one second to the left.

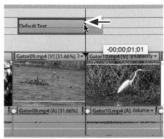

13 Following the instructions in the earlier "Applying fade-in and fade-out effects" section, fade the title that you just created in and out. In this case, the fade-in and fade-out effect should be fairly short—say, about five frames. You want to soften its appearance and disappearance, not make it noticeable or memorable.

14 Move the current-time indicator a few moments before the title you just created. Then press the spacebar to view the title. Press the spacebar to stop playback when you're finished.

15 Choose File > Save to save your work.

Using graphics

Graphics are a great way to add a polish to your productions, whether for a touch of whimsy or for a more comic element. We'll add the latter, staying in Expert view because there are many more graphics elements to work with, although you can access a subset in Quick view.

1 Move the current-time indicator to the start of Gator15.mp4, right after the short cross-dissolve transition.

2 On the far right of the Action bar, click Graphics ( Graphics) to open the Graphics panel. Click the pull-down menu, and choose the Thought And Speech Bubbles category.

3 Use the scroll bar on the right of the Graphics panel to scroll down to Speech Bubble 05-LEFT. Click and drag it to the Video 3 track right where it intersects the current-time indicator.

   Note that if you haven't used this graphic before, Adobe Premiere Elements may have to download it, which means you need to be connected to the Internet.

4 Double-click the graphic on the timeline to open it in title-editing mode.

5 Click in the text box, and drag your pointer over the default text to select it. Press the spacebar once, and type **Yuch!**. Then drag the pointer over the text again, and increase the font size to 120 to make the text fill the speech bubble.

6 Click the Applied Effects icon to open that panel; then click the disclosure triangle next to the Motion adjustment to expose those configuration options. Click and drag the Scale slider to the left to make the speech bubble smaller, and then click and drag the speech bubble upwards and to the right so it looks like it's coming from the baby alligator.

7 Shorten the speech bubble on the timeline so that it doesn't extend past Gator15.mp4. Click and drag the right edge of the speech bubble to the left until it reaches the right edge of Gator15.mp4.

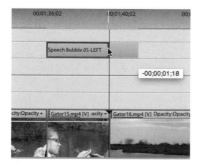

● **Note:** The speech bubble will always appear in the project where you first apply it. However, the speech bubble did not reliably reappear in subsequent projects created for later lessons from this project. For some reason, it doesn't seem to travel well to different projects in different folders, particularly on different systems. So don't be shocked if you don't see the speech bubble graphic in later projects, despite our best efforts.

8 Again following the instructions in the "Applying fade-in and fade-out effects" section, fade the title that you just created in and out. As with the title, in this case the fade-in and fade-out effects should again be about five frames, a subtle softening.

9 Move the current-time indicator a few moments before the title you just created. Then press the spacebar to view the title. Press the spacebar to stop playback when you're finished.

10 Choose File > Save to save your work.

OK, you're almost home. Let's add rolling credits, and you'll be done.

Working with animated titles

The titles you have created to this point have been static, but Adobe Premiere Elements can create animated titles as well. There are two types of animated titles: rolls and crawls. A *rolling* credit is defined as text that moves vertically up the screen, like the end credits of a movie. A *crawl* is text that moves horizontally across the screen, like a news ticker. In the following exercise, you'll create a rolling credit at the end of the project.

Creating a rolling credit

1 Press the End key to move to the end of the project.

2 In the Action bar, click Titles & Text (Titles & Text) to open the Titles & Text panel. Make sure that the General category is selected.

3 Click and drag the Default Roll title template to the Video 1 track, adjacent to Picture 8.jpg.

4 Using the Horizontal Type tool, select the Main Title text at the top of the Monitor panel. In the text options area of the Adjustments panel, click the Center Text ( ) icon to center the text. That way, whatever you type will continue to be centered. Make sure that the Main Title text is still selected, and type **Credits**.

5 Click the other text box, press Ctrl+A (Windows) or Command+A (Mac OS) to select all text, and then click the Center Text icon again to center the text.

6 In the second text box, if necessary, press Ctrl+A (Windows) or Command+A (Mac OS) to select all text, and do the following:

- Type **Filmed on location in the Louisiana Bayou:** and press Enter (Windows) or Return (Mac OS) *twice.*

- Type **Narration: Eleanor Rose** and press Enter (Windows) or Return (Mac OS) *twice.*

- Type **Eyeroll video: Elizabeth Whatley** and press Enter (Windows) or Return (Mac OS) *twice.*

- Type **Baby Alligator: Himself** and press Enter (Windows) or Return (Mac OS) *nine* times.

- Type **The End** and press Enter (Windows) or Return (Mac OS) *seven* times.

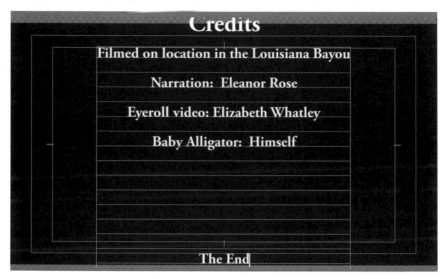

7 From the Adobe Premiere Elements main menu, choose Text > Roll/Crawl Options. The first few options are self-explanatory; here are descriptions of what the others specify (from Adobe Premiere Elements Help):

- **Start Off Screen**—The roll begins out of view and scrolls into view

- **End Off Screen**—The roll continues until the objects are out of view

- **Preroll**—The number of frames that play before the roll begins

- **Ease-In**—The number of frames through which the title rolls at a slowly increasing speed until the title reaches the playback speed

- **Ease-Out**—The number of frames through which the title scrolls at a slowly decreasing speed until the roll completes

- **Postroll**—The number of frames that play after the roll completes

8 Set up your page so that the credits start offscreen, quickly come into view, slow at the end, and then The End stays onscreen until the title fades out (which you'll do in the next exercise). To accomplish this, do the following:

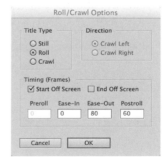

- Select the Start Off Screen check box (if not already selected).

- Leave the End Off Screen check box deselected (or deselect it).

- Set Preroll and Ease-In at **0** to make the title appear as quickly as possible.

- Set Ease-Out at **80** so the title slows as The End is rising.

- Set Postroll at **60** so The End stays static before it fades out.

9 Click OK to close the Roll/Crawl Options dialog box and apply your changes.

10 Place the current-time indicator just before the beginning of the rolling credits. Press the spacebar to play the rolling credits clip. If playback is too jerky, render the rolling credit title work area first.

When you play the clip, the text box with the credits will move—in the five-second default length of the title—from bottom to top across the monitor. This is a bit fast; we'll slow it down in the next exercise.

Changing the speed of a rolling title

When Adobe Premiere Elements creates a rolling title, it spreads the text evenly over the duration of the title. The only way to change the speed of a rolling title is to increase or decrease the length of the title clip. If you want the text to move more slowly across the screen, you need to increase the clip length.

1 In the timeline, place your pointer over the right end of the rolling title you just created, and click and drag the clip to the right. Note that as you drag, a small context menu shows you how much time you are adding to the clip. Add about five seconds to the length of the clip, and then release the pointer.

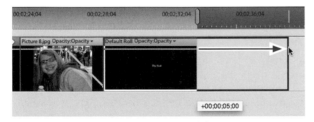

2 Following the instructions in the "Applying fade-in and fade-out effects" section, fade the title that you just created in and out. In this case, the fade-in and fade-out effects should each be about five frames in duration.

3 Place the current-time indicator just before the beginning of the rolling credits. Press the spacebar to play the rolling credits clip. Notice how your titles are now moving more slowly on the monitor and how The End stays onscreen until it fades out at the end. Pretty sweet, eh?

4 You're done here, so save your project as **Lesson08_End.prel**.

Exploring on your own

To increase your skill and versatility with titles, experiment with the different templates Adobe Premiere Elements provides. Keep in mind that you can modify elements like the color of text and the position of graphics. Here are a few steps to follow as you discover what's available:

1   Replace the custom title you created with a title created from a template.

2   Explore the drawing tools available to you when you're in title-editing mode.

3   Create an animated title. Remember that you can animate only titles with one line of text.

4   Place different transitions between your title clips and your video clips to view the various effects you can achieve.

Congratulations; you have completed the lesson. You've learned how to create a simple still title with text and graphics. You changed the style, size, alignment, and color of text. You've positioned and aligned text and graphic frames in the Monitor panel, and you've used one of the Arrange commands to change the stacking order of overlapping frames. You applied fade-in and fade-out effects to your titles. You know how to create rolling credits and how to use and customize title templates. It's time for a well-earned break. But before you stop, review the questions and answers that complete this lesson.

Review questions

1 How do you create a new title?

2 How do you exit title-editing mode, and how can you reenter it to make adjustments to a title clip?

3 How do you change the color of title text?

4 How do you add a fade-in or fade-out effect to a superimposed title clip?

5 What is a rolling credit, and how do you speed it up or slow it down?

Review answers

1 The easiest way to create a new title is to drag a title template to the desired location.

2 To exit title-editing mode, click anywhere in the timeline except on a title clip. To reenter title-editing mode, double-click any title on the timeline.

3 Double-click a title to enter title-editing mode in the Monitor panel. Select the text using the Horizontal Type tool. Then click the Color Properties button, and pick a new color in the Color Properties dialog box.

4 Select the title, and then click the Applied Effects button to open that panel. Under Opacity in Properties, click the Fade In or Fade Out button.

5 A rolling credit is text that scrolls vertically across your screen. Duration on the timeline controls scrolling speed. To slow scrolling speed, click and drag the title to make it longer. To increase scrolling speed, click and drag the title to make it shorter.

9 WORKING WITH SOUND

Lesson overview

The sound you use has a big impact on your movies. Adobe Premiere Elements provides you with the tools to narrate clips while previewing them in real time; to create, add, and modify soundtracks; and to control volume levels within clips. The project in this lesson helps you explore the basics of working with audio.

Specifically, you'll learn how to do the following:

- Create a custom-length background music track with music scores

- Add narration and normalize the volume of the narration

- Adjust volume and gain

- Use Smart Mix to automatically optimize the volume of your background music track and narration

- Adjust the volume of an audio track with and without keyframes

- Use the Audio Mixer

- Apply audio effects

 This lesson will take approximately 1.5 hours. Download the project files for this lesson from the Lesson & Update Files tab on your Account page at www.peachpit.com and store them on your computer in a convenient location, as described in the Getting Started section of this book. Your Account page is also where you'll find any updates to the chapters or to the lesson files. Look on the Lesson & Update Files tab to access the most current content.

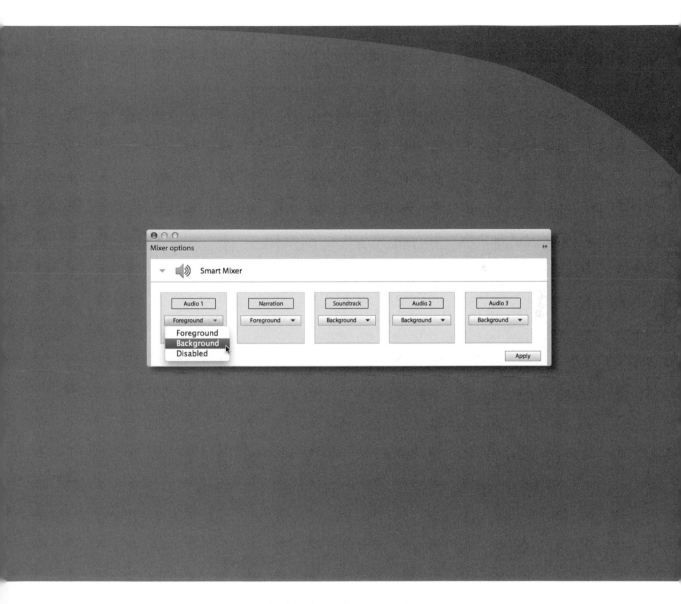

Applying Smart Mix to your project

Getting started

● **Note:** If you have not already downloaded the project files for this lesson to your computer from your Account page, make sure to do so now. See "Getting Started" at the beginning of the book.

● **Note:** If you see an error message asking for the location of Speech Bubble 05-LEFT. png, please press Skip. While content like the speech bubbles work well within a single project, sometimes they don't travel well when copied from project to project as we did for this book.

You'll modify this project by adding background music and narration and by adjusting the loudness of the audio on several of the clips. To begin, you'll open the Lesson09 project and prepare your Adobe Premiere Elements workspace.

1 Make sure that you have correctly copied the Lesson09 folder from your Account page onto your computer's hard drive. See "Copying the Classroom in a Book files" in the Getting Started section at the start of this book.

2 Launch Adobe Premiere Elements. If it's already open, choose Help > Welcome Screen in the Adobe Premiere Elements menu to return to the Welcome screen.

3 In the Welcome screen, click Video Editor, select Existing Project, and click the Open folder.

4 In the Open Project dialog box, navigate to the Lesson09 folder.

5 Within the Lesson09 folder, select the file Lesson09_Start_Win.prel (Windows) or Lesson09_Start_Mac.prel (Mac OS), and then click Open. If a dialog box appears asking for the location of rendered files, click the Skip Previews button.

Your project file opens.

6 Choose Window > Restore Workspace to ensure that you start the lesson in the default panel layout.

Viewing the completed movie before you start

To see what you'll be creating in this lesson, you can take a look at the completed movie. You'll have to be in Expert view to open the Project Assets panel to watch the movie, so if you're not, click Expert (Expert) to enter that view.

1 At the upper left side of the Adobe Premiere Elements window, click the Project Assets button (**Project Assets ▾**) to open that panel. Locate Lesson09_Movie.mov, and then double-click it to open the video into the preview window.

2 Click the Play button (▶) to watch the video about a boat ride in the bayou, which you'll continue to build in this lesson.

3 When you're done, close the preview window and click on Project Assets to close that panel.

Quick view or Expert view?

Although you can perform basic volume adjustments in Quick view, you'll have to work in Expert view for most other audio-related edits. For example, in Expert view, you can adjust audio volume, plus add keyframes to adjust volume over time. You also have access to normalization and gain controls, plus a range of useful audio effects that you can't apply or configure in Quick view.

Probably the biggest advantage of working in Expert view is the ability to see your audio files as waveforms, which instantly convey critical information about your audio files, like content and volume. You'll learn all about this in the "About waveforms" section later in this lesson.

If you're working in Quick view, to adjust volume, click the audio track, and then click Adjust ( ) at the upper right to open the Adjustments panel. Click the disclosure triangle to the left of the Volume adjustment to show the configuration screen, and then drag the Clip Volume adjustment to the right to increase volume or to the left to decrease volume. Or, click the numeric dB value (for decibels), type the desired adjustment, and press Enter (Windows) or Return (Mac OS).

Note that all adjustments increase or decrease the actual volume of the clip, so a dB level of 0.0 means no adjustment, not that the audio is set to 0.0dB. You can increase audio by a maximum of +6dB or drag the slider to –infinity (-∞), which brings the audio down to 0.0dB. To do more than change the volume of your clip, you'll have to switch over to Expert view, which is the view you'll be using for the rest of the lesson.

Workflow overview

Here's what you'll do during the bulk of this lesson: First, you'll add a background music track that adds flow to the project and helps maintain viewer interest through the slide show. Then, you'll add the Narration track and normalize it.

You'll be working with four tracks of audio: the audio captured with the video on the Audio 1 track, the audio captured with the greenscreen video on the Audio 2 track, the narration, and the background music. Once these tracks are on the timeline and optimized, you'll use the Smart Mix tool to automatically adjust the volume of all four tracks so they all play well together.

Adding background music with scores

To make it easier to add background music to your projects, Adobe Premiere Elements now includes 52 musical soundtracks, called *scores*, that you can customize to the length of your project. You access these scores via the Audio button in the Action bar. If you don't like the score that I chose for this video, feel free to sample the rest of the scores and choose your own. Here's the procedure, which you can also run through via a guided edit.

1 Press the Home key to move the current-time indicator to the beginning of the project.

2 At the right of the Action bar, click the Audio button (🎵 Audio) to open the Audio panel.

3 Click the menu to open the Music Score > Blues folder. Note that you can preview any score by hovering your pointer over the icon and clicking the Play button that appears.

4 Drag the Rainy Daydream score to the start of the Soundtrack track. Adobe Premiere Elements downloads the track.

5 In the Score Property dialog box, drag the Intensity slider to the third mark from the right.

Note that you can preview that intensity level by clicking the Preview button.

6 Select the Fit Entire Video option, and click Done to close the dialog box. Adobe Premiere Elements inserts the soundtrack and fits it to the length of the video.

7 Click the Collapse/Expand disclosure triangle to the left of the Soundtrack label to view the score.

Note the distinctive track pattern.

● **Note:** You can access the Score Property dialog box to change the Intensity level by double-clicking the score.

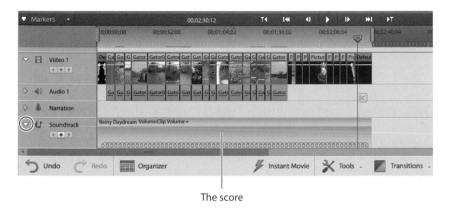

The score

8 Choose File > Save As, name the file **Lesson09_Work.prel**, and then save it in your Lesson 09 folder.

● **Note:** Scores are custom-built to the length of your video, which means that there are clear opening and closing sections. If you later adjust score duration, Adobe Premiere Elements will recalculate the optimal opening and closing sections, producing a good result in most instances. However, whenever you adjust score duration, you should preview to ensure that the score still has clear opening and closing sections. If not, start over, and reapply the score.

Adding narration

Now let's add the narration to the project.

1 Make sure that you are in Expert view.

2 Click the Project Assets button (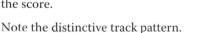) at the upper left to open the Project Assets panel.

● **Note:** In the Project
Assets panel, you can
use the Show/Hide
toggles to control what
kind of files you'll see. In
this figure, only Audio is
toggled to Show, which
is why the two audio
files are the only clips
showing in the panel.

3 Drag the narration.wav clip from the Project Assets panel, and drop it onto the start of the Narration track in the timeline.

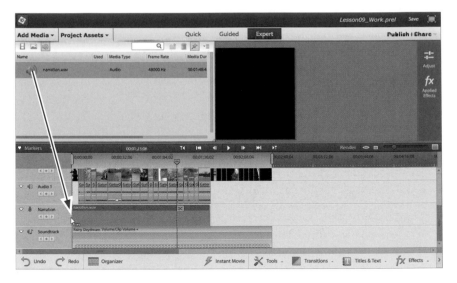

4 Press the spacebar to hear the voice-over added to the project.

Between the narration, background music, and ambient noise in the videos, you've got a royal audio mess on your hands. After learning a bit about waveforms, you'll fix that.

5 Choose File > Save to save your work.

Narrating a clip

In this exercise, you're working with a narration that I supplied, but of course at some point you may want to create your own narration. Using your computer's microphone, you can narrate clips while previewing them in the timeline. See Adobe Premiere Elements Help for a detailed procedure for narrating clips.

About waveforms

When you're working with audio, it helps to view the waveforms and make the tracks as large as possible, so you can see the details more clearly. Let's do that now, and then we'll talk about what waveforms are and what they tell you.

1 Hover your pointer over the dividing line between the timeline and the Monitor panel until it becomes a two-headed arrow. Then click and drag up to make the timeline taller.

2 In the Audio 1, Narration, and Soundtrack tracks, click the Collapse/Expand Track disclosure triangle to the left of the track name to expand the track and show the waveform.

3 To increase the height of the individual audio tracks, hover your pointer over the dividing line between the tracks until it changes to a two-headed cursor. Then click and drag up to make the track taller.

Note that this won't work until you have expanded the track as detailed in step 2.

4 If necessary, to see the track name in full, hover your pointer over the dividing line between the track descriptor and the timeline until it becomes a two-headed cursor. Then click and drag to the right to enlarge the track descriptor.

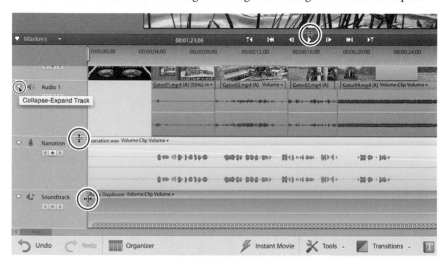

Now, to that discussion I promised you. Quite simply, a *waveform* is a graphic representation of the audio in the file. Each audio track in the project shows one component on top and the other on the bottom. The reason is that all of these audio files are stereo, and therefore have left and right channels, and the visuals correspond to those channels—the left channel is shown on the top and the right on the bottom. If the files were mono, you would see only one waveform for the entire track; if the files were recorded in 5.1 surround sound, you would see six.

Volume is represented graphically, hopefully intuitively, in each channel. When volume is low, the bushy line representing the waveform narrowly surrounds the centerline, or isn't visible at all. For example, in the Narration track, the first four seconds or so are flatlined, and then the waveform starts. This tells you that the first four seconds have no narration. If you play the project from the start to about ten seconds in, you'll hear what your eyes are telling you.

In the Audio 1 track, notice that the Gator01.mp4 audio is very, very low, whereas Gator04.mp4, when we're motoring over the river, is more substantial. If you drag your current-time indicator over each track and play the project, you'll hear that Gator04.mp4 is loud and Gator01.mp4 has little audible volume.

How can you tell when the audio volume is acceptable? That depends on the track. For example, the audio in the Narration track should be much louder, because it's the most important audio in the project, and it must be heard. However, the wave-form is clustered around the centerline, which tells you that the audio is low. When the audio is sufficient, the tips of the audio waveforms approach the outer edges of the graph area, but never touch for long. You'll fix this low audio in a moment with normalization.

As mentioned previously, the score in the soundtrack displays the distinct score pat-tern, and doesn't have a waveform. We'll adjust the volume of that track in a moment.

Although not excessive within the context of a standalone audio file, the audio in Gator04.mp4 is also supposed to be in the background, lower than the narration and background music. So it's definitely too loud, and must be adjusted, which you'll do using the Smart Mix tool.

Adjusting audio volume

Adobe Premiere Elements offers multiple mechanisms for adjusting the loudness of a clip, but they all use one of two adjustments: *volume* and *gain*. Although there are some slight technical differences between volume and gain adjustment, they both accomplish the same thing: adjusting the loudness of your audio. But they use different toolsets; we'll discuss these toolsets and their implications in this and the following section. Let's experiment with the two approaches on the Narration track, starting with volume adjustments.

In Lesson 6, you learned how to adjust clip opacity on the timeline by dragging the Opacity connector line upward and downward. You can adjust the volume of any audio clip the same way. We'll adjust the volume of the Narration track using this technique.

1 Preview the audio volume before making any adjustments. Move the current-time indicator over Gator01.mp4, right around 00;00;04;00. Press the spacebar to play the file. You can certainly hear the narration, but it could benefit from a volume boost. When you're ready, press the spacebar to stop playback.

2 In the Narration track, place your pointer over the yellow volume graph line on narration.wav at any location in the clip. The pointer changes to a double-arrow icon (⇕).

3 Click and drag the volume graph upward to the limit (about 6.02dB), and then release it.

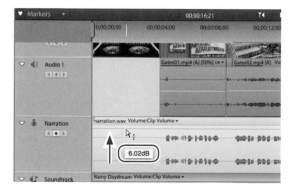

● **Note:** Adjusting the volume line doesn't change the waveform display. However, as you'll see in the next exercise, adjusting gain directly does change the waveform. Although adjusting the volume line is easier and more accessible than adjusting gain directly, if you overboost volume, you can produce distortion without being able to view the clipping in the waveform.

4 Shift the current-time indicator back to the start of Gator01.mp4, and press the spacebar to play the movie.

The loudness of the narration clip has increased substantially.

A few notes on volume adjustments

Volume adjustments are keyframable, which means you can vary volume over the duration of the clip. With gain, which you'll explore in the next exercise, all adjustments are for the entire clip.

Because volume is keyframable, it's the mechanism used by Adobe Premiere Elements in the Smart Mix tool, which varies clip volume over time. You can also use keyframes to fade in the volume of a clip at the start and fade it out at the end.

Adjusting loudness via volume adjustments does have some negatives, however. First, volume adjustments don't change the waveform, so you're flying blind in terms of whether volume is sufficient or if you've boosted volume too much and caused distortion. This is the reason you're limited to an increase of 6dB, which may not be enough for some audio files. Second, you can adjust the volume of only one clip at a time; with gain controls, you can adjust multiple clips simultaneously.

Third, with volume adjustments, there's no concept of *normalization*, a magical adjustment that ensures that the audio is as loud as possible without causing distortion. More on this in the next exercise.

Adjusting audio gain and normalization

Now let's experiment with adjusting audio gain.

1 Click Undo at the lower left () to undo the volume adjustment you made in the previous exercise.

2 Right-click narration.wav in the Narration track, and choose Audio Gain. Adobe Premiere Elements opens the Clip Gain dialog box.

3 Click Gain Level to make it active, and type **25**. Or, click on the number and drag it to the right to about the same level.

4 Click OK to apply the gain adjustment and close the Clip Gain dialog box.

The waveform expands dramatically, and much of the waveform is flattened against the top and bottom of the track. This is called *clipping*, and in moderate-to-extreme cases, clipping will distort your audio. If you preview the video now, you'll hear that distortion (but turn down the volume on your computer first, because this video will be very loud).

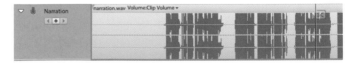

On occasion, manual volume adjustments can cause distortion if you boost the levels too high. When you use the Gain control, you get a visual indicator of clip volume and know when you've overcooked your audio.

5 Click Undo to undo this adjustment.

6 Right-click narration.wav again, choose Audio Gain to open the Clip Gain dialog box, and click the Normalize button. Adobe Premiere Elements closes the dialog box.

This time, the waveform expands out with little or no clipping (some areas may look clipped, but if you zoom in to the timeline to examine the waveform more closely, you'll see that they aren't). The reason is that normalization boosts clip volume as much as possible without introducing distortion into the clip. By definition, normalization can't cause clipping. This makes Normalization a superior option for volume adjustments, because other adjustments can distort your audio and don't show you when they do. When you adjust gain, either manually or via normalization, Adobe Premiere Elements updates the waveform, so you can see if you've boosted volume to the point where it might cause distortion.

● **Note:** To see how many decibels Normalization boosted the gain, right-click narration.wav, and choose Audio Gain again to open the Clip Gain dialog box. You'll see that Adobe Premiere Elements boosted audio volume by about 10dB.

7 Choose File > Save to save your work.

Volume, gain, or normalize?

So now you know the pros and cons of volume and gain adjustments. Which should you use? Although there are no hard-and-fast rules, here are some suggested workflows.

Normalize when increasing loudness

When you're adjusting clip volume upward, use normalization to avoid distortion. The only problem with normalization comes when you have a single long clip with extreme low and high volumes. Let's say you were shooting a wedding and didn't get close enough (or mic the bride, groom, or officiant) to capture the vows at sufficient volume. As a result, the levels are very low when the bride and groom are speaking. However, when the crowd starts applauding, the levels are quite high.

If you apply normalization to this clip, Adobe Premiere Elements won't boost the volume of the applause beyond the point of causing distortion, which might mean that it won't boost the volume of the vows at all. Your best option in this case is to split the clip into low- and high-volume regions—vows in one and applause in another—and apply normalization separately to each, or only to the vows section.

Of course, you can apply both functions—normalization, which is a form of gain, and volume adjustments—to the same clip. So if you need to fade a clip in and out, normalize first to achieve optimal levels, and then fade in and out via volume controls.

Normalize when decreasing loudness on multiple clips

If your project has multiple clips that are too loud, you can adjust them all en masse via the gain control. Select all the clips, right-click, and choose Audio Gain to open the Clip Gain dialog box. Specify the desired gain adjustment, and click OK. Adobe Premiere Elements lowers the gain of all clips by the adjustment value.

Adjust volume for fades and Smart Mix

As mentioned earlier, gain adjustments aren't keyframeable. For this reason, Adobe Premiere Elements uses volume adjustments for fade ins and outs, and for Smart Mix.

OK, now that you've boosted narration volume to the ideal level, let's adjust the volume of the entire project with Smart Mix.

Adjusting project volume with Smart Mix

Note: I boosted narration volume first because Smart Mix never increases volume: It works by adjusting the volume of background tracks downward. So if any clip needs to be louder, fix that before using Smart Mix.

You now have three audio tracks: the audio included with the videos on Audio 1 track, the background music score, and the normalized narration. Typically, when present, the narration takes precedence, and needs to be heard over the other two tracks. Let's use Smart Mix to do just that.

1 Press the Backslash key (\) to show the entire project. Adjust the interface so you can see all three audio tracks.

2 Press the Home key to move the current-time indicator to the start of the project.

3 In the Action bar, click the Tools button (✕ Tools) to open the Tools panel. Scroll down until you see the Smart Mix button.

Note: At times, the Smart Mixer opens in a truncated window that shows only a portion of the first audio track. If this happens, click and drag the lower right edge to the right to display the full window, as in the figure below.

4 Click Smart Mix to open the Smart Mixer.

Here's where you tell Adobe Premiere Elements which audio tracks to place in the foreground and which to place in the background.

5 Adobe Premiere Elements assumes that Audio 1—the audio shot with the video—should be in the foreground, which, in many instances, it should be. However, here it should not, so click the Audio 1 pull-down menu, and choose Background. Make sure that Narration is set to Foreground, and Soundtrack is set to Background. Then click Apply. Adobe Premiere Elements analyzes all audio tracks and applies the Smart Mix.

Note: In some instances, Smart Mix may not be effective for one track but will be quite effective on the others. If this happens, choose Disabled for the track that's not working well, run Smart Mix for the other tracks, and adjust the excluded track via volume or gain controls.

Adobe Premiere Elements prioritizes the Narration and Audio 2 tracks by reducing the volume of the Soundtrack and Audio 1 tracks with keyframes in the Soundtrack and some files on Audio 1.

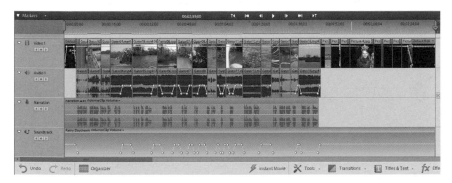

Raising and lowering volume with keyframes

You learned about working with keyframes in video in Lesson 6 in a section titled (appropriately enough) "Working with keyframes." Audio keyframes operate identically to the video-related keyframes discussed in that lesson. To refresh your memory, a keyframe is a point in the timeline where you specify a value for a particular property—in this case, it'll be the audio volume. When you set two keyframes, Adobe Premiere Elements interpolates the value of that property over all frames between those two keyframes. As you saw in the previous exercise, Adobe Premiere Elements uses keyframes in the Smart Mix function to vary volume over time.

For some properties, including opacity for video and volume for audio, you can create keyframes in the timeline by pressing the Ctrl (Windows) or Command (Mac OS) key and then clicking the associated graph with your pointer. You then drag the keyframe upward or downward to adjust its value, or to the left or right to adjust its location. To delete keyframes in the timeline, click to select them, right-click, and then choose Delete.

In this exercise we'll review these procedures. Specifically, you'll add keyframes to fade in the volume of the soundtrack at the beginning of your movie. It's probably not essential for this particular project, because the score has a definite starting section, but it's a valuable skill you'll use frequently in your own productions.

1 Drag the current-time indicator near the start of the project, around the 00;00;01;00 mark.

2 Click to select the Rainy Daydream clip in the timeline's soundtrack.

3 Click Zoom In (=) until you can see the 00;00;01;00 timecode in the timeline and spacing looks like the following figure.

4 With the current-time indicator at the 00;00;01;00 mark, position the pointer over the yellow volume graph of the Rainy Daydream clip at the current-time indicator. The pointer needs to change to a white arrow with double arrows (⬉), not the Trim Out tool (🔲). Press Ctrl (Windows) or Command (Mac OS); the pointer changes to the Insert Keyframe pointer (⬉₊). Click the volume graph to add a keyframe at the 00;00;01;00 mark.

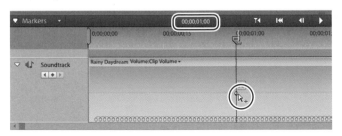

5 Press the Home key to move the current-time indicator to the beginning of the movie. If necessary, use the Zoom slider to zoom in for more detail.

6 Using the procedure detailed in step 4, create another keyframe at the 00;00;00;00 mark.

7 Drag the new keyframe all the way down to create the start of the fade in. The text box should display –oodB to resemble the mathematical symbol –∞ for negative infinity.

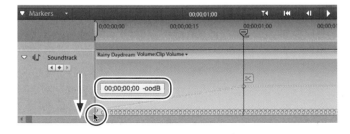

● **Note:** You can easily fade your audio in and out by right-clicking any audio track and choosing Fade > Fade In Audio or Fade Out Audio, whichever applies. This inserts the selected effect using the duration selected as the default for audio transitions.

8 To hear this change, press the Home key, and then press the spacebar to play. You'll hear the soundtrack fade in over the first second of the production rather than starting at full strength.

9 Save your project as **Lesson09_Work.prel**.

Working with the Audio Mixer

If, for some reason, Smart Mix doesn't produce the result you want, you have an alternative: the Audio Mixer. Using the Audio Mixer, you can adjust the volume and balance of the different audio tracks as the audio plays, so you can make sure your audience members hear what you want them to hear. For example, you can lower the volume for the soundtrack during the narration and increase it again during the slide show at the end of the project when the narration is complete.

Let's start fresh by reloading the Lesson09_Start project file and the narration and background music clips.

1   Choose File > Open Project. Navigate to your Lesson09 folder, and select the project file Lesson09_Start_Win.prel (Windows) or Lesson09_Start_Mac.prel (Mac OS). Click the Open button to open your project.

2   Press the Home key to move the current-time indicator to the start of the clip.

3   Click the Project Assets button to open that panel. Then drag the narration.wav clip from the Project Assets panel, and drop it onto the start of the Narration track in the timeline.

4   Normalize the audio volume in narration.wav: Right-click narration.wav, and choose Audio Gain to open the Clip Gain dialog box. Then click the Normalize button.

5   Add the background music track again: Click the Audio button, and then click the menu to open the Music Score > Blues folder. Drag the Rainy Daydream score to the start of the Soundtrack track, drag the intensity slider to the third mark from the right, select the Fit Entire Video option, and click Done to close the dialog box.

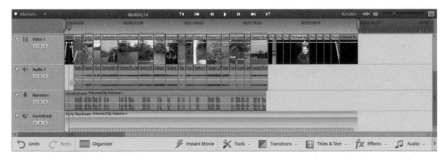

6   If it isn't there already, press the Home key to place the current-time indicator at the beginning of the movie. Press the spacebar to begin playing your video. You should hear the same familiar mess that you started with.

● **Note:** At times, the Audio Mixer opens in a truncated window that shows only a portion of the first audio track. If this happens, click and drag the lower right edge to the right to display the whole window, as shown in the figure below.

7 When you're finished previewing the movie, press the spacebar, and then press the Home key again to set the current-time indicator right at the beginning of the video, which is where you want to start mixing audio.

8 In the Action bar, click the Tools button (✕ Tools) to open the Tools panel. Click Audio Mixer to open the Audio Mixer.

Your Audio Mixer panel shows five audio tracks, but only the first three—Audio 1, Narration, and Soundtrack—contain audio. You can ignore Audio 2 and Audio 3.

9 Press the spacebar to begin playback.

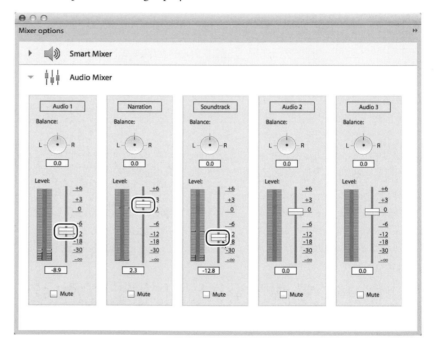

10 Grab the Level handles for Audio 1, Narration, and Soundtrack, and adjust them as desired while the video plays.

Note that all adjustments made via the Audio Mixer will be reflected as keyframes on the audio track, but will become visible only after you stop playback.

11 When you're done making adjustments, press the spacebar to stop playback, and then close the Mixer Options window.

Edit to the beat of your favorite song

You can use the Adobe Premiere Elements Beat Detect tool to automatically add markers at the beats of your musical soundtrack. Beat detection makes it easy to synchronize slide shows or video edits to your music.

1. Add an audio clip or a video clip that includes audio to the Soundtrack track. My example file is the Rainy Daydream score.

2. Right-click the audio track, and choose Beat Detect. The Beat Detect Settings dialog box opens.

3. In the Beat Detect Settings dialog box, specify the settings as desired, and click OK (in most instances, the default settings should be fine).

4. Adobe Premiere Elements opens a Beats track beneath the timescale, with markers corresponding to the beats in the soundtrack. To "edit to the beat," make sure that your cuts from shot to shot or picture to picture occur at a marker.

Working with audio effects

In most projects, the primary audio-related variable that you'll adjust is volume, and in this lesson you've explored a number of techniques to accomplish that. In addition, Adobe Premiere Elements has multiple audio effects that you can use to further enhance your projects, including controlling the volumes and frequencies of the different channels in your audio files, detecting and removing tape noise, eliminating background noise, and adding reverberation to give ambience and warmth to the audio clip. If you have any audio clips with excessive background noise, or hiss or hum, you should give these effects a try.

You can find the audio effects in the Effects panel by choosing Audio Effects from the menu, but only in Expert view. You apply audio effects by dragging them onto the target audio clip. You can then configure them in the Applied Effects panel. If any of the effects look particularly interesting, you can search Adobe Premiere Elements Help for more details.

Working with sound effects

In addition to audio effects, Adobe Premiere Elements includes dozens of sound effects that you can access via the Audio button on the Action bar. These include effects like crashes, explosions, impacts, weather, and more, that can be the perfect touch of polish for that action movie you've been contemplating. Use the effects like any other content—just drag them onto any audio track on the timeline, and edit as desired.

Exploring on your own

Great news: You've finished another lesson and learned the basics of working with sound. Specifically, you learned to create a custom-length soundtrack, add narration to your projects, use Smart Mix to adjust audio gain directly, and create and adjust keyframes.

But you're not finished yet. The best way to master the audio tools in Adobe Premiere Elements is to continue to explore them. Try the following:

- Experiment with different scores. Think of some upcoming projects (birthdays, holidays, vacations), and try to find the appropriate tracks for those videos.

- Try out various audio effects, such as Delay and Channel Volume. Check out the "Audio Effects" section of Adobe Premiere Elements Help.

- As you did for the fade-in of the soundtrack, create a fade-out for the soundtrack at the end of your project.

Review questions

1 What are waveforms, and why are they so important?

2 What is Smart Mix, and when should you use it?

3 What is the Audio Mixer, and how do you access it?

4 How would you change the volume of a clip over time using keyframes?

5 What is normalization, and how is it different from adjusting audio volume directly?

Review answers

1 Waveforms are graphical representations of audio in a file. They're important because they instantly reveal details about the clip's content and volume that direct many loudness adjustments.

2 Smart Mix is a feature that lets you identify which audio track(s) you want in the foreground and which ones you want in the background. It automatically adjusts the volume of the background clips to ensure that the foreground clip—usually speech or narration—is clearly audible. You should use Smart Mix whenever you're trying to mix two or more audio tracks, especially when one contains narration or other dialogue and the other contains ambient noise and/or background music.

3 Using the Audio Mixer, you can easily adjust the audio balance and volume for different tracks in your project. You can refine the settings while listening to audio tracks and viewing video tracks. Each track in the Audio Mixer corresponds to an audio track in the timeline and is named accordingly. You can access the Audio Mixer by clicking Tools in the Action bar.

4 Each clip in the Adobe Premiere Elements timeline has a yellow volume graph that controls the keyframes of the clip. To add keyframes, Ctrl-click (Windows) or Command-click (Mac OS) the line. You must have at least two keyframes with different values to automatically change the volume level of an audio clip. You can also use the Audio Mixer to set keyframes to change the volume of your audio clip over time.

5 Normalization boosts the audio volume of all samples of an audio clip the same amount, stopping when further volume increases would produce distortion in the loudest sections of the clip. When you boost volume manually, you run the risk of causing distortion.

10 CREATING MENUS

Lesson overview

In this lesson, you'll create a menu for a movie to be recorded on a DVD, Blu-ray, or AVCHD disc, or to a web DVD. You can follow along with most of this lesson, even if your system does not have a disc recorder, although it will be helpful if it does. Specifically, you'll learn how to do the following:

- Add menu markers to your movie

- Create an auto-play disc

- Use templates to create disc menus

- Customize the look of the menus

- Preview a disc menu

- Record a DVD, Blu-ray, or AVCHD disc

- Create and upload a web DVD

This lesson will take approximately two hours. Download the project files for this lesson from the Lesson & Update Files tab on your Account page at www.peachpit.com and store them on your computer in a convenient location, as described in the Getting Started section of this book. Your Account page is also where you'll find any updates to the chapters or to the lesson files. Look on the Lesson & Update Files tab to access the most current content.

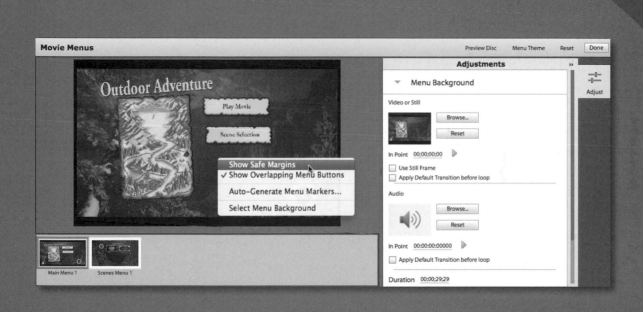

Creating a DVD with menus using the Outdoor
Adventure template

Getting started

To begin, launch Adobe Premiere Elements, open the Lesson10 project, and review a final version of that project.

● **Note:** If you purchased the downloadable version of Adobe Premiere Elements, using the menus demonstrated in this chapter will involve an additional download that could be lengthy depending on the speed of your Internet connection. For example, on a connection with about 10Mbps download speed, the required components downloaded in about five minutes. If possible, start running the first exercise to download these materials in advance of the time you actually intend to work on and complete the exercise. That way, the materials that you need will already be downloaded. If you can't, we apologize in advance for any delays.

1   Make sure that you have correctly copied the Lesson10 folder from your Account page onto your computer's hard drive. See "Copying the Classroom in a Book files" in the Getting Started section at the beginning of this book.

2   Launch Adobe Premiere Elements. If it is already open, choose Help > Welcome Screen in the Adobe Premiere Elements menu to return to the Welcome screen.

3   In the Welcome screen, click Video Editor, select Existing Project, and click the Open folder.

4   In the Open Project dialog box, navigate to the Lesson10 folder that you copied to your hard drive, select the file Lesson10_End_Win.prel (Windows) or Lesson10_End_Mac.prel (Mac OS), and then click Open. If a dialog box appears asking for the location of rendered files, click the Skip Previews button.

A finished version of the project file you will create in this lesson opens. You may review it now or at any point during the lesson to get a sense of what your project should look like.

5   In the Action bar at the bottom of the Adobe Premiere Elements workspace, click Tools (✖ Tools) to open the Tools panel. Click Movie Menu to open the Menu Theme panel.

6   At the top of the Menu Theme panel, choose Travel from the pull-down menu to open that folder, and choose Outdoor Adventure. At the bottom left of the Menu Theme panel, click Add Menu Markers Automatically For Me, if necessary, to make sure that it is *not* selected. Then click Continue. If the template isn't installed on your system, Adobe Premiere Elements will automatically download it. As noted above, download time will depend on your Internet connection speed, but should take no more than 5–10 minutes. Once the menu downloads, Premiere Elements will enter the Disc Layout workspace.

● **Note:** If you have not already downloaded the project files for this lesson to your computer from your Account page, make sure to do so now. See "Getting Started" at the beginning of the book.

● **Note:** You can create menus in Quick or Expert view, but since by now you're probably comfortable in Expert view, you'll work in that for this lesson.

● **Note:** If you see an error message asking for the location of Speech Bubble 05-LEFT.png, please press Skip. While content like the speech bubbles work well within a single project, sometimes they don't travel well when copied from project to project as we did for this book.

● **Note:** With the prerelease software, the download occurred normally, but Adobe Premiere Elements displayed a Media Not Found error message. In the unlikely event that you see this error message, click Done at the upper right of the Movie Menus panel, and repeat step 6. The error message should disappear.

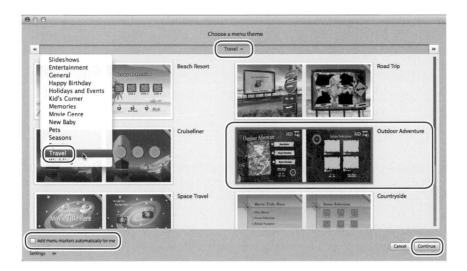

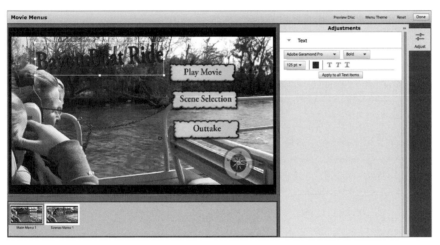

7 At the upper right of the Disc Layout workspace, click Preview Disc (Preview Disc) to open the Preview Disc window.

The Preview Disc window allows you to view and test your menus as they will appear when played on an optical disc or web DVD.

8 In the Preview Disc window, click the Scene Selection button in the main menu to switch to the Scene Selection menu. Click either chapter to begin playing the scene. As with chapters in a Hollywood DVD, these are links to scenes on the timeline that you'll create in the first exercise.

9 Press the spacebar to stop playback, and then close the Preview Disc window by clicking the Exit button (EXIT) in the lower right corner of the window.

10 After reviewing the finished file, choose File > Open Project, and select the file Lesson10_Start_Win.prel (Windows) or Lesson10_Start_Mac.prel (Mac OS). Click No when asked if you want to save changes to the file. If a dialog box appears asking for the location of rendered files, click the Skip Previews button.

11 Choose Window > Restore Workspace to ensure that you start the lesson in the default layout.

Understanding DVD, Blu-ray, and AVCHD discs, plus web DVDs

Before we actually start creating menus and approaching project completion, it's not a bad idea to be familiar with the basic formats and media that support the whole process.

DVD is a generic term that encompasses a few different formats. The format you'll work with in Adobe Premiere Elements is commonly referred to as DVD-Video. In terms of disc content and playability, this is the same type of DVD that you can purchase or rent and play on a DVD player connected to your TV set or on a computer fitted with the appropriate drive. Adobe Premiere Elements can burn single-layer (4.7GB) and dual-layer (8.5GB) DVD media.

A Blu-ray Disc—often abbreviated as BD—is an optical disc format that can store 25GB on a single-layer disc or 50GB on a dual-layer disc. It gets its name from the blue-violet laser that a Blu-ray player uses to read it (as opposed to the red laser used by CD and DVD players and drives).

An AVCHD disc is a traditional DVD that contains HD video in AVCHD format. AVCHD discs are playable on Blu-ray players and some computers but not traditional DVD players. The key benefit of the AVCHD disc is that it enables you to burn HD content to inexpensive DVD media without purchasing a Blu-ray Disc recorder, which makes it a convenient, affordable way to view and share your HD content on Blu-ray players.

To make a DVD, Blu-ray, or AVCHD disc in Adobe Premiere Elements, you must have a compatible DVD or Blu-ray Disc burner. It's important to note that although your system may have a DVD or Blu-ray Disc *player*, it may not be a recordable drive, also known as a DVD or Blu-ray Disc writer or burner. A computer drive that's described as DVD-ROM or BD-ROM will only play DVDs or Blu-ray Discs, not record them. (But a BD-ROM/DVD-R/CD-R drive will play Blu-ray Discs, play and record DVDs, and play and record CDs.) Check your computer's system specifications to see which drive (if any) you have. Drives capable of recording DVDs and Blu-ray Discs are also available as external hardware. Often, such external recordable drives are connected through your system's IEEE 1394 port, although some drives connect through the USB port.

Note that the process of authoring your projects or creating menus and menu markers is identical for all optical discs. You'll designate which type of disc to record just before you burn the disc in the final exercise of this lesson.

In contrast to the other disc-based options mentioned above, a web DVD is a collection of files that you upload to a website to display your content online—complete with the menus and interactivity available for disc-based output. As you'll learn in the section "Creating web DVDs," you create the files using a separate option in the Publish+Share panel, and then upload them to a website for hosting. In previous versions of Adobe Premiere Elements, you had the option to host the files on Photoshop.com, but that service has been discontinued.

Physical media

The type of disc onto which you'll record your video is important. You should be aware of two basic formats: recordable (DVD-R and DVD+R for DVD and AVCHD discs, BD-R for Blu-ray Discs) and rewritable (DVD-RW and DVD+RW for DVDs and AVCHD discs, BD-RE for Blu-ray Discs). Recordable discs are single-use discs; once you record data onto a recordable disc, you cannot erase the data. Rewritable discs can be used multiple times, much like the floppy disks of old.

Also available are dual-layer DVD-Recordable discs (DVD-R DL and DVD+R DL) that offer 8.5GB of storage space instead of the 4.7GB of standard DVD-R, DVD+R, DVD-RW, DVD+RW discs, and dual-layer BD-R discs featuring 50GB of storage space.

So which format should you choose? The first thing to note is that for recording purposes, DVD-R and DVD+R discs are not 100% interchangeable. While most newer drives can record to both formats, some older drives cannot. On the playback side, all drives should be able to play both DVD-R and DVD+R recorded media. It's the same with DVD-RW and DVD+RW; if you have an older drive, you should check to see which format(s) it can record to before buying blank media.

If you're recording optical media, you should recognize that playback compatibility is one of the major issues with recordable disc formats. For example, on the DVD side, many older DVD players may not recognize some rewritable discs created on a newer DVD burner. Compatibility is also more of a concern with dual-layer media than with single-layer discs. Another issue is that, as of this writing, the media for recordable discs is less expensive than the media for rewritable discs (usually much less than $0.40 per disc). However, if you make a mistake with a recordable disc, you must use another disc, whereas with a rewritable disc you can erase the content and use the disc again. For this reason, I suggest using rewritable discs for making your test discs and then using recordable discs for final or extra copies.

On the Blu-ray Disc side, playback compatibility is at least a minor issue with all media. But because the BD-R and BD-RE formats were developed at the same time, BD-RE discs are just as likely to play in a given player as their BD-R counterparts. That said, BD-R discs have come down in price to around a dollar in quantities of

25+, whereas BD-RE discs remain quite a bit more expensive, so you'll probably find BD-R discs more cost-effective, even though they can't be erased and reused. Dual- or double-layer BD-R discs sell online for as little as $3 per disc, but you have to shop carefully to find these prices, and you'll pay much more for faster recording speeds.

Manually adding scene markers

Note: This project is only about two minutes long due to necessary limitations on the file size. Most projects would likely be longer, but the basic principles remain the same.

Note: When you click the Add Marker button in Quick view, the Menu Marker dialog box opens automatically (you don't have to choose Menu Marker). This is because the other two marker-related options available in Expert view—TimeLine Markers and Beat Markers—are not available in Quick view, so the only kind of marker you can create in Quick view is a Menu Marker.

When you're watching a DVD or Blu-ray Disc movie, you normally have the option to jump to the beginning of the next chapter by pressing a button on the remote control. To specify the start of such chapters or sections in your project, you must add *scene markers*. In this exercise, you will place scene markers at the beginning of each of the two main sections of the project, so your viewers can access these sections more easily during playback. You'll start by adding the marker for the videos.

1 Scroll through the entire movie in the timeline.

2 Click anywhere in the timeline, and then press the Home key to move the current-time indicator to the start of the movie. Then press the Page Down key to move to the start of Gator01.mp4.

3 At the top left of the timeline, click the Markers pull-down menu (), and choose Menu Marker > Set Menu Marker. The Menu Marker dialog box opens.

4 You'll work more with this panel later in this lesson; for now, just click OK to close the dialog box.

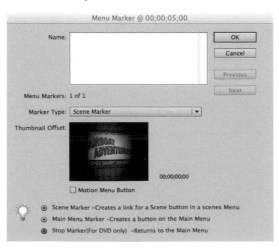

5 Notice the pale green scene marker icon that has been added on the time ruler.

● **Note:** You may have to move the current-time indicator and zoom in on the video project to better see the green scene marker. For example, in the figure, the current-time indicator is at the start of the project.

6 At the top of the Monitor panel, click the Quick button to switch to Quick view. Notice that the marker looks identical in this view.

7 Click the Expert button at the top of the Monitor panel to return to that view.

8 Drag the current-time indicator to the start of the slide show.

9 Right-click the time ruler at the current-time indicator, and choose Set Menu Marker. Click OK to close the Menu Marker dialog box.

You should now have two markers in your project—one for each section of this short movie.

Creating an auto-play disc

Most professional DVDs and Blu-ray Discs have menus to help viewers navigate through the disc content. You will work with menus shortly, but there is a quick and easy way to produce a disc without menus: creating an *auto-play disc*. An auto-play disc is similar to videotape: When you place the disc into a player, it begins playing automatically. There is no navigation, although viewers can jump from scene to scene—as defined by the markers you just added—using a remote control.

Auto-play discs are convenient for short projects that don't require a menu or as a mechanism for sharing unfinished projects for review. For most longer or finished projects, you'll probably prefer to create a menu.

As you'll see, the procedure for creating an auto-play disc is simple: Just burn the disc without applying a menu.

1 On the extreme upper right of the main window, click Publish+Share (**Publish+Share ▾**), and choose Disc.

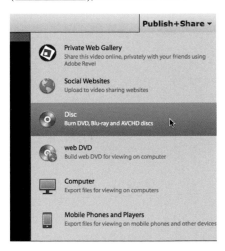

2 Adobe Premiere Elements opens the Missing Disc Menu dialog box. To burn an auto-play disc, click No.

3 The disc burning panel opens. We'll cover the options in this panel near the end of this chapter in the section "Burning DVD, Blu-ray, and AVCHD discs." To actually burn a disc now, jump ahead to that section. To continue on to the next exercise, click the Back button, and then click the Publish+Share button to close that panel.

● **Note:** There's no need to preview before burning an auto-play disc, but if you'd like to, here's how: Add a menu, as detailed in "Creating a disc with menus" section. Then, above the Adjustments panel at the upper right, click Reset to remove the menu. Use this same procedure to create a disc with automatically generated scene markers. When you're ready to burn the disc, follow the same procedure detailed in this exercise.

4 Choose File > Save As, and save this project file to your Lesson10 folder as **Lesson10_Work.prel**.

Automatically generating scene markers

Manually placing markers in the timeline, as you did in the first exercise in this lesson, gives you ultimate control over the placement of your markers. For long videos, however, you may not want to place all the markers by hand. To make the process of placing markers easy, Adobe Premiere Elements can create markers automatically based on several configurable parameters.

1 Choose File > Save As, and save Lesson10_Work.prel in your Lesson10 folder as **Lesson10_Markers.prel**. You'll return to Lesson10_Work.prel after you finish exploring the automatic generation of scene markers in your newly created copy.

2 In the Action bar at the bottom of the Adobe Premiere Elements workspace, click Tools (✕ Tools) to open the Tools panel. Click Movie Menu to open the Choose A Menu Theme panel.

3 In the lower left corner of the Menu Theme panel, click Settings (Settings ▸▸) to expose the scene marker options.

4   To automatically create menu markers, select the Add Menu Markers Automatically For Me option. Then choose one of the following three options:

- Select At Each Scene to place a marker at the start of each video clip in your project. Leave this option selected for now.

- Select Every *X* Minutes, and enter the duration in minutes to insert a marker at the designated interval in the project. Do not select this option for this exercise.

- Select Total Markers, and enter the number of markers in the designated field. Adobe Premiere Elements will insert the designated number of markers at even intervals in the project. Do not select this option for this exercise.

5   Select Clear Existing Menu Markers to remove the markers you created manually earlier.

6   At the top of the Menu Theme panel, click the Change Category pull-down menu, and choose Travel. Then click the Outdoor Adventure theme.

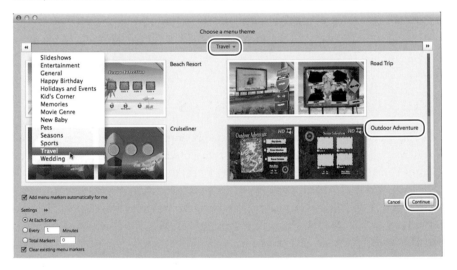

7   At the bottom right of the Menu Theme panel, click Continue. If you haven't downloaded the Outdoor Adventure Theme previously, Adobe Premiere Elements will download it now, so you must be connected to the Internet. After downloading is complete, Adobe Premiere Elements applies the theme, adds the automatic menu markers at the start of each video clip, and enters the Disc Layout workspace.

8   At the upper right of the Disc Layout workspace, click Preview Disc (Preview Disc) to open the Preview Disc window.

9 In the Preview Disc window, click Play Movie to begin playing your project. Once the first video clip begins playing, click the Next Scene button (▶▶) repeatedly, and notice how the video jumps from scene to scene.

10 Click the Exit button (⊠ EXIT) at the bottom right of the Preview Disc window to close it.

11 At the upper right of the Movie Menu workspace, click Menu Theme (Menu Theme) to reopen that panel. Click Settings to expose the automatic marker settings.

12 Select Add Menu Markers Automatically For Me (if it's not already selected), select Total Markers, type **4** into the number field, and select Clear Existing Menu Markers. Then click Continue.

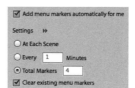

Four markers are now evenly spread out across the timeline.

Using the Total Markers option may be preferable to creating a marker for every clip to reduce the number of scenes in your movie.

13 Choose File > Save to save Lesson10_Markers.prel. Then choose File > Open Recent Project > Lesson10_Work.prel to return to the project file from the previous exercise.

Creating a disc with menus

Building an auto-play disc as you did in the previous exercise is the quickest way to go from an Adobe Premiere Elements project to an optical disc you can watch in your living room. However, auto-play discs lack the ability to jump directly to different scenes, as well as other navigational features that most users expect when watching a DVD, Blu-ray Disc, or AVCHD disc. You can quickly create such navigation menus in Adobe Premiere Elements using a variety of templates designed for this purpose.

1 In the Action bar at the bottom of the Adobe Premiere Elements workspace, click Tools (✂ Tools) to open the Tools panel. Click Movie Menu to open the Menu Theme panel.

2 At the top of the Menu Theme panel, click the Change Category pull-down menu, and choose Travel. Then click the Outdoor Adventure theme.

Adobe Premiere Elements ships with many distinctive menu templates—predesigned and customizable menus that come in a variety of themes and styles. The Outdoor Adventure template is a good thematic fit for our project, and once you finish customizing it, it will look and sound entirely appropriate. For your own projects, you should be able to find a template with a theme that matches your content, particularly for family-related events.

3 At the bottom left of the Menu Theme panel, make sure Add Menu Markers Automatically is *not* selected. You want to use the markers that you manually created in a previous exercise.

4 At the bottom right of the Menu Theme panel, click Continue. If you haven't downloaded the Outdoor Adventure theme previously, Adobe Premiere Elements will download it now, so you must be connected to the Internet. After downloading the theme, Adobe Premiere Elements will apply the theme and enter the Disc Layout workspace.

Each template contains a main menu and a Scene Selection menu. The main menu is the first screen that the viewer sees when the disc is played. The Scene Selection menu is a secondary panel accessed when the viewer clicks the Scene Selection button in the Main menu (or the equivalent of that button in other templates).

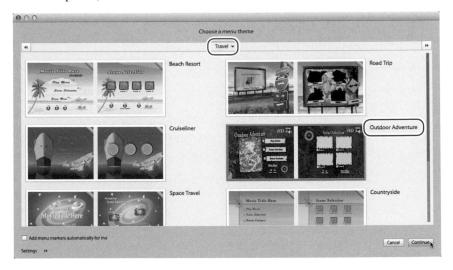

● **Note:** To replace a template after you've selected it, click the Menu Theme button on the far upper right of the Disc Layout workspace to reopen the Menu Theme panel. Choose a different theme in that panel, and click Continue; Adobe Premiere Elements replaces the existing theme with the newly selected theme. Be sure to recheck your Menu Marker settings when changing themes, because Adobe Premiere Elements seems to select the Add Menu Markers Automatically option each time you open the Menu Theme panel.

5 At the bottom left of the Disc Layout workspace, click to select Main Menu 1 if it's not already selected.

You see three text objects in the WYSIWYG preview area: Outdoor Adventure, Play Movie, and Scene Selection. The first is a simple text title that you'll customize to match the project. The second two are button links that your viewers will use to access the content in the project, clicking Play Movie to start the video playing from the start and Scene Selection to access the Scene Selection menu. The text in both is fine, so you'll leave them alone.

6   Make sure your safe zones are showing. If they're not, right-click in the WYSIWYG preview area, and choose Show Safe Margins.

Safe zones for titles can be important when you're producing an optical disc.

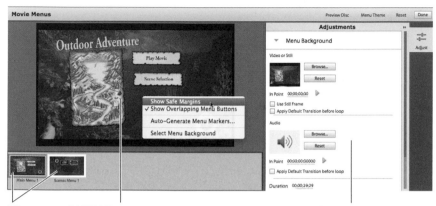

Disc menus   WYSIWYG preview area   Adjustments panel

7   Customize the movie title: In the preview area of the Disc Layout workspace, click the Movie Title Here text once. A thin, white rectangle appears around the button, indicating that it is selected.

8   Double-click the Outdoor Adventure text to open the Change Text dialog box. If the Movie Title Here text is not already highlighted, select it now, and then type **Bayou Boat Ride**. Click OK to close the Change Text dialog box and to apply the change.

9   Let's make the text smaller so it fits within the Title Safe area: Back in the preview window, click the text to make it active, and then on the right in the Adjustments panel, click the Font Size pull-down menu, and choose 84 pt. Note that you can also change the font, font color, and other attributes, which you'll do to some button text later in the lesson.

10 Click and drag the text so that it's centered over the picture beneath the text.

Note: Rollover effects like the circles in this example vary from template to template. Sometimes they are a symbol, sometimes a color change; however, there will always be some visual cue as to which button is about to be selected.

11 On the extreme upper right of the Disc Layout workspace, click the Preview Disc button (Preview Disc) to preview the main menu. Place your pointer over the Play Movie and Scene Selection buttons, but don't click them yet. Notice the yellow square that appears to the left of each button as the pointer passes over the text. This rollover effect is part of the menu template and shows viewers which button they're selecting. Click the Play Movie button; the movie begins to play.

12 As the movie is playing, you can use the DVD-remote-like controls below the preview window to control playback. To return to the main menu of your project during testing, click the Main Menu button ( ) at the bottom of the Preview Disc window.

13 Click the Exit button (✕ EXIT) on the bottom right of the Preview Disc window to close it.

14 Choose File > Save to save your project file.

So now you've changed the text in the title and resized it to fit within the text background. Next, you'll customize the Scene Marker buttons, and then you'll insert a video into the drop zone in the main menu and add a soundtrack to the main menu.

Modifying Scene Marker buttons

One of the benefits of optical discs and web DVDs is the ability to jump quickly to specific scenes in a movie. For each scene marker you add in the timeline, Adobe Premiere Elements automatically generates a Scene Marker button on the Scene Selection menu. If you have more scene markers than the number of scenes that will fit on a single Scene Selection menu, Adobe Premiere Elements creates additional Scene Selection menu pages and navigational buttons to jump back and forth between the pages.

If the template that you selected has image thumbnails on the Scene Selection menu (as the menu you're working with now does), Adobe Premiere Elements automatically assigns an image thumbnail to it. You can customize the appearance of a Scene Marker button by providing a name for the label and changing the image thumbnail used to identify the scene.

Changing button labels and image thumbnails

1 Click the Scenes Menu 1 thumbnail in the lower left corner of the Disc Layout workspace to view the Scene Selection menu.

► **Tip:** When you're using menu templates, one- or two-word titles fit best into the text boxes. Otherwise, they become ungainly in the menu.

Adobe Premiere Elements has generated the two Scene Marker buttons and their image thumbnails based on the scene markers you added in the first exercise. By default, Adobe Premiere Elements named the Scene Marker buttons Scene 1 and Scene 2, although this will vary according to the template. You'll customize these for your content shortly.

In addition, by default, the thumbnail in the Scene Marker button is the first frame of the clip the button links to. This doesn't work well for the first thumbnail, because it's obscured by the vignetting effect, so viewers can't easily discern the content of the scene. You'll fix that in a moment.

Note: You opened the Menu Marker dialog box briefly when you were creating markers on the timeline in the first exercise. Had you customized the Name field then, Adobe Premiere Elements would have used the name that you entered, not the default name. If you know the button name you want to use when you create the menu marker on the timeline, it's more efficient to enter it then. Just keep it short.

2 In the Disc Layout workspace, double-click the Scene 1 button to open the Menu Marker dialog box for the first marker. In the Name field, type **Videos**.

3 In the Thumbnail Offset section, notice that the timecode is set to 00:00;00;00. Place your pointer over the timecode, drag to the right to about 00;00;02;00, and then release the pointer to freeze the movie at that location. Or, click the time counter, and enter the timecode directly. Click OK. Adobe Premiere Elements updates the button name and image thumbnail in the Scene Selection menu.

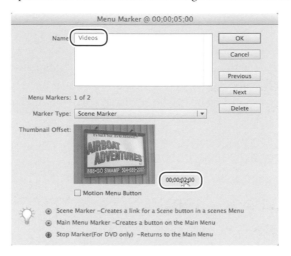

Next, you'll change the name of the remaining button.

4 Double-click the second button, Scene 2, to open the Menu Marker dialog box. Type **Slideshow** into the Name field, and click OK. (You'll leave this image thumbnail on the default frame.) Adobe Premiere Elements updates the button name in the Scene Selection menu.

5 Click the Preview Disc button at the upper right to open the Preview Disc window. Click the Scene Selection button to navigate to the Scene Selection menu. Notice that Adobe Premiere Elements has updated the button names and thumbnails.

6 At the bottom of the Preview Disc window you can see a group of navigation buttons that simulate the controls on a DVD remote control. Click any of the arrows to advance through the Scene Menu buttons, and click the center circle (the Enter button) to play the selected scene. Because Adobe Premiere Elements automatically controls the navigation of all menu buttons, you should preview all scenes on the disc to ensure that you placed your markers where you want them. When you're done, click the Exit button (⊠ EXIT) to close the Preview Disc window.

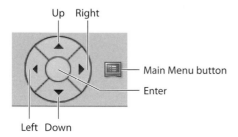

Adding submenus and menu links to bonus clips

Before you start customizing menu appearance, you should be aware of some other navigation and button placement options. For example, on the DVDs of many Hollywood movies, you'll find a link on the main menu to bonus or outtake clips sections, accessed via submenus. Adobe Premiere Elements lets you create this kind of submenu button on your main menu by adding a special menu marker.

In addition, by default, once a viewer starts watching any portion of the movie, the video will continue on to the end, even if there are intervening scene markers. In the project you've been working on, this isn't a problem, but with other projects, you may want to stop playback after a scene completes, and return the viewer to the menu. You can accomplish this by using a *stop marker*.

In this exercise, you'll add a stop marker to your project and a button on the main menu linking to a bonus video clip.

1 In the lower left corner of the Disc Layout workspace, click to select Main Menu 1. Currently, two buttons are in this menu: the Play Movie and Scene Selection buttons.

2 Click in the timescale above the timeline to select the timeline. Press the End key to move the current-time indicator to the end of the last clip.

You will now add a special marker to the end of your movie.

3 Right-click the time ruler at the current-time indicator, and choose Set Menu Marker. The Menu Marker dialog box opens.

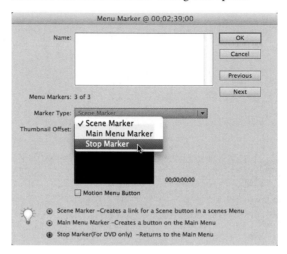

4 Choose Stop Marker from the Marker Type menu.

When a stop marker is reached during playback, the viewer will be returned to the main menu.

5 Click OK to add the stop marker.

In the timeline, stop markers are colored red to help differentiate them from the green scene markers and the blue main menu markers. You will learn more about main menu markers later in this lesson.

Next, you'll add a clip named Outtake.mp4 to the end of the timeline. This clip will be a bonus clip that users can access from the main menu but is not part of the main movie. You can't do this from the Disc Layout workspace, so you'll have to exit that first.

6 In the upper right corner of the Disc Layout workspace, click Done (Done) to close that workspace and return to the main Adobe Premiere Elements workspace. Use the slider bar on the bottom and the zoom controls to configure your interface like the next figure, so you can see the end of the project and have room to drag a file onto the Video 1 track.

7 In the upper left corner of the workspace, click Project Assets (Project Assets ▾) to open that panel, and scroll down to locate Outtake.mp4. Then drag the Outtake.mp4 clip into the Video 1 track after the credit title sequence at the end of your timeline. Be sure to place the clip a few seconds after the last clip, leaving a gap between the clips.

In case you're wondering, the outtake video is the fabulous eye roll video that we trimmed out in Chapter 5. Alligators and bayous notwithstanding, that really was the best shot of the day, proving that in videography as in life, sometimes it's better to be lucky than smart.

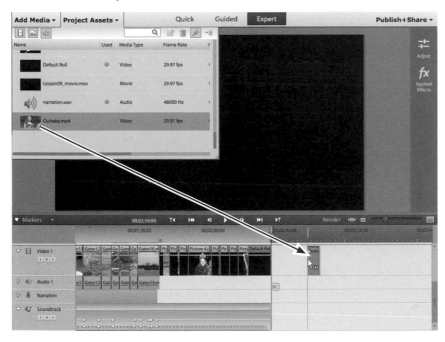

8 Press the Page Down key to advance the current-time indicator to the beginning of the added Outtake.mp4 clip, and then right-click, and choose Set Menu Marker to open the Menu Marker dialog box.

9 In the Menu Marker dialog box, choose Main Menu Marker from the Marker Type menu. In the Name field, type **Outtake**, and then click OK to close the Menu Marker dialog box.

   Adobe Premiere Elements adds a button named Outtake to Main Menu 1 in the Disc Layout workspace.

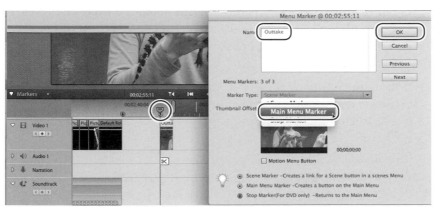

10 In the Action bar at the bottom of the Adobe Premiere Elements interface, click Tools (✖ Tools) to open the Tools panel. Click Movie Menu to enter the Disc Layout workspace.

11 Click the Preview Disc button, and then click the Outtake button to play that video. When the clip has finished playing, the main menu appears.

If you play the main movie from start to finish, the video stops after the credits because of the stop marker you added, and you will not see the Outtake.mp4 clip.

12 Close the Preview Disc window.

13 Choose File > Save to save your project file.

Three types of menu markers

There are three types of menu markers that you can apply to the timeline in Adobe Premiere Elements. Each one appears and functions differently within the interface and your projects, as described here:

- **Scene markers (◉)** automatically add a Scenes button to the Scene Selection menu of your disc. Scene Selection menus are secondary to the main menu. A Scene Selection button on the main menu will link to the Scene Selection menu.

- **Main menu markers (◉)** automatically add a button to the main menu of your disc. Most templates have space for either three or four buttons on the first menu page. The Play Movie button and the Scene Selection button are present by default. This will leave you with space for one or two more buttons, depending on the template you've chosen. If you add more main menu markers to your movie, Adobe Premiere Elements will create a secondary main menu.

- **Stop markers (◉)** force Adobe Premiere Elements to stop playback of your timeline and return the viewer to the main menu. Use stop markers to control the viewer's flow through the movie. For example, if you want the viewer to return to the main menu after each scene, insert a stop marker at the end of each scene. You can also use stop markers to add bonus or deleted scenes after the main movie, linking to this content using either scene or main menu markers.

Customizing menus with video, still images, and audio

You can customize your menus in Adobe Premiere Elements by adding a still image, video, or audio to the menu. You can also combine multiple items, such as a still photo and an audio clip. Alternatively, you can add a video clip and replace the audio track with a separate audio clip.

Keep in mind that any customizations you make to disc menus will not be saved back to the template; they apply only to the current project.

Adding a still image or video clip to your menu

When you're adding visual content to a menu, you'll use the same procedure regardless of whether it's a still image or a video clip. In this exercise, you'll insert a video clip into a menu. By default, when you insert a video, the audio plays with the video as well, although you can change this by inserting a separate audio file, as you'll do later.

Note that some menu templates have drop zones—regions within the menu where you can insert videos or still images. The menu template that we're working with does not, so still images or videos added to the background fill the complete background.

● **Note:** Follow this procedure to use your still image or video either in a drop zone or as a full-screen background image.

1 In the Action bar at the bottom of the Adobe Premiere Elements window, click Tools (✖ Tools) to open the Tools panel. Click Movie Menu to enter the Disc Layout workspace.

2 In the lower left corner of the Disc Layout workspace, click to select Main Menu 1, and then click anywhere on the menu background to open the Menu Background controls in the Adjustments panel.

3 In the Adjustments panel, in the Menu Background area, click the Browse button, navigate to the Lesson10 folder, and choose Menu.mp4. Click Open to close the dialog box and to insert the clip into the menu.

4 Note the Menu Background options available in the Adjustments panel. Specifically, you can do the following:

- Play the video by clicking the green Play triangle (▷).

- Choose an In point for the video to start, either by dragging the time counter or by typing in the timecode for the desired starting point.

- After choosing an In point, select Use Still Frame to use the current frame as the background or within the drop zone.

- Apply the default transition to the video clip before the menu starts to loop by selecting Apply Default Transition Before Loop. Note that the maximum duration for video menus is 30 seconds; the menu will loop indefinitely after that time.

For this exercise, leave the options at their default settings, and click Preview Disc to preview the menu. If it looks a bit jerky, don't worry; it will look much smoother once it is rendered for your optical disc or web DVD.

5 Let's add the same video as background for the Scenes Selection screen. In the lower left corner of the Disc Layout workspace, click to select Scenes Menu 1, and then click anywhere on the menu background to open those controls in the Adjustment panel. Follow steps 3 and 4 to add the video to this menu.

6 Choose File > Save to save your project file.

As mentioned earlier, when you add a video to a menu with a drop zone, the video plays within that drop zone. When you add a video to a menu without a drop zone, the video plays in the background of the menu, as it does here. Sometimes this works out well right out of the box; sometimes it would benefit from some tweaking. For example, on the new background, the Bayou Boat Ride text would be more readable in a different color. You'll learn how to make that kind of change later in this lesson.

In some cases, but not here, some critical regions of the video may be obscured by menu graphics that you can't delete or replace. Accordingly, to create a menu with your own full-screen still image or video in the background, choose a template without a drop zone or other graphic content that will obscure a video or still image.

If you opt to customize a menu with a full-screen background image or video, you can click the Apply To All Menus button in the Menu Background Adjustments panel to apply the background to all menus. You can also insert a different still image or video clip as a background in each menu, or simply use the background image included with the menu template.

Adding an audio clip to the background

Let's substitute a separate audio clip for the audio included with the Menu.mp4 video clip. Use this same procedure to add audio to any menu template, whether it is modified with a custom video or image background or used as is.

1 Click Main Menu 1 in the Disc Layout workspace to open the Adjustments panel.

2 Click the Browse button in the audio section, select the menuaudio.aiff clip in the Lesson10 folder, and then click Open.

3 If you want to add a fade-out so the audio loops nicely, select Apply Default Transition Before Loop.

4 In the Disc Layout workspace, click the Preview Disc button. You can see the video and hear the audio track you selected for the main menu background.

   If the Audio controls are not showing, click the menu background in the Disc Layout workspace to reveal them.

5 Close the preview window.

6 If you want to remove the audio portion from the menu background, click the Reset button next to the speaker icon in the Audio section of the Adjustments panel (but for the purposes of this task, don't actually do this).

7 To insert the same video and audio file combination as background for your other menu, click the Apply To All Menus button in the Adjustments panel. Don't do this in this case, because the video will be obscured by the graphic in the Scene Selection menu.

8 Save your project.

Note: You may have noticed that the background music track was the score that we integrated into the project back in Chapter 9. To create the 30-second iteration, I created a project with a single still image that stretched to 30 seconds on the timeline via the Time Stretch function. Then I applied the score, fit it to the video, and exported the audio track using controls you can read about in Chapter 11.

Animating buttons

If the menu template that you select uses thumbnail scene buttons like the one we're using, you can elect to animate the buttons. With an animated button, a designated duration of video from the linked scene will play within the thumbnail while the menu displays. The main menu for this project does not include any buttons with image thumbnails. However, the Scene Selection menu does have image thumbnails. Let's animate these thumbnails.

Animating thumbnails

1 In the lower left corner of the Disc Layout workspace, select the Scenes Menu 1 thumbnail.

2 Click the Videos button to select it.

   Currently, this button displays a still frame extracted from the video clip at the 00;00;02;00 mark.

3 In the Adjustments panel, in the Menu area, scroll down if necessary to see all of the Poster Frame section, and then select the Motion Menu Button option. Click Apply To All Marker Buttons to animate all marker buttons.

Note: You can't set the Out point or the end of clips in the Adjustments panel, but you can set all of your motion menu buttons to be the same duration, as explained in the following steps.

4   If you want to change the In point of the video clip and play a different segment in the animated thumbnail, drag the time counter (which currently reads 00;00;02;00) to the desired spot.

Now let's set the duration of the motion menu buttons.

5   To access the Duration control, click an empty area of the background menu. This deselects the current scene button, and the Adjustments panel switches to display the Menu Background properties. Scroll down to the bottom of the Adjustments panel, if necessary, to locate the Motion Menu Buttons area. If necessary, click the disclosure triangle to reveal the Duration control.

6   Note that the default duration for the Motion Menu Buttons is 00;00;04;29, which you can shorten, but not lengthen.

7   Click the Preview Disc button in the Disc Layout workspace. In the main menu, click the Scene Selection button to access the Scene Selection menu. Both buttons should now be animated. Since the animations are so short, they tend to be irritating, so I almost never use this feature.

8   Close the Preview Disc window.

● **Note:** All animated buttons share the same duration.

9   If you want to pick a different In point for your thumbnail video, select the Motion Menu Buttons option, and choose a suitable In point for the other scene button. If you didn't click Apply To All Marker Buttons in step 3, you must individually activate scene buttons to animate them.

10 Deselect Motion Menu Buttons for this project by clicking each button and deselecting the Motion Menu Button option box for each.

11 Save your project.

Customizing button size and location

Beyond adding still images, video, and audio to your menu, you can also change the size and location of buttons and text on your menus. In this exercise, you'll adjust text size and button location.

1   Make sure you're in the Disc Layout workspace; if not, click Tools (✕ Tools) in the Action bar at the bottom of the Adobe Premiere Elements window, and then click Movie Menu to enter the Disc Layout workspace.

2   In the Movie Menus workspace, click the Main Menu 1 thumbnail to make sure the main menu is loaded.

3 Enlarge the Bayou Boat Ride title: Click the text; an eight-point bounding box appears. Place your pointer on the lower right corner of the box, and drag to the right to make the text larger.

● **Note:** Scaling text boxes in this manner can be tricky, because the width and height do not scale proportionally. Text can easily become distorted.

4 Move the three buttons on the menu to the right: Click the Play Movie button to make it active, and then drag it to the right, closer to the title-safe zone. Do the same for the other two buttons.

5 Save your project.

● **Note:** All buttons and titles within Adobe Premiere Elements templates are designed to fall within the title-safe zone. If you plan to resize or move buttons or text on the menu, you should enable Show Safe Margins in the Disc Layout workspace, as we did here, by right-clicking the menu and choosing Show Safe Margins.

Overlapping buttons

Buttons on a disc menu should not overlap each other. Someone using a pointer to navigate and click the menu may not be able to access the correct button if another one is overlapping it. Overlap can easily occur if button text is too long or if two buttons are placed too close to each other.

In some instances, you can fix overlapping buttons by shortening the button name or simply by moving the buttons to create more space between them. By default, overlapping buttons in Adobe Premiere Elements are outlined in red in the Disc Layout workspace. You can turn this feature on or off by right-clicking in the Disc Layout workspace and choosing Show Overlapping Menu Buttons.

Changing menu button text properties

The Adjustments panel lets you modify the font, size, color, and style of your menu buttons, and you can automatically apply changes made to one button to similar buttons. You can modify the text attributes of five types of objects:

- **Menu Titles**, which are text-only objects that aren't linked to clips or movies

- **Play buttons**, which link to the beginning of your main movie

- **Scene Marker buttons**, which link to the Scene Selection menu

- **Marker buttons**, which directly link to a menu marker on the timeline

- **Navigational buttons**, such as the link back to the main menu in the Scene Selection menu

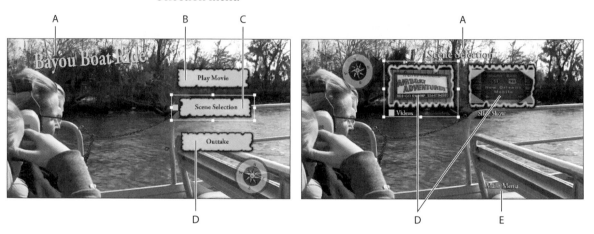

A. Text
B. Play button
C. Scenes button

D. Scene Marker button
E. Navigational button

You need to know about these different designations because any time you change a single item (say, a Marker button), you can apply the same change to all like items (in this case, all Marker buttons). However, this won't affect other button or text types, like Play or Navigational buttons. So if you wanted to change *all* text and buttons to the same color, you'd have to change all five categories to effect the change.

1   Under Disc Menus in the Disc Layout workspace, click the Scenes Menu 1 thumbnail.

2   Click the Videos button. The Adjustments panel updates automatically and shows that this is a Scene Marker button.

3   In the Text area of the Adjustments panel, click the font menu. Note that you can change the font of this or any text in the menu. The Adobe Garamond Pro font looks fine here, so let's leave that selected. But let's make the text a bit larger.

4 Click the Change Text Size pull-down menu beneath the font selector, and choose 60 pt. Then click Apply To All Marker Buttons to apply the change to all other Scene Marker buttons.

The Slide Show button text looks great. What about the Scene Marker button on Main Menu 1? Let's have a look.

5 Under Disc Menus in the Disc Layout workspace, click the Main Menu 1 thumbnail.

You can barely see the text in the Outtake button. That's because when we applied the change to all Scene Marker buttons, we changed the font color here as well as the size. Oops—unintended consequences. Let's fix that.

6 Click Undo, and then click the Scenes Menu 1 thumbnail to return to that menu. Click the Slide Show button, and manually change the font size to **60**.

7 While we're here, let's make the Main Menu navigational button larger. Click the Main Menu text to make it active, and choose 60 points for the font size. This is the only navigational button in this menu set, but if you had multiple Scene Selection menus, you would click Apply To All Navigational Buttons to apply the change to all navigational buttons.

8 Let's change the text color to make it more readable: Click the Main Menu 1 icon to return to that menu.

9 The brown font in the buttons on the right should work well for the menu text. To identify that color, click the Play Movie button, and then the color chip next to 45-point font size. Note the RGB color values in the color picker (R: 101, G: 53, B: 24). Let's change the menu text to that color.

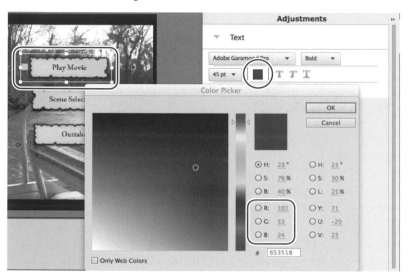

● **Note:** Using Apply To All Text Items will work well here, since the menu title is too small on that menu (don't these menu designers have grandparents?!), though you may have to move the title and some buttons down to stay in the title safe zone.

10 Click the Bayou Boat Ride text in the menu, and then the color chip next to the font size. Enter the RGB values from step 9. Then click Preview Disc to preview the new color. It's not a slam dunk, but it appears more readable than the original yellow text in most places in the motion menu. You make the call: keep it, click Undo to return to the original color, or choose a new color. Don't forget to do the same to the text title in the Scenes Menu.

One last set of changes: The text in the buttons is too small, so let's make it larger. Note that each button is a different type (Play, Scenes, and Marker button, top to bottom respectively), so you can't use the respective "Apply to" buttons.

11 Click each button, and change the font size to 60 points. Much better. Hopefully, your main menu looks close to that shown in this figure.

12 Choose File > Save As, and save this project file to your Lesson10 folder as **Lesson10_End.prel**.

Creating web DVDs

Web DVDs create the DVD experience within a web page, complete with menus, links, and high-quality video. If you have your own website or FTP access to someone else's, you can create files to upload and present from there, and invite friends and family to watch it. This exercise will take you through the file-creation and upload workflows for a web DVD.

1 In the upper right corner of the Disc Layout workspace, click Done to close the workspace and return to the main Adobe Premiere Elements workspace.

2 Save your current project. It's always a good idea to save your Adobe Premiere Elements project file before rendering your project.

3 In the upper right corner of the main workspace, click Publish+Share, and then click web DVD.

In the web DVD: Choose Location And Settings workspace, you'll notice that your only option is Save To Folder On Computer.

4 Choose the appropriate preset from the Presets menu. In this case, you have three choices:

- HD provides the best overall quality, but only viewers with fast connection speeds will be able to play the videos without stopping.

- SD High Quality NTSC is the best-quality, highest-bandwidth option in SD mode.

● **Note:** After you choose a preset, Adobe Premiere Elements will display its parameters below the Presets menu. The HD NTSC preset uses a frame size of 1280x720 at 29.97fps and produces a presentation with a total size of 62.42MB.

- SD Medium Quality NTSC creates an experience that can be viewed most smoothly by the broadest range of viewers, but will have the lowest frame quality.

When you're choosing, try to select the quality level that best matches the connection speed of your intended viewers.

5 Type **Bayou_Boat_Ride** in the Project Name field.

6 Click the Browse button, and save the presentation in the Lesson10 folder.

● **Note:** You can create SD web DVDs from HD content, but you shouldn't try to create HD web DVDs from SD content, because the video will likely look pixelated and/or blurry.

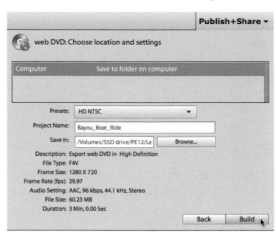

● **Note:** Rendering time depends on the speed of your computer, but could take 5–10 minutes or longer. Check the Build In Progress screen to gauge time to completion.

7 Click Build to continue. Adobe Premiere Elements renders the menus and content, and, when complete, displays a Build Completed message with a clickable link to the content just saved to your hard drive. Click the link to display the web DVD in your browser.

8 Open Windows Explorer (Windows) or File Manager (Mac OS), and navigate to the Bayou_Boat_Ride subfolder in the Lesson10 folder.

Here you'll find the files that Adobe Premiere Elements just created. To make this presentation available on a website, you have to upload all of the files to a website and send your viewers a link to the Play_web DVD.html file. To do this, you need FTP access to a website and an FTP upload utility like Filezilla, which is free and available on Windows and Macintosh platforms.

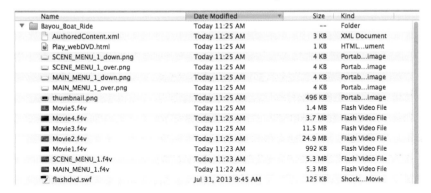

The following figure shows Filezilla uploading the web DVD files to the PRE12 folder on my website at www.doceo.com. I created the PRE12 folder to reduce clutter on the root content directory on my website, but that's not essential.

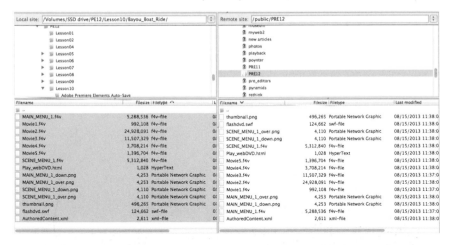

9 To play the web DVD, go to www.doceo.com/PRE12/Play_webDVD.html.

   I used the HD preset, so after clicking the link, wait a few moments for the necessary bits to download to your computer.

10 Click Done to close the web DVD window and return to Adobe Premiere Elements.

Burning DVD, Blu-ray, and AVCHD discs

After you've previewed your disc and have checked the menus and button names, you're ready to record the project to a DVD, AVCHD, or Blu-ray Disc. As noted at the beginning of this lesson, you must have a DVD recorder to produce a DVD or AVCHD disc, or a Blu-ray Disc writer to record a Blu-ray Disc.

When you're making any of these discs, Adobe Premiere Elements converts your video and audio files into a compressed format. Briefly, compression shrinks your original video and audio files to fit them on a disc. For example, a 60-minute video in AVCHD, DSLR, DV, or HDV format requires approximately 13GB of hard-disk space. However, a DVD-Video has only 4.7GB of space. So how do you fit a 13GB video onto a 4.7GB disc? Through compression!

Compressing video can take a long time, particularly if you're working from HD source material, so you should allow quite a bit of time for this process. For example, 60 minutes of video may take 4–6 hours to compress and record onto a DVD, and compressing and recording video onto a Blu-ray Disc can take even longer. For this reason, it may be a good idea to initiate the disc-burning process (which begins with compressing the video) at a time when you don't need your computer.

To maintain maximum quality, Adobe Premiere Elements compresses a movie only as much as is necessary to fit it on the disc. The shorter the movie, the less compression required, and the higher the quality of the video on the disc.

1   Save your current project. It's always a good idea to save your Adobe Premiere Elements project file before burning a disc.

2   In the upper right corner of the main Adobe Premiere Elements workspace, click Publish+Share, and then select Disc.

3   Choose DVD at the top of the Disc: Choose Location And Settings panel. Encoding parameters for Blu-ray and AVCHD discs are covered in the sidebar "Choosing Blu-ray and AVCHD disc quality options."

● **Note:** With AVCHD and Blu-ray Discs, you may be able to play content from a USB drive by plugging the drive into the USB port of a Blu-ray player. To create these files, burn your content to a folder, and then copy the content to the USB drive.

4   In the Burn To pull-down menu, choose Disc. If you don't have a disc recorder on your editing workstation, you can burn the project to a 4.7 or 8.5GB folder, copy that folder to another computer with a recorder, and burn the content to disc there using another program.

5 In the Disc Name field, type **Bayou_Boat_Ride**. Software playing DVDs or Blu-ray Discs on a personal computer may display this disc name.

6 Choose the desired DVD or Blu-ray Disc burner from the Burner Location menu. If you don't have a compatible disc burner connected to your computer, the Burner Location menu is disabled, and the Status line reads "No burner detected."

7 If you want to create a DVD, AVCHD, or Blu-ray Disc, ensure that you've inserted a compatible blank or rewritable disc in the disc burner. If you insert a disc after you start this process, click Rescan to have Adobe Premiere Elements recheck all connected burners for valid media.

8 In the Copies field, select the number of discs you want to burn during this session. For this exercise, choose 1.

When you select multiple copies, Adobe Premiere Elements prompts you to insert another disc after the writing of each disc is completed until all the discs you specified have been burned.

9 From the Presets menu, choose NTSC_Widescreen_Dolby DVD.

Adobe Premiere Elements is also capable of burning a project to the PAL standard (used in Europe, parts of Africa, South America, the Middle East, Australia, New Zealand, some Pacific Islands, and certain Asian countries) in normal or widescreen format.

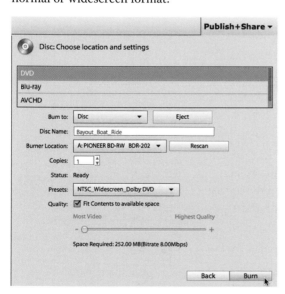

10 Select Fit Contents To Available Space to ensure that Adobe Premiere Elements maximizes the quality of your video based on disc capacity.

11 To burn a disc at this point, click the Burn button. If you don't want to burn a disc, click the Back button.

● **Note:** This exercise ends with the burning of a DVD. If you don't want to create a DVD, follow the steps of the exercise only up to the point of writing the disc. If you will be creating a DVD, I suggest using a DVD-RW or DVD+RW (rewritable) disc, if you have one available, so that you can reuse the disc later.

● **Note:** Adobe Premiere Elements detects only burners that are connected and turned on at the time you started Adobe Premiere Elements. If you connected and turned on any burners after that point, Adobe Premiere Elements will not recognize them until you restart the application.

Congratulations! You've successfully completed this lesson. You learned how to manually and automatically add scene markers to your movie, create an auto-play disc, and—by applying a menu template—create a disc with menus. You added a submenu for an outtake clip and learned about stop and main menu markers. You customized the disc menus by changing text attributes, background images, button labels, and image thumbnails. You added sound and video clips to the menu background, and activated (and then deactivated) motion menu buttons. You created a web DVD to upload to the web and share with the world, and you learned how to burn your movie onto a DVD, Blu-ray, or AVCHD disc.

Choosing Blu-ray and AVCHD disc quality options

When you're burning to a Blu-ray or AVCHD disc, you have multiple resolution and video standard options. If you're producing your video for playback in the United States or Japan, choose NTSC; otherwise, choose PAL.

When you're choosing a target resolution, use the native resolution of your source footage. For example, HDV has a native resolution of 1440x1080, so if you recorded in HDV, you should produce your disc at that resolution. If you're shooting in AVCHD, you may be recording in native 1920x1080, so use that resolution for your disc. If you're not sure what resolution you're recording in, check the documentation that came with your camcorder. Ditto if you're shooting with a DSLR or other capture device.

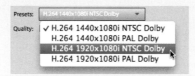

Review questions

1 What is an auto-play disc? What are one advantage and one disadvantage of creating such a disc?

2 How do you identify separate scenes for use in your disc menu?

3 What is a submenu, and how would you add one to your disc menu?

4 Which menu button text properties can you change, and how do you modify these properties?

5 Which type of menu template should you choose if you want to insert a still image or video file as a full-screen background for your disc menus?

6 What is a web DVD, and when should you use one?

7 What are the key benefits of burning an AVCHD disc?

Review answers

1 An auto-play disc allows you to create a DVD or Blu-ray Disc quickly from the main movie of your project. The advantage of an auto-play disc is that it can be created quickly and easily; the disadvantage is that it doesn't have a menu for navigation during playback.

2 Separate scenes can be defined by placing a scene marker on a specific frame in the timeline. You set scene markers in the timeline using the Add Menu Marker button.

3 A submenu is a button on your main disc menu that points to a specific section of your project, such as a credit sequence or a bonus clip. You create submenus by adding a main menu marker to your timeline.

4 You can change the font, size, color, and style of your text buttons. You change these text properties in the Adjustments panel for objects selected in the Disc Layout workspace.

5 You should choose a template that does not include a drop zone. If you insert a still image or video into a menu template with a drop zone, Adobe Premiere Elements will display that content only within the drop zone.

6 A web DVD presents a DVD-like experience on the web, complete with menus, themes, and high-quality video. Use web DVDs to share your productions with friends and family without having to burn and send them a physical DVD.

7 The key benefit of an AVCHD disc is the ability to record HD video onto a standard DVD-Recordable or rewritable disc using a standard DVD recorder. The resulting disc will play only on a Blu-ray player.

11 SHARING MOVIES

Lesson overview

In this lesson, you'll learn how to do the following:

- Upload a video file to YouTube

- Export a video file for subsequent viewing from a hard drive

- Export a video file for viewing on an iPad

- Export a single frame as a still image

- Save a custom preset to reuse preferred encoding parameters

Sharing movies works identically in Quick and Expert views, so you can choose the view you're most comfortable with for this lesson.

Adobe supplements the list of presets and their configuration options dynamically online. So don't be surprised if the screens that you see have more presets and different configuration options than are shown on these pages.

 This lesson will take approximately 1.5 hours. Download the project files for this lesson from the Lesson & Update Files tab on your Account page at www.peachpit.com and store them on your computer in a convenient location, as described in the Getting Started section of this book. Your Account page is also where you'll find any updates to the chapters or to the lesson files. Look on the Lesson & Update Files tab to access the most current content.

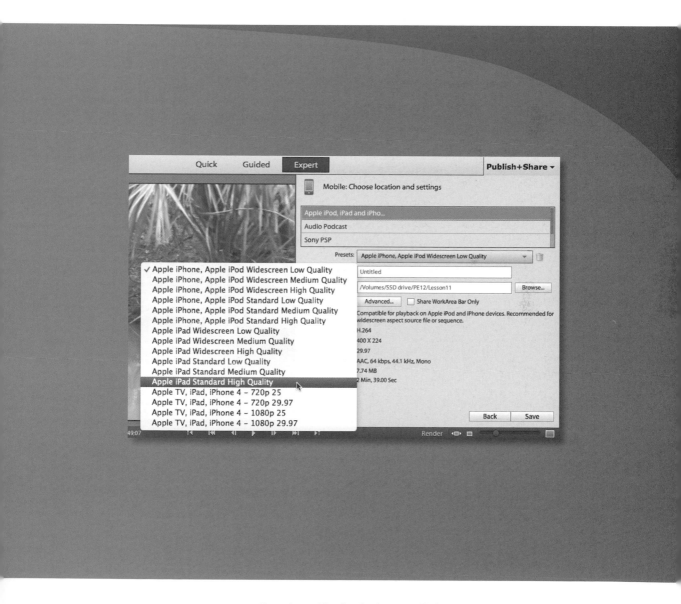

Exporting a video for viewing on an iPad

Sharing and exporting video

● **Note:** If you have not already downloaded the project files for this lesson to your computer from your Account page, make sure to do so now. See "Getting Started" at the beginning of the book.

Apart from creating web DVDs and the various optical disc formats supported by Adobe Premiere Elements, you can export and share movies, still images, and audio in a variety of file types for the web, computer playback, mobile devices, and even videotape. The Publish+Share panel (**Publish+Share ▾**) is the starting point for exporting your finished project, where you choose your target and configuration options.

Selecting any of the Publish+Share options opens a view in the panel that provides output-specific options and settings. The panel simplifies sharing and exporting by providing presets of the most commonly used formats and settings. With some presets, if you want to specify unique settings for any format, you can make changes in an Advanced options area. Other formats, particularly those targeted at video sharing websites (online) and devices (mobile phones and players), may be locked down to ensure that your file conforms to the requirements of the target service or device.

The first step for all sharing is choosing the desired target. The exercises in this lesson walk you through examples of the available targets in the Publish+Share panel.

Getting started

To begin, you'll launch Adobe Premiere Elements and open the project used for this lesson.

1   Make sure that you have correctly copied the Lesson11 folder from your Account page onto your computer's hard drive. See "Copying the Classroom in a Book files" in the Getting Started section at the start of this book.

2   Launch Adobe Premiere Elements. If it is already open, choose Help > Welcome Screen to return to the Welcome screen.

3   In the Welcome screen, click Video Editor, select Existing Project, and then click the Open folder.

4   In the Open Project dialog box, navigate to the Lesson11 folder you copied to your hard drive.

5   Within the Lesson11 folder, select the file Lesson11_Start_Win.prel (Windows) or Lesson11_Start_Mac.prel (Mac OS), and then click Open.

Your project file opens.

6   Choose Window > Restore Workspace to ensure that you start the lesson in the default panel layout.

Viewing the completed movie for the first exercise

To see what you'll be exporting in this lesson, press the spacebar to play the completed movie. If the movie looks familiar, that's because it's the project you finished back in Lesson 9 after adding a soundtrack and narration. Now it's time to share the fruits of your hard work with the world!

Rather than duplicating the project file and content from Lesson 9 to Lesson 11, I provided the rendered file that you just played onto the timeline, because it simulates the Lesson 9 project completely and saves a few hundred megabytes in the content that accompanies this book. The experience will be *the same* as if you were working with the original content and project file.

Still, if you want to work with the original assets, load the Lesson09_ Work.prel file that you created in Lesson 9, or load the Lesson09_Start_Win.prel (Windows) or Lesson09_Start_Mac.prel (Mac OS) file if you didn't work through that lesson. Obviously, those projects would be in the Lesson09 folder, not the Lesson11 folder. In your shoes, I would simply use the project file you currently have loaded, but feel free to work with the original content if that's your preference.

Uploading to YouTube

In addition to uploading to Adobe Revel, Adobe Premiere Elements provides presets for three online destinations—Facebook, Vimeo, and YouTube. The workflow is very similar for all of them: A simple wizard guides your efforts. In this exercise, you'll work through uploading to YouTube. It's faster if you already have an account with YouTube, but if not, you can sign up as part of the process.

1   In the upper right corner of the main Adobe Premiere Elements workspace, click Publish+Share (**Publish+Share ▾**), and then click Social Websites. If this is your first time clicking this option, it may take Adobe Premiere Elements some time to download the presets.

2 Choose Upload Video To YouTube.

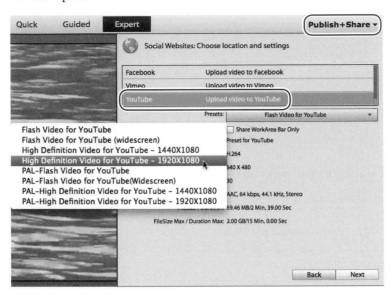

3 Choose the Flash Video For YouTube (widescreen) preset.

If you've shot in 720p resolution with your AVCHD or DSLR camera, as we did with this project, I recommend that you try uploading using both Flash Video For YouTube (widescreen) and High Definition Video For YouTube 1920x1080, and then retaining the video that looks the best. Then again, by the time you work through this exercise, there might be a 720p output preset.

● **Note:** For your SD projects, use Flash Video For YouTube for standard definition (SD) 4:3 projects and Flash Video For YouTube (widescreen) for (SD) 16:9 projects. When you're working with HD video, to upload high-definition (HD) video to YouTube, choose the preset that matches your source footage, which will be High Definition Video for YouTube - 1440X1080 for HDV and AVCHD camcorders that don't have the "FullHD" seal emblazoned on the side, and High Definition Video for YouTube – 1920X1080 for most "FullHD" AVCHD camcorders and most DSLR cameras.

4 If desired, select the Share WorkArea Bar Only option to upload only the Work Area bar.

5 Click Next.

6 Adobe requests authorization to manage your YouTube account. If the computer you're working on is not logged in to your YouTube account, you'll be asked to log in. Please do so. If this is your first time uploading to YouTube, click Sign Up Now and register.

If you are logged in, you'll go directly to the permissions screen. Once there, click Accept.

Return to Adobe Premiere Elements, and click the Complete Authorization button.

7   Enter the required information about your project: Title, Description, Tags, and Category, and then click Next.

8   Select a category for your project, and choose whether you want to allow the public to view your project or to keep it private. Then click Upload. Adobe Premiere Elements renders the project and starts uploading to YouTube. Status messages advise you of the progress during each step.

9 When the upload is complete, the URL appears in the Publish+Share panel. You can choose View My Shared Video to open YouTube and watch your video, or choose Send An E-mail to alert friends to your new posting.

10 Click Done to return to the Publish+Share panel.

Sharing on your personal computer

In the previous exercise, you exported an Adobe Premiere Elements project to YouTube. In this exercise, you'll export your project as a standalone video file to play on your own system, upload to a website, email to friends or family, or archive on DVD or an external hard drive.

As you'll see in a moment, Adobe Premiere Elements lets you output in multiple formats for all these activities. Each file format comes with its own set of presets, available on the Presets menu. You can also customize a preset and save it for later reuse, which you'll do in this lesson.

See the sidebar "Choosing output formats" for more information on which preset to choose. In this exercise, you'll use the QuickTime format.

1 In the upper right corner of the main Adobe Premiere Elements workspace, click Publish+Share (**Publish+Share ▾**), and then click Computer.

2 From the list at the top of the Publish+Share panel, scroll down if necessary, and choose QuickTime.

3 From the Presets menu, choose NTSC DV 16:9. After you complete the lesson, the custom preset that you create will be available via this menu.

4 Enter **Lesson11_SharePC** in the File Name field, and then click Browse to select the Lesson11 folder as the Save In folder.

5 Click the Advanced button (Advanced...) below the Save In field. Adobe Premiere Elements opens the Export Settings dialog box.

The NTSC DV 16:9 preset is great if you want to edit the file further in a Mac-based program, but the files are too large to easily email to friends and family. You'll create a custom preset that creates more compact files.

6 Click the Video Codec menu, and choose the H.264 codec.

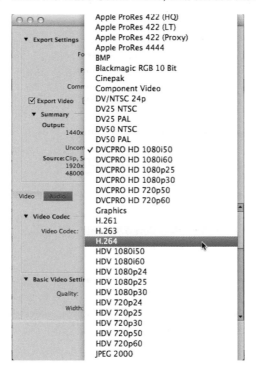

7 In the Basic Video Settings area, if a link icon appears to the right of the Width and Height values, click to remove that box, and then click to insert **640** in the Width field and **360** in the Height field. Then make the following selections to set the other parameters of your preset:

• Leave the Frame Rate at 29.97.

• Click the Field Order pull-down menu, and choose Progressive.

• Click the Aspect pull-down menu, and choose Square Pixels (1.0).

- Click the Render At Maximum Depth option to render at the highest possible quality. While this will extend rendering time somewhat, it's usually worth it.

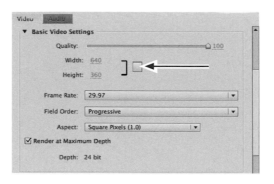

● **Note:** Look for a link icon (▦) in the box next to Width and Height. When the link is present, Adobe Premiere Elements links the width and height to maintain the aspect ratio of the source footage. Most of the time, that constraint is the right decision. But sometimes you'll want to change the aspect ratio, and the presence of the link prevents you from entering the desired values. In these cases, simply click the link to disable this option. The box should not be selected when you're using the preset that you selected, but if it is, click the box to deselect it.

8 Scroll down in the Export Settings dialog box, and click the disclosure triangle next to Advanced Settings (if necessary) to reveal those controls. Leave all settings deselected.

9 Click the disclosure triangle next to Bitrate Settings (if necessary) to reveal that control. Select the Limit Data Rate To check box, click the text field, and type **3000**.

10 Click the Audio tab in the Export Settings dialog box to open the Audio controls. From the Audio Codec pull-down menu, choose AAC. Set Sample Rate to 48000Hz and Channels to Stereo, as shown in the figure below.

11 Click OK to close the Export Settings dialog box; the Choose Name dialog box opens. Type **H.264 640x360 3 Mbps preset** into the name field, and click OK to close the dialog box.

12 Back in the Publish+Share panel, note that Adobe Premiere Elements has inserted the preset that you just created into the Presets menu.

The movie you're exporting will be produced using the parameters that you just selected, and the next time you click that menu, the new preset will be available with the other custom presets.

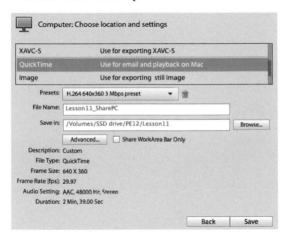

13 If desired, select the Share WorkArea Bar Only option.

14 To start exporting your movie, click Save.

Adobe Premiere Elements begins rendering the video, and displays a progress bar and an estimated time to complete the rendering process. Click Cancel at any time to stop the exporting process. Otherwise, you'll see a Save Complete! message when the rendering is complete.

15 Click Done to return to the Publish+Share panel. To play the movie, open Windows Explorer (Windows) or File Manager (Mac OS), navigate to the file you just created, and double-click it. The default player for the MOV format, typically the QuickTime Player, should open and play the file.

Choosing output formats

The output format you choose is often dictated by how you plan to distribute your video, whether you're exporting it for user playback or further editing in other systems, or what kinds of computers your target audience will use to play it. Here's a rundown of the output formats available in Adobe Premiere Elements, how compatible they are with various playback environments, and where they're typically used.

• **Adobe Flash Video:** Adobe Flash Video is a very high-quality format that's used by the majority of sites on the Internet for playback via the ubiquitous Adobe Flash Player. Use this format if you're producing files to be distributed from a website. However, for playback from hard drives, the FLV or F4V files produced by this format require a standalone player that many viewers don't have. Accordingly, the format is not appropriate for creating files to view on other computers outside the browser environment, whether by email, file transfer protocol (FTP), or via a Universal Serial Bus (USB) drive.

• **MPEG:** MPEG is a widely supported playback format, although it is used almost exclusively for desktop or disc-based playback rather than for streaming. Use MPEG to create files for inserting into Blu-ray or DVD projects produced in other programs. For most casual hard-drive-based playback, however, QuickTime offers better quality at lower data rates, making it a better option for files shared via email or FTP.

• **AVCHD:** AVCHD is a high-definition format that you can burn to a DVD to play on a Blu-ray player (as you learned in Lesson 10). AVCHD is also a good choice for archiving a high-quality version of your edited video for long-term storage or for playing back on a computer that has software that can play AVCHD files. Although very high quality, AVCHD is not a good medium for sharing video files, because the files are quite large and difficult to transfer.

• **XAVC-S:** XAVC is an ultra-high-resolution format used by some consumer camcorders. If you're editing XAVC video, use presets in this category to archive your footage or to produce files that you can watch on your 4K TV sets or monitors.

• **AVI (Windows only):** Use DV presets to archive standard-definition (SD) productions or to produce SD files for further editing in other programs. But note that DV AVI files are too large for casual distribution via email or FTP, and although many Mac OS programs can import AVI files, QuickTime is a better choice when you're planning to edit your projects further on the Mac platform. You can also access other AVI codecs via the Advanced button in the preset, but again, QuickTime is generally a better choice for distributing files because of near universal compatibility on both Windows and Macintosh computers.

(continues on next page)

Choosing output formats (continued)

- **Windows Media (Windows only):** Windows Media files—whether distributed via a website, email, or FTP—can be played by virtually all Windows computers via the Windows Media Player. Quality is good at low bitrates, making Windows Media a good choice for producing files to be distributed via email to other Windows users. However, Macintosh compatibility may be a problem, because Microsoft hasn't released a Windows Media Player for OS X, forcing users to download a third-party solution from Flip4Mac. When you're producing files that may be viewed on Macintosh or Windows computers, use the QuickTime format.

- **QuickTime:** QuickTime is the best choice for files intended for viewing on both Macintosh and Windows computers, whether distributed via the web, email, or another technique. All presets use the H.264 codec, which offers very good quality but can take a long time to render.

- **Image:** Use Image to export images from your project.

- **Audio:** Use Audio to export audio from your project.

When you're producing a file for uploading to a website like Yahoo Video or Blip.tv, check the required file specifications published by each site before producing your file. Typically, a QuickTime file using the H.264 codec offers the best blend of high quality at modest data rates and near universal compatibility.

Exporting to mobile phones and players

Adobe Premiere Elements also includes an option for producing files for mobile phones and players, such as the Apple iPod, iPad, and iPhone, and the Sony PlayStation Portable. Note that most of these devices have very specific and inflexible file and format requirements; changing any parameters in the Export Settings window may produce a file that's unplayable on the target device.

In this exercise, you'll learn how to create a file for an iPad; if you're producing a file for a different device, just choose that device and preset in the appropriate steps.

1   In the upper right corner of the main Adobe Premiere Elements workspace, click Publish+Share (**Publish+Share ▾**), and then select Mobile Phones And Players.

2   From the list at the top of the Publish+Share panel, choose Apple iPod, iPad And iPhone.

3 From the Presets pull-down menu, choose a preset that matches your target device, aspect ratio (widescreen or standard), and desired output quality. Note that high-quality files produced for an iPad may not load on older iPhones or iPods. For the purposes of this exercise, choose Apple iPad Widescreen High Quality.

4 Next to File Name, enter **Lesson11_iPad**, and then click Browse to select your Lesson11 folder as the Save In folder.

5 If desired, select the Share WorkArea Bar Only option.

6 To start exporting your movie, click Save.

Adobe Premiere Elements starts rendering the video, and displays a progress bar and an estimated time to complete each phase of the rendering process. Click Cancel at any time to stop the exporting process. Otherwise, you will see a Save Complete! message when the rendering is complete.

7 Click Back to return to the Publish+Share panel.

After producing the file, transfer it to your device in the appropriate manner. For example, use iTunes to upload the file to your iPod or iPhone.

● **Note:** If you produce your movies using video captured from DV or HDV tape, you may want to archive your project back to tape. For instructions regarding this process, search Adobe Premiere Elements Help for "Sharing to Videotape."

Exporting a frame of video as a still image

Occasionally, you may want to grab frames from your video footage to email to friends and family, include in a slide show, or use for other purposes. In this exercise, you'll learn how to export and save a frame from the project.

1 In the timeline, drag the current-time indicator to timecode 00;01;19;09, or click the current timecode box at the lower left of the Monitor panel, type **11909**, and press Enter (Windows) or Return (Mac OS).

2 In the Action bar on the bottom of the Adobe Premiere Elements interface, click Tools (✖ Tools), and then select Freeze Frame.

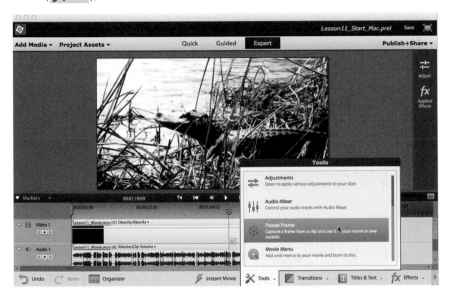

3 In the Freeze Frame dialog box, click Export to create a separate still image, which is what you want to do here.

Note the Insert In Movie option, which you would use to insert the frame into the movie if that's why you were grabbing the image. If you have Adobe Photoshop Elements installed, you can also elect to edit the captured frame in Adobe Photoshop Elements if you choose the Insert In Movie option.

4 In the Export Frame dialog box, locate the Lesson11 folder, and name your file **gator.bmp**. Click Save to save the still image to your hard drive and to close the Freeze Frame dialog box.

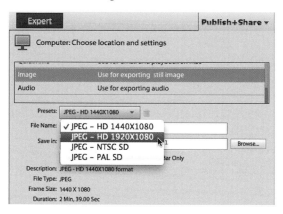

▶ **Tip:** The snapshot export function is very quick and easy, but outputs only BMP files at the resolution of your current project. For more control over export size and formats, click Publish+Share, click Computer, and then choose Image, which exposes multiple presets that you can customize by clicking the Advanced button.

Congratulations! You've completed the penultimate lesson in this book! You've learned how to export your finished movies to YouTube, create compatible files for playback on iPads and other mobile devices, and compress movies in various formats for distribution via email and FTP and playback on Windows and Macintosh computers. And you've also learned how to grab still images from your video and export them in the format of your choice. On to Lesson 12, where you'll learn how to fine-tune and enhance those images in Adobe's companion program for still-image editing, Photoshop Elements.

Review questions

1   What's the best format to use for creating files to view on Windows computers or to share with other viewers with Windows computers?

2   Why shouldn't you change any encoding parameters for files produced for iPods or other devices?

3   What is Adobe Revel?

4   What's the easiest way to upload your movie to a website, such as YouTube or Facebook?

5   When might you want to export a file into AVCHD format?

Review answers

1   Windows Media is the best format for Windows because it combines small file size with high quality. Although virtually all computers can play MPEG-1 or MPEG-2 files, the files are usually too large for easy transport. QuickTime files may pose a problem, because not all Windows computers support QuickTime (but most do), and Adobe Flash Video files with the .flv extension require a standalone player, which not all computers have installed.

2   Devices have very specific playback requirements, and if you change a file parameter and deviate from these requirements, the file may not load or play on the target device.

3   Adobe Revel is a new online sharing service for still pictures and videos. Adobe Premiere Elements can export directly to Adobe Revel.

4   Open the Publish+Share panel, and then click the Social Websites button. Choose YouTube, Facebook, or Vimeo, and then follow the instructions for your selected destination site to render and upload your movie.

5   You might want to export a file into AVCHD format for subsequent burning to a Blu-ray Disc or as a high-quality archive of the project.

12 WORKING WITH ADOBE PHOTOSHOP ELEMENTS

Lesson overview

Adobe Photoshop Elements and Adobe Premiere Elements are designed to work together and let you seamlessly combine digital photography and video editing. You can spice up your video projects with title images created in Adobe Photoshop Elements, or select images in the Elements Organizer and send them to Adobe Premiere Elements to create a slide show.

To work on the following exercises, you must have Adobe Photoshop Elements installed on your system. In this lesson, you will learn several techniques for using Adobe Photoshop Elements together with Adobe Premiere Elements. Specifically, you'll learn how to do the following:

- Add single and multiple images from the Elements Organizer to an Adobe Premiere Elements project

- Create a Photoshop file optimized for video

- Edit a Photoshop image from within Adobe Premiere Elements

 This lesson will take approximately one hour. Download the project files for this lesson from the Lesson & Update Files tab on your Account page at www.peachpit.com and store them on your computer in a convenient location, as described in the Getting Started section of this book. Your Account page is also where you'll find any updates to the chapters or to the lesson files. Look on the Lesson & Update Files tab to access the most current content.

A cool title created in Adobe Photoshop Elements for use in Adobe Premiere Elements

Viewing the completed movie before you start

Note: If you have not already downloaded the project files for this lesson to your computer from your Account page, make sure to do so now. See "Getting Started" at the beginning of the book.

To see what you'll be creating, let's take a look at the completed movie.

1 Before you begin, make sure that you have correctly copied the Lesson12 folder from your Account page onto your computer's hard drive. See "Copying the Classroom in a Book files" in the Getting Started section at the start of this book.

2 Navigate to the Lesson12 folder, and double-click Lesson12_Movie.mov to play the movie in your default application for watching QuickTime files.

Getting started

Note: To sort images in the Organizer, Adobe Photoshop Elements uses the date and time information embedded in the image file by the digital camera. In the Organizer menu, choose Sort By: Newest to show new files first, and to enable you to create a slide show in chronological order when transferring the photos to Adobe Premiere Elements.

You'll open Adobe Photoshop Elements 12 and import the files needed for the Lesson12 project. Then you'll create an Adobe Premiere Elements project from images, much like you created a video project using videos back in Lesson 1. Let's review that procedure quickly.

If you have a project open in Adobe Premiere Elements when you use this technique, the Organizer will add the selected files to the current project at the end of the current timeline. If no project is open, the Organizer will create a new project, which is the workflow you'll follow in this exercise. Accordingly, if you have a project open in Adobe Premiere Elements, please close it (after saving if necessary) before starting this exercise.

1 Launch Adobe Photoshop Elements. If it is already open, choose Help > Welcome screen to open the Welcome screen.

2 In the Welcome screen, click the Organizer button to open the Elements Organizer.

3 If you've previously used Adobe Photoshop Elements, your Organizer may be displaying the photos in your current catalog. If this is the first time you've launched Adobe Photoshop Elements, you may receive a message asking if you want to designate a location to look for your image files. Click No to close the dialog box.

4 Choose File > Get Photos And Videos > From Files And Folders. Navigate to your Lesson12 folder and select—but do not open—the Images subfolder. Then click Get Media. Adobe Photoshop Elements imports the photos.

⬤ **Note:** If you've worked through previous projects from this book, there's a good chance that Adobe Premiere Elements will refuse to reimport some or all of these images. In this case, you can work with any eight images already in the Elements Organizer. Or, if you click the Show Panel icon (⬛) at the extreme lower left, you should see folders from previous lessons, which may contain the images previously imported. Select the various folders, and you may see the images as they're shown in this book's figures. Either way, the content of the images shouldn't impact the skills you'll learn in this lesson; any eight should do.

5 If a message appears telling you that only the newly imported files will appear, click OK. In the Organizer, you should see eight images from the bayou boat ride project. Thumbnail images are small versions of the full-size photos. You'll be working with the full-size photos later in this lesson.

6 Take these steps to make sure your Organizer looks the same as the figure:

- Choose View > Media Types. Make sure Photos is selected and all other media types are deselected.

- Choose View > Details and View > File Names to show these elements.

- In the Sort By menu on top of the Organizer's media browser, make sure Name is selected.

7 Press and hold the Ctrl (Windows) or Command (Mac OS) key, and then, in the Photo Browser, click the first seven images to select them (Picture 1.jpg–Picture 7.jpg). The Organizer highlights the gray area around the thumbnail to indicate a selected image.

8 In the Tools panel at the bottom of the Organizer, click the triangle next to the Editor icon, and choose Video Editor. A dialog box may appear informing you that the files will be inserted at the end of your timeline and that the Adobe Premiere Elements defaults will be used. Click OK. If Adobe Premiere Elements is not already open, it will launch automatically. If Adobe Premiere Elements opens the Smart Fix dialog box and asks if you want to fix quality problems in the clips, click No.

An Adobe Premiere Elements project is created, and the images you selected in Adobe Photoshop Elements are now visible in the timeline. The first image is displayed in the Monitor panel. If desired, click the Backslash key (\) to spread the images over the open timeline.

Slide show length: Don't assume!

Although you might assume that the total length of the slide show is equal to the number of images multiplied by the default duration for still images, it's actually less than that. The reason is that Adobe Premiere Elements inserts the transition effect between the images by overlapping the clips by the default length of the transition effect. Note that you can change the default still-image duration and transition duration in the Adobe Premiere Elements Preferences panel. See the section "Working with project preferences" in Lesson 2 for more details.

9 Select all scenes in the timeline, and choose Clip > Group to place the entire group onto one target that can be moved as a single clip. Then choose Clip > Ungroup to treat each still image as its own scene in the timeline.

10 Press the spacebar to play your project. Adobe Premiere Elements uses the default duration of five seconds for each still image, and applies a cross-dissolve as the default transition between each clip.

11 Return to the Organizer by clicking the Organizer button at the lower left of the workspace or by holding down Alt (Windows) or Command (Mac OS) and pressing Tab until you see the icon for the Elements Organizer. Release the Alt (Windows) or Command (Mac OS) key. The Elements Organizer opens.

12 Click to select only one image, the one named Picture 8.jpg, and then choose Edit > Edit With Premiere Elements Editor. Click OK to close the Edit With Premiere Elements dialog box if it appears. If the Smart Fix dialog box appears, Click No and do not fix the quality problems. Adobe Premiere Elements becomes your active application, and the image is placed at the end of your timeline.

13 Choose File > Save As, and save this project file in your Lesson12 folder as **Lesson12_Work.prel**.

● **Note:** Because you're sending only a single image from Adobe Photoshop Elements to Adobe Premiere Elements, no transition has been placed on the image. In this case, if you wanted to add a transition, you would have to do so manually, but do not add one at this time. See Lesson 7 for more information about adding transitions.

Creating a new Photoshop file optimized for video

The first part of this lesson focused on importing image files from the Organizer into Adobe Premiere Elements. In this exercise, you'll create a new still image and modify it in Adobe Photoshop Elements, and then use it in your Adobe Premiere Elements project.

1 In Adobe Photoshop Elements, choose File > New > Blank File. In the New dialog box, type **Title**. Then click the Preset menu, and choose Film & Video.

2 Click the Size pull-down menu, and choose HDTV 1080p, which matches the resolution of the project you should have open in Adobe Premiere Elements. If you're working on a different project, choose the size that matches the resolution of your current Adobe Premiere Elements project. If you don't know or have forgotten the resolution of the project, in Adobe Premiere Elements click Edit > Project Settings > General to view your project settings.

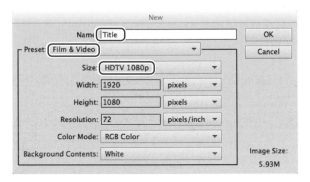

3 Click OK to create the file.

4 Save the file in the Lesson12 folder. Choose File > Save As, and in the Save As dialog box, check to make sure that you named the file **Title.psd**; then navigate to your Lesson12 folder, and click Save.

Customizing a title in Adobe Photoshop Elements

Now that you have your Photoshop file, you'll add the background that you captured in the previous lesson, customize the background, and then add some text.

1 Still in Adobe Photoshop Elements, at the top of the Editor, make sure Expert (Expert) is selected.

2 If necessary, choose View > Guides to hide the title- and action-safe guides, which you don't need because you're not producing a DVD with this project or otherwise producing a file that will be viewed on a television set.

3 In Adobe Photoshop Elements, choose File > Open. The Open dialog box opens. Navigate to the Lesson12 folder on your hard drive, choose gator.bmp, and click Open to load the image into Adobe Photoshop Elements.

4 Choose Select > All to select the image, and then choose Edit > Copy to copy the image to the clipboard.

5 Click Title.psd to make it active, and choose Edit > Paste to paste the copied gator.bmp image into Title.psd. If you see an error message about the background of the image being locked, click OK to enable the procedure.

6 To adjust the size of the pasted image to fit Title.psd, click and drag any of the eight small squares on the edges and sides of the bounding box.

If you don't see the squares, click to select the Move tool in the Select area in the upper left of the Tools panel. Position the image so that it fills the white area of Title.psd. Then click the Commit Current Operation check mark on the lower right to set the adjustment.

7 At the bottom right of the Adobe Photoshop Elements workspace, click Effects (_fx_) to open that panel. At the upper right, click Filters, and choose Sketch from the pull-down menu.

8 Drag the Water Paper effect onto Title.psd, and release the mouse button. Adobe Photoshop Elements applies the effect to the image.

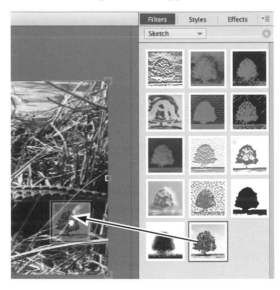

Next, we'll add a text title to Title.psd.

9 Click the Horizontal Type tool () in the Draw section of the Tools panel on the extreme left.

10 In the Text tool options bar, choose Rockwell Extra Bold. Type **150** into the font size field, and center the text alignment. If you don't have that font on your system, choose a different font that's very wide, like Cooper Std or Impact. If the font isn't wide, you'll have a hard time seeing some of the effects you'll apply below.

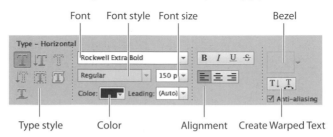

Now let's change the font color.

11 Click the Text Color chip, and then click the Bring Up Color Picker icon in the Color Swatches dialog box to open the color picker.

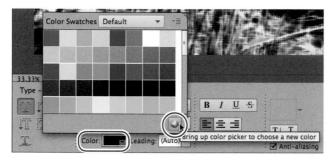

12 In the Select A Color To Add To The Palette dialog box, you see RGB values on the lower right. Type R: **242**, G: **174**, B: **54**, which is the orange color you used when creating the opening title. Then click OK to close the Select A Color To Add To The Palette dialog box.

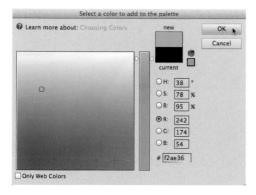

13 Click the image on the top left, and type **Bayou Boat Ride**.

14 Click the Move tool ( ) in the Tools panel to return to the selection arrow. Position the text to approximately where it's shown in the figure (if necessary). Now let's make the text more legible. To do this, right-click the text box, and choose Edit Layer Style. The Style Settings dialog box opens.

15 Make the following adjustments in the Style Settings dialog box:

- Select the Drop Shadow option to add a drop shadow.

- Select the Stroke option to add a stroke, and drag the size to 8px, as shown in the figure.

- Click OK to close the Style Settings dialog box.

The text is much more legible and distinctive. Now let's warp the text.

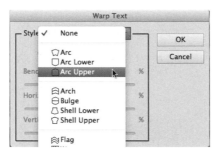

16 Double-click the text box to select all text, and then click the Create Warped Text icon in the Type Tools panel.

17 In the Warp Text dialog box, click the Style pull-down menu, and choose Arc Upper. Make sure that Bend is set to +50. Click OK to close the dialog box.

18 Click the Move tool ( ) in the Tools panel to return to the selection arrow. Position the text to approximately where it's shown in the figure (if necessary).

19 Choose File > Save to save Title.psd.

20 Switch to Adobe Premiere Elements by holding down the Alt (Windows) or Command (Mac OS) key and pressing Tab until you see the icon for Adobe Premiere Elements. Release the Alt (Windows) or Command (Mac OS) key; Adobe Premiere Elements opens.

Now you're in position to import the file into Adobe Premiere Elements.

21 Make sure that you're in Expert view. Then click the Add Media button, and choose Files And folders. The Add Media dialog box opens. Navigate to the Lesson12 folder, click to select Title.psd, and then click Open (Windows) or Import (Mac OS). Adobe Premiere Elements imports the file and displays it in the Project Assets panel, although you may need to scroll down to see the imported file.

22 Drag Title.psd from the Project Assets panel to the beginning of the movie, waiting for about two seconds for the other images to shift to the right. Then release the pointer. If Adobe Premiere Elements opens the Smart Fix dialog box, click No.

Adobe Premiere Elements inserts Title.psd at the start of the movie and shifts all other content to the right.

23 Save your work.

Editing a Photoshop image in Adobe Photoshop Elements

You can edit an Adobe Photoshop Elements image (or any image, for that matter) while you're working in Adobe Premiere Elements by using the Edit In Photoshop Elements command. Once you save your image, changes you make to the image in Adobe Photoshop Elements will be updated in Adobe Premiere Elements, even if the clip is already placed in your timeline.

1 Right-click the Title.psd clip in the timeline, and choose Edit In Adobe Photoshop Elements. The Title.psd file opens in Adobe Photoshop Elements.

2 If necessary, click the Move tool (⊹) in the Tools panel to choose the selection arrow. Then right-click the text box, and choose Edit Layer Style.

3 In the Style Settings dialog box, click the color chip next to the stroke controls to open the Select Stroke Color dialog box. Change the RGB values to R: **255**, G: **0**, B: **0**. Then click OK to close the Select Stroke Color dialog box, and click OK again to close the Style Settings dialog box.

4 Choose File > Save As. Click the file Title.psd in the Lesson12 folder. In the Save As dialog box, deselect Save In Version Set With Original. Click Save, and then click OK (Windows) or Replace (Mac OS) to overwrite Title.psd.

5 Switch to Adobe Premiere Elements.

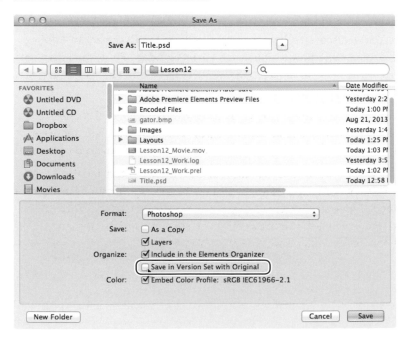

The changes made to the Title.psd file in Adobe Photoshop Elements have automatically been updated in the Adobe Premiere Elements project. This is very useful because it eliminates the need to re-import an image file every time a change is made.

6　Click the top of the timeline to select it, and then press the Home key to place the current-time indicator at the beginning of the timeline. Press the spacebar to play your project. When you're finished reviewing, save your work.

Congratulations! You've finished the lesson on working with Adobe Photoshop Elements. You've discovered how to get photos from the Organizer to Adobe Premiere Elements and how to enhance them using Adobe Photoshop Elements. You've also learned how to create a title in Adobe Photoshop Elements for use in Adobe Premiere Elements.

This is the last lesson in this book. We hope that you have gained confidence in using Adobe Premiere Elements 12, developed some new skills, and increased your knowledge of the product and the many creative things you can accomplish with it.

But this book is just the beginning. You can learn more by studying the Adobe Premiere Elements 12 Help system that is built into the application. Simply choose Help > Adobe Premiere Elements Help, and browse or use the search functionality to find what you need. Also, don't forget to look for tutorials, tips, and expert advice on the Adobe Systems website at www.adobe.com.

Review questions

1 What's the best way to make sure that an image you create in Adobe Photoshop Elements matches the video that you'll be adding it to?

2 How can you edit an image included in an Adobe Premiere Elements project in Adobe Photoshop Elements?

3 What are the advantages of creating your titles and editing your images in Adobe Photoshop Elements compared to Adobe Premiere Elements?

Review answers

1 Make sure that you create the file using the same dimensions as your video project.

2 Right-click the image in the Adobe Premiere Elements timeline, and choose Edit In Adobe Photoshop Elements from the contextual menu.

3 Adobe Photoshop Elements has many more still-image effects and several more advanced text-related adjustments than Adobe Premiere Elements.

INDEX

H

H.264 codec, 285, 289
hard drives
    considerations, 10, 33, 55, 59
    fragmentation, 55
    importing content from, 47, 60
    loading video files from, 9
    sharing/exporting video, 280–281
    sufficient space on, 55
    transferring media to, 51, 55
HD mode, 271–272
HD (high-definition) video, 127
HDV camcorders
    capturing/importing video from, 10, 33, 48, 53–59
    connectors on, 54–55
    setting up, 55
High Definition Video For YouTube preset, 282
high-definition. *See* HD
History panel, 22
Home key, 96
Horizontal type tool, 202–203, 207
HSB (Hue, Saturation, and Brightness), 189
HSL (Hue, Saturation, and Lightness), 189
Hue, Saturation, and Brightness (HSB), 189
Hue, Saturation, and Lightness (HSL), 189

I

IEEE 1394 ports, 53–54, 55
IEEE 1394 standard, 53–54
Image format, 289
images
    adding to titles, 208–209
    composite, 126
    graphics elements, 19, 215–217
    graphics library, 18, 19
    reframing with Motion controls, 148–149
    slide shows, 113–115
    still. *See* still images
importing video. *See* capturing/importing video

In points. *See also* Out points

In points. *See also* Out points
    adjusting, 100, 110
    anchoring to, 165
    described, 100
    setting in Preview window, 68, 69, 70
    for thumbnail videos, 264, 266
Information panel, 22
Insert In Movie option, 291
Instant Movie panel, 18
InstantMovies, 51, 84–88
"Insufficient media" error message, 193–194
Interest Level slider, 116–117
interlaced video, 37
iPad, exporting video to, 289–290

J

J-cuts, 118

K

keyframes, 156–162
    adjusting, 162–163
    adjusting volume with, 231, 235–236
    animating effects with, 18, 156–159
    audio, 235
    considerations, 157
    creating fade-outs with, 159–163
    deleting, 162
    described, 156, 235
    modifying, 162–163
    presets, 164, 165–166
    scaling, 165
    showing/hiding, 156
keyframing, 156
keyword tagging, 72, 78–80
keywords, 78–80

L

laptop computers, 54
layering, 104
layers, adjustment, 24, 169–170
L-cuts, 118
letterboxing, 31, 34

libraries, 18, 19
lighting adjustments, 133–134
lighting effects, 130, 133–134
Lightning Effects, 127
linked video, 118
live video capture
    vs. clip-based import, 47–48
    procedure for, 47–48, 53–57

M

main menu markers, 262
margins, 206
marker buttons, 268
Maximum Project Versions setting, 39
media
    cache, 39, 40
    capturing. *See* capturing/importing video
    not found, 244
    optical. *See* optical media
    preferences, 40
    sorting, 11
    specifying location for, 51
    types of, 71
Media Not Found error message, 244
Media Types option, 71
Menu Background options, 264
Menu Marker dialog box, 248–249, 258
menu markers, 262
Menu Theme panel, 251–253
menu titles, 268
menus, 242–276
    adding audio, 264–265
    adding visual content, 263–265
    backgrounds, 264
    bonus clips, 259–262
    creating, 253–256
    customizing, 263–265
    getting started, 244–246
    looping, 264
    submenus, 259–262
    templates, 253–254, 257
microphones, 52
midtone adjustment, 134–135
Missing Disc Menu dialog box, 250

Mobile Phones and Players option, 21
Monitor panel
    adjusting size, 41, 42
    centering elements in, 205
    overview, 12–13, 16
    playing movies in, 94
    video editing in, 93–97
    zooming in/out, 95
monitors, dual, 42
Motion controls, 146–149
motion effects, 125, 127, 144–145
motion menu buttons, 266
motion tracking, 21, 23, 125, 174–176
MOV format, 287
Movie Menu tool, 20
movies. *See also* video
    Entire Movie button, 167–168
    InstantMovies, 51, 84–88
    moving to specific points in, 95–96
    playing. *See* playback
    positioning CTI at beginning/end of, 96
    sharing. *See* exporting video
    themes. *See* themes
    YouTube, 281–284
MPEG format, 288
music
    background, 24, 87, 226–227, 237
    beat detection, 238–239
    themes, 87
Music option, 87
musical soundtracks, 226–227

N

Name option, 71
narration, adding, 227–228
Narration tool, 21
Narration track, 93
navigation, 259
navigational buttons, 268, 269
New Project command, 33, 34
New Project dialog box, 29
Next Scene control, 57
Normalization option, 231, 232–233
notebook computers, 54

Step Forward button, 95
Still Image Default Duration setting, 38
still images
    adding to menus, 263–265
    duration of, 200, 201
    exporting video frames as, 291–292
    viewing in Organizer, 71
stop markers, 259–260, 262
stop-motion video, 51
stopwatch icon, 157, 159
storyboard-style editing, 97
streaming playback, 187
submenus, 259–262
Summer Day FilmLook, 169, 170

T

tagging clips
    to Events, 75–77
    Organizer techniques for, 70–72
    to Places, 72–74
    removing tags, 83
tags, 11
Tags/Info icon, 11
Tags/Information panel, 11
tape-based video capture, 10, 33, 48, 53–59
Temperature and Tint effect, 130
templates
    menus, 253–254, 257
    titles, 19, 200, 202
text. See also titles
    animating, 211
    centering, 205
    changing alignment/style/size, 204–205
    color, 207–208, 270
    gradient, 207–208
    overview, 199–201
    scaling, 267
    size, 268–269
    Speech Bubbles, 215–217
text library, 18, 19
Text track, 201
Theme Content option, 87
Theme Music option, 87

themes
    choosing, 85–86
    fitting clips to, 86
    music, 87
    titles, 200
thumbnails
    animating, 265–266
    scene markers, 257–259
Time Remapping effect, 21, 125, 141–145
Time Stretch effect, 21, 149
timecode, 56, 97
timecode format, 56
timecode numbers, 56
timecode-based scene detection, 56, 57
time-lapse video, 51
Timeline panel, 13, 41
Title Safe area, 255
Title track, 93
titles. See also text
    adding images to, 208–209
    animated, 211, 217–219
    backgrounds, 211–214
    centering, 205
    considerations, 257
    crawls, 217
    creating, 201, 202–203
    customizing, 255–256
    duration of, 200, 209, 214
    editing, 201
    fade-in/fade-out, 209–210
    full-screen, 200, 202–203
    modifying text in, 203–205
    overlay, 200, 201, 211–214
    overview, 199–201
    rolling credits, 217–219
    safe zones, 255
    Speech Bubbles, 215–217
    superimposing over video clips,
        211–214
    templates, 200, 202
    text alignment/style/size, 204–205
    themes, 200
    using graphics with, 215–217
titles library, 18, 19

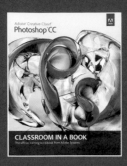

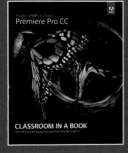

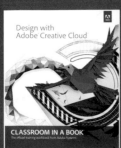

The fastest, easiest, most comprehensive way to learn
Adobe Creative Cloud™

Classroom in a Book®, the best-selling series of hands-on software training books, helps you learn the features of Adobe software quickly and easily.

The **Classroom in a Book** series offers what no other book or training program does—an official training series from Adobe Systems, developed with the support of Adobe product experts.

To see a complete list of our Adobe Creative Cloud titles go to: www.adobepress.com/adobecc

Adobe Photoshop CC Classroom in a Book
ISBN: 9780321928078

Adobe Illustrator CC Classroom in a Book
ISBN: 9780321929495

Adobe InDesign CC Classroom in a Book
ISBN: 9780321926975

Adobe Dreamweaver CC Classroom in a Book
ISBN: 9780321919410

Adobe Flash Professional CC Classroom in a Book
ISBN: 9780321927859

Adobe Premiere Pro CC Classroom in a Book
ISBN: 9780321919380

Adobe After Effects CC Classroom in a Book
ISBN: 9780321929600

Adobe Audition CC Classroom in a Book
ISBN: 9780321929532

Adobe SpeedGrade CC Classroom in a Book
ISBN: 9780321927002

Digital Video with Adobe Creative Cloud Classroom in a Book
ISBN: 9780321934024

Design with the Adobe Creative Cloud Classroom in a Book
ISBN: 9780321940513

AdobePress

WATCH
READ
CREATE

Unlimited online access to all Peachpit, Adobe Press; Apple Training, and New Riders videos and books, as well as content from other leading publishers including: O'Reilly Media, Focal Press, Sams, Que, Total Training, John Wiley & Sons, Course Technology PTR, Class on Demand, VTC, and more.

No time commitment or contract required! Sign up for one month or a year. All for $19.99 a month

SIGN UP TODAY
peachpit.com/creativeedge